On This DAY in HISTORY

DAN SNOW

JOHN MURRAY

First published in Great Britain in 2018 by John Murray (Publishers)
An Hachette UK company

This paperback edition published in 2019

8

Copyright © Dan Snow 2018

The right of Dan Snow to be identified as the Author of the
Work has been asserted by him in accordance with the
Copyright, Designs and Patents Act 1988.

Maps by Rodney Paull

A CIP catalogue record for this title is available from the British Library

Paperback ISBN 978-1-473-69130-8
eBook ISBN 978-1-473-69128-5

Typeset in Janson Text LT Std by Palimpsest Book Production Limited,
Falkirk, Stirlingshire

Printed and bound by Clays Ltd, Elcograf S.p.A.

John Murray policy is to use papers that are natural,
renewable and recyclable products and made from wood grown in
sustainable forests. The logging and manufacturing processes are expected
to conform to the environmental regulations of the country of origin.

John Murray (Publishers)
Carmelite House
50 Victoria Embankment
London EC4Y 0DZ

www.johnmurray.co.uk

To my little Wolf.
Explore the past, shape your future.

Contents

Introduction　ix

History Hit　xv

Maps　xvi

January　1

February　35

March　67

April　101

May　135

June　169

July　203

August　237

September　271

October　305

November　339

December　373

Timeline　406

Bibliography　410

Acknowledgements　412

Introduction

Anniversaries matter. A child's year (and that of a strange number of adults) revolves around the day on which they were born. Canada Day in Ottawa plunges you into an ocean of patriotic revellers in red and white drinking Canadian beer, while remaining scrupulously polite, under a hot July sun. St Patrick's Day in March is a rather more raucous celebration of Irishness that literally turns the Guinness green around the world. 26 January is special in both Australia and India, where it is Australia Day and Republic Day respectively. The former celebrates the arrival of the British, the latter, their departure.

Crowds of us in the UK cheer every Bonfire Night as the autumnal darkness echoes with the thump of exploding gunpowder and an umbrella of fireworks fills the sky. Very few of us pause to think about why we are told to 'Remember, remember the fifth of November'. Why do we still burn effigies of unsuccessful terrorist Guy Fawkes on bonfires all over Britain, four centuries after his foiled mass murder attempt and his own grisly death?

On This Day in History is an attempt to explore our past, though these anniversaries, and provide a little more context about the events we choose to remember, and others that we have forgotten.

My family live and breathe history. It runs through us like a genetic marker. My aunt is a professor of history, my Welsh grandmother, 'Nain' as we called her, was an oral historian, my mum, dad, siblings, we were all brought up with one eye on the past. My parents were journalists who explained current affairs through a deep understanding of how the world had got there. And then they spent their weekends and holidays taking us kids to battlefields and castles. (It was a habit their children found deeply irksome, and yet we now in turn inflict it on our children.) I knew growing up that I was immensely lucky: I was born into an economically and emotionally secure family, I was half Canadian with a tribe of wonderful cousins with cooler accents and clothes across the Atlantic, and I happened to be a native English speaker, a language that was, usefully, spoken across the world. I was, in short, a product of the past. And, if it hadn't been for a chance meeting of a British and Canadian journalist at an Ottawa press conference on a particular day in 1973, I would not have existed.

I never doubted that history mattered. How could it not? History was everything that had gone before. Just as our adult lives are shaped by the circumstances of our early years, so our lives, and the nature of the societies in which we live, are shaped by what has happened in the past. And my parents were always going off to cover these anniversaries, heading off to Cadiz for the 500th anniversary of the departure of Columbus and to the beaches of Normandy for D-Day. For one day, these long-past events reasserted themselves, elbowed their way into the newspapers and evening bulletins before they were lost again for another year.

Scanning the calendar at the start of every year became a Snow family tradition. When I was eight, I spotted that the 200th anniversary of Waterloo was approaching. Dad humoured me and agreed that he would take me to the bicentennial re-enactment. I roared with laughter at the very idea that one day I would be as old as thirty-six; it was less funny when, twenty-eight years later, that birthday duly came around, but as a present, my Dad did indeed take me over to Belgium, where we watched, in wonder, as thousands of re-enactors surged across the battlefield.

Families don't always talk about the effects of history. I'm so glad mine did. My Nain told me of how her husband, my 'Gramps', had almost fallen victim to Hitler's wolf packs in the north Atlantic, as he escorted convoys back and forth to supply Britain's food and war materiel. Her father had narrowly escaped a shell-blast in Gallipoli in 1915. Her grandfather had been David Lloyd George, Britain's wartime prime minister. He was party to decisions that changed the world. He laid the foundations for a welfare state in the UK; threw his weight behind war with Germany in 1914; agreed to the establishment of a Jewish homeland in Palestine; shaped the Versailles settlement and encouraged the disastrous Greek attack on Turkey after the First World War. Each decision had enormous, often unimagined consequences, many of which we are still living with, yet each began as a conversation, a signature on a piece of paper, a single moment on a particular day.

Anniversaries offer a moment to take stock and remind ourselves that what we see in the present has its genesis in the past. Events do not spring from a vacuum. They form and evolve over time and their present nature is a reflection of their histories. It is deeply affecting to study the slaughter of the first day of the Somme, the sinking of the *Titanic* or the cataclysmic Great Lisbon Earthquake, but it always feels different, more immediate on the day of the year it happened.

Throughout my career – across television, radio, podcasts, online video, social media posts, articles and books – I have repeatedly seen anniversary stories go viral, be shared by tens of thousands online, and be watched by millions. The first programme I ever made covered the sixtieth anniversary of the start of the battle of El Alamein and when it was broadcast on the exact night in October when Montgomery's heavy guns opened fire in the Western Desert, it really struck a chord with the audience.

I have been lucky to be present at so many anniversaries since. I helped to drop a wreath from the deck of a British frigate into choppy seas off the tip of Cape Trafalgar exactly 200 years to the hour since the British, French and Spanish ships opened fire in that climactic naval battle. I have stood on the Somme battle-field at dawn looking at a landscape of rolling fields flecked with wild flowers, 100 years to the minute after a thousand whistles sent an army of young men out of their trenches. I have watched galloping, mail-clad horsemen charging up the slope at Battle in Sussex, during a huge re-enactment in 2006, with the largest number of people packed onto that field since the first Battle of Hastings exactly 940 years before.

Watching those events, I have often asked myself why this particular date should drive us to engage with these moments in our past. They remain just as important, relevant, fascinating or tragic on any day of the year. Yet an anniversary is a direct link that forces us to stop and acknowledge the past. On the eleventh hour of the eleventh day of the eleventh month in 1918 the guns of Europe fell silent. After four years of the most bitter and devastating fighting, The war to end all wars was finally over. The Armistice was signed at 5 a.m. in a railway carriage in the Forest of Compiegne, France on November 11, 1918. On 7 November 1919, George V issued a proclamation calling for a two-minute silence, where 'all locomotion should cease, so that, in perfect stillness, the thoughts of everyone may be concentrated on reverent remembrance of the glorious dead'. Now, over eighty years later, a two-minute silence is still observed throughout the country. The formal end of the First World War is still marked 'lest we forget', not just to remember the appalling losses of that conflict but those who have been killed or injured in the line of duty ever since. Remembrance is something we should always be mindful of, but we cannot all think about everything all the time and having a special day ensures that each year we will be reminded of our debt to those who fought on our behalf and our obligations to those who continue to struggle with the consequences of war.

This book is my attempt to harness that connection and explore some of the most important and interesting moments from our past. Each entry gives a short precis of a day which continues to influence our present and future. Some, like Armistice Day and the Ides of March, you might have heard of; some I hope will come as a surprise. The day, for instance, that Napoleon ran away from a group of rabbits showed that the Great Emperor's supposedly inexorable rise to power was stoppable, whilst 2 August 1343, when Jeanne de Clisson became a pirate and single-handedly declared war on the king of France, is a vivid example that we don't have to be the victims of history – we can choose to make our own. Each entry is the merest tip of the iceberg; each page could be a book in its right and whole books have been written about each (sometimes many).

I relished the opportunity, while studying history at university or writing my previous books, of submerging myself into a particular period and concentrating on a limited group of characters, but this book has allowed me to roam from medieval Japan to modern California and from our hominid ancestors to Kellogg's breakfast cereals (and their strange inspiration), the Great Beer Flood of 1814 or the fateful meeting between Ada Lovelace and Charles Babbage that led to the invention of the first computer program). In the space I have I've tried to offer a flavour of 366 key stories – some well known, some less; some hilarious, some tragic – that I hope add up to an alternative history of the world.

There is so much more to history than battles and the deaths of kings. It is everything that has ever happened to anyone who has ever lived, it is the sum total of human experience, the darkest, weirdest, funniest, most remarkable, tragic or inspirational things any of us have ever done. Science, engineering, literature, politics, war, natural disasters and more; the past is a vast reservoir of stories that we can learn from.

Many, but not all, of these things can be explored through one day on which a decisive turning point occurred. Take, for example, 9 May 1941, when a handful of Royal Navy sailors boarded a sinking U-boat in the Atlantic and managed to secure an Enigma decryptions device and codebooks. This was the tool that Bletchley Park desperately needed to decipher the supposedly unbreakable German military communications and save countless lives. The brave actions of those sailors on that one day changed the outcome of the bloodiest war in human history.

My ambition has been to choose days whose events continue to reverberate today. From the birth of the NHS, the USA or Google to the death of Chinese naval exploration or the British Raj, there are particular days on which the tectonic plates of our politics or culture shifted. It has been fascinating researching accounts of participants and witnesses. Some knew that history was being made, such as the many crowding into Versailles to watch the Peace Treaty signing in 1919, while others had no idea that the day's events mattered, like the unimpressed readers of a scientific journal in which Charles Darwin's thesis on evolution was first published.

It is easier to spot the seismic shifts with hindsight, but

history is viewed from an ever-shifting perspective. A decade ago there might have been less Chinese history in a general book like this one, for example; now the rise of the Middle Kingdom has sent us rushing to search for lessons, clues and character-forming moments in its past. There may well have been less engineering and science in favour of treaties and coronations. But that's not always where the big changes are now being made. Today politicians seem unwilling or unable to make radical decisions for societies, the big shifts in how we live are emerging from the tech corporations who have transformed the way we eat, find partners, exercise, work, communicate and spend our leisure time. I hope many of the entries provoke reflection about the present. There are examples of financial crashes, and the failure to learn their lessons, there is an entry on the rise of fascism in Italy, featuring a 'strongman' who promised radical solutions that he insisted he alone could deliver. There is the resignation of a corrupt US president. There are too many examples of leaders blundering into wars which they then hoped they could control, only for the chaos and cost of the conflicts to overwhelm them. There is climate change, religious terrorism, fake news and nationalism. Though much has changed, much has stayed the same. If we are going to make better decisions about the challenges that face us, we could start by reminding ourselves how our forebears dealt with similar situations – and choose to act differently. The ambition, curiosity, fear, greed, altruism and love that shape our actions today are the same forces that drove the semi-mythical Agamemnon and Menelaus to the gates of Troy (the book's earliest story) thousands of years ago.

:H HISTORYHIT.TV

Before you get cracking into the book, a little something.

Two years ago I started a history club called History Hit. Amazingly, it has become the UK's leading destination for history fans and has served over 10,000 happy members.

I started it because I was frustrated that there didn't seem to be a place that history buffs could really indulge their passion for the past.

We offer our members access to hundreds of history documentaries, interviews and exclusive podcasts. They also get a weekly newsletter from me, exclusive events, extraordinary travel experiences and brilliant member offers.

I would love to offer you 3 months of free membership to see if you like what we are doing.

Just head to www.HistoryHit.tv and enter the code 'book' when completing your subscriber details for access to all of our great shows.

That's enough internet stuff. Enjoy the book and thank you for reading it.

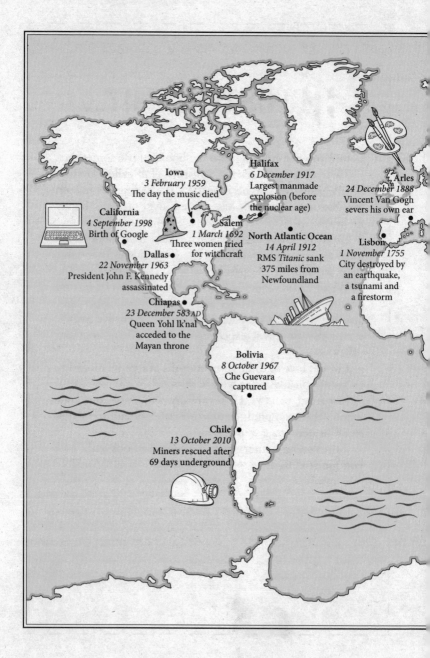

California
4 September 1998
Birth of Google

Iowa
3 February 1959
The day the music died

Salem
1 March 1692
Three women tried
for witchcraft

Halifax
6 December 1917
Largest manmade
explosion (before
the nuclear age)

Arles
24 December 1888
Vincent Van Gogh
severs his own ear

Dallas
22 November 1963
President John F. Kennedy
assassinated

North Atlantic Ocean
14 April 1912
RMS *Titanic* sank
375 miles from
Newfoundland

Lisbon
1 November 1755
City destroyed by
an earthquake,
a tsunami and
a firestorm

Chiapas
23 December 583 AD
Queen Yohl Ik'nal
acceded to the
Mayan throne

Bolivia
8 October 1967
Che Guevara
captured

Chile
13 October 2010
Miners rescued after
69 days underground

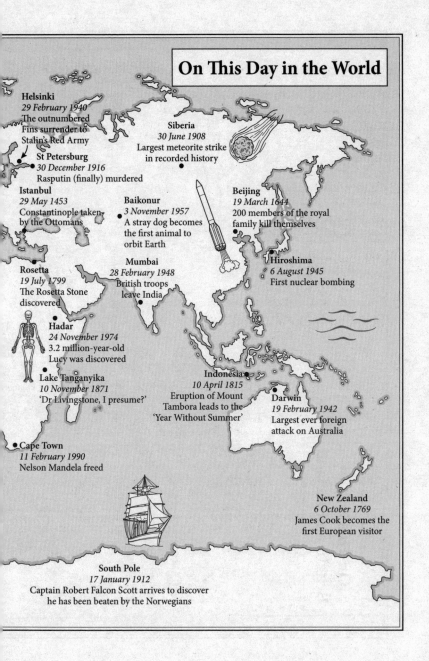

On This Day in the World

Helsinki
29 February 1940
The outnumbered
Fins surrender to
Stalin's Red Army

St Petersburg
30 December 1916
Rasputin (finally) murdered

Siberia
30 June 1908
Largest meteorite strike
in recorded history

Istanbul
29 May 1453
Constantinople taken
by the Ottomans

Baikonur
3 November 1957
A stray dog becomes
the first animal to
orbit Earth

Beijing
19 March 1644
200 members of the royal
family kill themselves

Rosetta
19 July 1799
The Rosetta Stone
discovered

Mumbai
28 February 1948
British troops
leave India

Hiroshima
6 August 1945
First nuclear bombing

Hadar
24 November 1974
3.2 million-year-old
Lucy was discovered

Lake Tanganyika
10 November 1871
'Dr Livingstone, I presume?'

Indonesia
10 April 1815
Eruption of Mount
Tambora leads to the
'Year Without Summer'

Darwin
19 February 1942
Largest ever foreign
attack on Australia

Cape Town
11 February 1990
Nelson Mandela freed

New Zealand
6 October 1769
James Cook becomes the
first European visitor

South Pole
17 January 1912
Captain Robert Falcon Scott arrives to discover
he has been beaten by the Norwegians

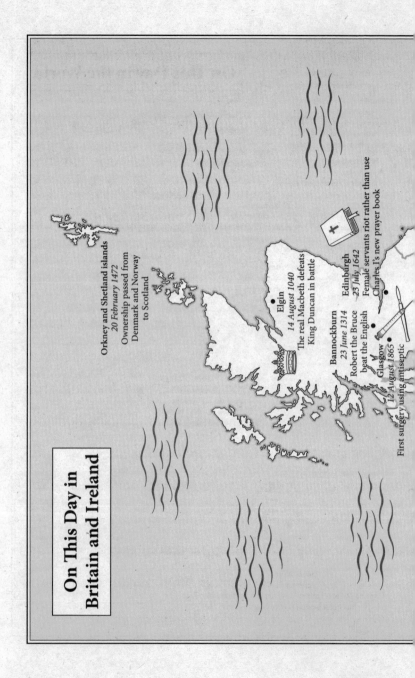

On This Day in
Britain and Ireland

Orkney and Shetland islands
20 February 1472
Ownership passed from
Denmark and Norway
to Scotland

● Elgin
14 August 1040
The real Macbeth defeats
King Duncan in battle

Bannockburn
23 June 1314
Robert the Bruce
beat the English

Edinburgh
23 July 1642
Female servants riot rather than use
Charles I's new prayer book

● Glasgow
12 August 1865
First surgery using antiseptic

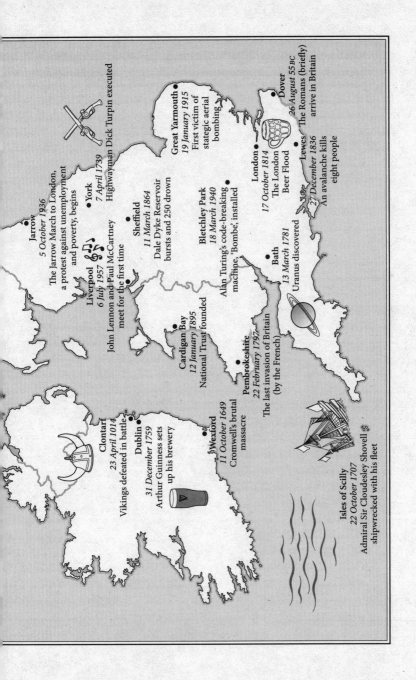

Jarrow
5 October 1936
The Jarrow March to London, a protest against unemployment and poverty, begins

York
7 April 1739
Highwayman Dick Turpin executed

Liverpool
6 July 1957
John Lennon and Paul McCartney meet for the first time

Sheffield
11 March 1864
Dale Dyke Reservoir bursts and 250 drown

Great Yarmouth
19 January 1915
First victim of stategic aerial bombing

London
17 October 1814
The London Beer Flood

Dover
26 August 55 BC
The Romans (briefly) arrive in Britain

Lewes
27 December 1836
An avalanche kills eight people

Bletchley Park
18 March 1940
Alan Turing's code-breaking machine, 'Bombe', installed

Bath
13 March 1781
Uranus discovered

Cardigan Bay
12 January 1895
National Trust founded

Pembrokeshire
22 February 1797
The last invasion of Britain (by the French)

Clontarf
23 April 1014
Vikings defeated in battle

Dublin
31 December 1759
Arthur Guinness sets up his brewery

Wexford
11 October 1649
Cromwell's brutal massacre

Isles of Scilly
22 October 1707
Admiral Sir Cloudesley Shovell shipwrecked with his fleet

JANUARY

1 January

On New Year's Day 1886, Lord Randolph Churchill, the Secretary of State for India, presented Queen Victoria with an extravagant gift: Burma.

Like his son Winston, Randolph was charismatic, single-minded and hugely ambitious. Although his Queen Empress already commanded the largest empire the world had ever seen, encompassing 20 per cent of the landmass of the globe and 25 per cent of the population, he saw no reason to stop. The once mighty kingdom of Burma was the latest ancient state outside Europe to collapse in the face of gunships, rifles, medicine and telegraphy. Its demise is a case study in British imperial aggrandisement spurred on by economic opportunity and racist thinking.

By the end of 1887, France, Britain's old adversary, was pushing its claims in northern Vietnam. Meanwhile British merchants in Rangoon railed against the Burmese authorities who resisted exploitation of their valuable teak forests. How could Britain stand by, they argued, as the French strengthened their hand in South East Asia, and British merchants practising free trade were subjected to petty bureaucracy and humiliation by a savage race?

When the Burmese authorities had the effrontery to fine the British for illegal logging, Churchill did not hesitate. In went the gunboats. The Burmese had no hope of stopping the imperial superpower. General Harry Prendergast marched into the palace in Mandalay and gave the royal family a night to pack. The most valuable royal jewel, the huge Nga Mauk ruby, disappeared, possibly into the pocket of a British officer.

As the royal family were loaded into bullock carts and taken into captivity between lines of red-coated imperial troops, British officers transformed the palace into a social club, building a bar and moving billiard tables into the queen's throne room.

Back in Britain Queen Victoria noted in her diary that New Year's Day was, 'Alas! a wretched dull, rainy morning.' She went for a drive in a carriage in the afternoon and answered a few telegrams. She did not mention Burma.

2 January

Something did not seem right. Late tonight in 1981, Constable Robert Hydes saw a car parked in the driveway of an industrial park in Sheffield and he suspected criminal behaviour involving drugs or vice. He ran a check on the number plate and it came up false. Hydes approached the car, and ordered the occupants out. A 24-year-old sex worker and a middle-aged man with a black beard emerged. The latter identified himself as Peter Sutcliffe. Hydes arrested him for driving with false number plates. Little did he know, he had just nabbed one of the twentieth century's most prolific serial killers.

Back at the police station, other officers quickly noticed the fact that Sutcliffe fitted the description of the so-called Yorkshire Ripper, as the press had dubbed the murderer who had been attacking women across the county between 1975 and 1980. The Ripper's victims had been assaulted with a hammer and then horribly mutilated. Some had been stabbed dozens of times. Sutcliffe was searched and found to be wearing a V-neck sweater under his trousers, the arms were pulled up his legs, the neck area exposed his genitals, the elbows were padded to act as kneepads.

The following day officers returned to the scene of the arrest and found a knife, hammer and rope, which he had dumped when he had convinced Constable Hydes that he was 'bursting for a pee'. The questioning intensified and two days later he admitted that he was the Ripper. He claimed that he had murdered the women because he had heard the voice of God urging him to do so.

At his trial, his legal team claimed a defence of diminished responsibility, but the judge rejected it and a jury found that he was guilty of thirteen murders and seven more attempted murders. The judge gave him twenty concurrent life sentences, and today he is one of only a handful of British prisoners who will never be released.

3 January

It is one of the greatest examples of unintended 'blowback' in intelligence history. Today in 1925 Benito Mussolini announced the final dismantling of Italian democracy. In a typically truculent and bizarre speech to the Italian Parliament, the prime minister confirmed what many had long feared, that fascism was a revolutionary force that was now in total control of the Italian state. He had come a long way since his first foray into politics, when he had been paid £100 a week by the British security agency, MI5, to produce propaganda taking on opponents of Italy's costly involvement in the First World War. A decade later, the former British agent had seized control of his country and sought to transform it into a military superpower capable of challenging his former paymasters for control of the Mediterranean basin.

Mussolini's speech was a response to a crisis that threatened his young government. The King of Italy had made him prime minister in 1922 in the hope that this bellicose, supremely confident strongman could overcome Italy's deep political schism that many feared would lead to civil war. A conservative establishment chose to ignore Mussolini's bluster and thought that he would protect their economic interests. Over the following months he dismantled the free press, the electoral system and had opponents murdered. It was his obvious responsibility for the assassination of one opposition politician that shook his regime in late 1924 and provoked his theatrical speech in January. In it he admitted that, 'if Fascism has been a criminal association, then I am the chief of that criminal association'; 'I alone,' he went on, 'assume political, moral, and historical responsibility for all that has happened.'

Following the speech he abolished all elections, made himself 'Head of the Government' and turned Italy into a police state. Italy became the first of western Europe's dictatorships, a beacon to those like Adolf Hitler, who saw in Mussolini a template for resurgent nation states united by political and racial purity and military might.

4 January

His owner signed the paperwork with great reluctance. But eventually today in 1853 Solomon Northup was granted his freedom after more than a decade as a slave.

Solomon was from New York, and had been born free, the son of a freed slave. He had married, loving his wife, he said, with a passion 'sincere and unabated'. The couple had three children, and while he was a farmer, they supplemented their income, he working as a fiddler, she as a cook. While doing this work, in 1841, he was lured by the prospect of a job in a circus, which took him to Washington, DC, a place where slavery remained legal. Despite the paperwork proving his freedom he was drugged then sold into slavery by 'monsters in the shape of men'.

He was shipped to New Orleans, and became a slave for twelve years – for most of his children's childhoods. His first owner, he wrote later, was at bottom a kind man, blinded by the world around him 'to the inherent wrong' of slavery, but he was sold on to crueller masters. Then he overheard the abolitionist views of a Canadian carpenter and told him his story. This man assisted him at great personal risk.

Later, with the help of a local writer, Solomon Northup published a memoir, *Twelve Years a Slave*. It became a bestseller, though legal action against his kidnappers failed. He rejoined his family and became an active abolitionist. Though his own end is unknown his memoir became a central tract of abolitionism, and today is a priceless source describing the institution of American slavery from within.

5 January

The Duke of Burgundy died within sight of his enemy's capital. Today in 1477, outside the walled town of Nancy in what now is north-eastern France, the final battle was fought that led to the disappearance of a significant European domain: the odd-shaped, fractured Duchy of Burgundy.

At Nancy the final Duke of Burgundy – Charles the Bold (or Charles the Reckless, depending upon the translation) – was brutally killed by Swiss mercenaries. He was short, stout and dark-haired, and had a fierce temper, from which his description as '*temeraire*' – bold, rash, reckless – derives. After the battle he was found in a frozen pool of water, his body pierced and his head split apart, recognisable as much from his long, ingrown toenails as from his face.

To modern eyes, used as we are to contiguous states, his territory looks bizarre, divided into separate northern and southern segments. But of course this was a personal fiefdom, accrued by marriage and warfare, not a region unified by any modern notion of 'nationality'. The duke's scattered holdings stretched from the North Sea coast, down through Luxembourg and parts of Alsace and Lorraine, to what is still called Burgundy in France. It would not have seemed so strange to people at the time, even if they were accustomed (which of course they weren't) to looking at territory on a map.

After his death, without any successor, his lands were shared between his rising and more powerful neighbours, France and the Habsburg Empire. Burgundy is more than a historical curiosity, its rise and falls illustrate the haphazard and transient nature of our European borders. Frontiers, which can feel like ancient, natural faultlines, are more often the product of a marriage bargain made or a battle lost.

6 January

For the only time in its thousand-year history, Westminster Abbey hosted a royal burial and a coronation on the same day, today in that most dramatic of years, 1066.

The abbey was the passion of King Edward the Confessor, the fulfilment of a promise he made to the Pope that he would erect a great shrine to St Peter in his western outpost of Christendom. Built in the Norman style he had so admired during his long exile in Normandy as a young man, it was the first magnificent Romanesque building in the kingdom of the Anglo-Saxons. It was completed a week before his death in late 1065.

Edward left no children. There was a vacancy on the throne of one of Europe's richest kingdoms, and several ambitious men determined to fill it. Home advantage was vital. Harold Godwinson, Earl of Wessex, moved fast. Edward was buried in his new abbey in the morning, and that very afternoon Harold crowned himself king. He was a warlord, fabulously wealthy and through a hastily arranged dynastic marriage to the sister of the most powerful family in the north, a unity candidate for those who wanted the throne to go to an Englishman.

Harold hoped that his speedy coronation would deter foreign rivals. He was wrong. William, Duke of Normandy, Edward's cousin, flew into a rage when he heard about the events in the abbey, and in Norway, the giant Viking, Harald Sigurdsson, the 'Hardrada' or 'Hard Ruler', started planning a massive Viking assault on England.

Westminster Abbey would host another royal coronation before the tumultuous year was out.

7 January

The first cross-Channel flight took place today in 1785 as a Frenchman and an American flew a balloon from Dover Castle to Calais. Just.

Jean-Pierre Blanchard came from a poor family outside Rouen and had seized on the new enthusiasm for ballooning as his road to fame and fortune. In the scientific ferment of the eighteenth century, French thinkers had realised that capturing hot air would provide enough lift to carry humans. In 1783 the first ascent in a hot-air balloon shocked Paris and Blanchard rode a wave of balloon-mania to London. After a few ascents he teamed up with American exile John Jeffries in a bid to cross the Channel.

At one o'clock the balloon rose gently from the castle grounds, as a crowd of spectators roared, and it drifted on the north-westerly breeze out over the Channel. Blanchard and Jeffries waved from a boat beneath the balloon, ready to man the oars which they hoped would enable them to steer the balloon. They were dressed in frock coats, stockings and wore ostrich feathers in their hats. It could be considered the first airmail as they carried letters from British aristocrats to their French counterparts.

It was a harrowing journey; several times they almost ditched. They jettisoned every piece of cargo they had and finally hurled their own clothes into the sea. It worked. After two and half hours they landed, shivering and somewhat traumatised, just outside Calais. The world's first international flight was complete.

8 January

The man who helped to birth modern science died today in 1642. Galileo Galilei – a man who pioneered the modern scientific method – continued to receive visitors and discuss his work until just before his death of fever and heart failure at the age of seventy-seven. On the same date, precisely three centuries later, perhaps the most brilliant scientific mind of his generation, Stephen Hawking, was born.

Galileo, as he is usually known, has been seen as the father of astronomy, of physics, and of the scientific method – quite a reputation. He is famous too for the denunciation his views received from the Church: for his trial by the Inquisition and his forced recantation. His ideas were revolutionary, and like all revolutionaries he seriously ruffled feathers.

As a youth, ironically, he had contemplated entering the Church himself until his father dissuaded him. His inquisitive mind and ceaseless experimentation saw him go on to teach, first in his home city of Pisa (where, famously, he dropped objects of differing weight from the top of the Leaning Tower to disprove Aristotle's claim that the speed of their fall was proportional). He also made telescopes. Armed with a telescope, Galileo showed that the heavens were imperfect – as the moon's irregularity showed – and that Copernicus's heretical argument that planets circled the sun must be right.

News that Stephen Hawking has died is breaking as I write. Having been born on the date of Galileo's death, the date of his own death, 14 March, is the anniversary of the birth of Albert Einstein. Coincidence, he would surely insist, but a pleasant circularity all the same.

9 January

Government and taxation have been locked in a symbiotic embrace since the dawn of time. The latter pays for the former. According to the Book of Genesis wealthier ancient Egyptians paid the pharaoh 20 per cent of their farm yields; the poor had to pay with their labour. Today in 1799 the British government introduced a sophisticated new form of taxation that was now possible thanks to the development of modern business practices, a cash economy and complex bookkeeping.

Faced with the costs of waging the most expensive war the British state had ever faced, Prime Minister William Pitt introduced a tax on income. If you earned over £60 you paid less than 1 per cent, but for the two or three per cent of families who earned more than £200 it rose to 10 per cent.

He promised it was temporary. And it was. Initially.

When peace came in 1802 it was abolished. But it was a pause, not an end to the conflict. In 1803, when Britain went back to war with Napoleon, income tax was reintroduced and lasted until 1816 by which time Napoleon was safely imprisoned in the South Atlantic. The tax was not popular. Opponents demanded that all government records be destroyed, and they were very publicly burned, but copies were kept in the archives, obviously.

In 1842 Sir Robert Peel turned to income tax to deal with a budget deficit. It was still temporary but governments of both stripes found it too lucrative, and slowly it was embedded at the heart of a modern revenue system. Today income tax is the largest single source of government revenue from Britain to the United States, Australia and beyond.

10 January

In 1901 on this day the Age of Oil dawned as a massive blowout in Texas sent black gold spurting fifty metres into the sky. It was a personal triumph for the tireless prospector Anthony Lucas (born in Croatia as Antun Lučić).

People had always known there was oil in Texas. It bubbled up in pools. Native Americans had used it as a remedy. Spanish conquistadors had waterproofed clothing with it. At the end of the nineteenth century the market for oil was growing. Private homes and public streets were lit by kerosene and the newly invented internal combustion engine had the potential to change the world if a supply of cheap fuel could be found.

Lucas became fixated on Spindletop Hill in north-east Texas where there was a network of sulphurous springs and gas seeping from the ground, which would burst into flame when lit. Investors came and went as he tried to cobble together the means to drill. Three attempts had to be abandoned. By the end of 1900 he was just another hopeless dreamer pumping money into a hole in the ground.

Then on 10 January 1901, while drilling at a depth of over 300 metres, great bubbles of mud were suddenly forced up to the surface. Minutes later six tons of drilling pipe was thrown into the air and the filthy roughnecks manning the rig sprinted to safety. Next there was a blast of gas, followed by an eruption of oil. Lucas and his team had provoked the world's first gusher.

It took nine days and nearly 1 million barrels of oil blasting out before Lucas could tame the well. Thousands of people had gathered to watch and overnight the nearby village of Beaumont was transformed as hordes of speculators moved in. It was the start of one of the most profound changes in history, making a huge impact on our way of life, and our planet.

11 January

It was the first-ever National Lottery – 'a very rich Lottery General' – and the winners were finally drawn today in 1569, three years after the tickets had been sold, at the old St Paul's Cathedral.

The first prize was the vast sum of £5,000, paid partly in cash but also in plate, in tapestries as well as in 'good linen cloth'. Across the country publicity posters were put up showing drawings of the prizes.

The aim of the lottery was to fund repair of the country's ports, with an emphasis on building for the nation's defence. (Since Henry VIII's time there had been concerns over the 'ruin and decay' of coastal towns.) England's Protestant identity and aspiration to Great Power status made its naval defences seem increasingly important.

In the case of this lottery, the value of the prizes equalled the total money raised. So how did the organisers make any profit? Well, tickets were sold some time earlier, in 1566 – meaning that the government was effectively granted an entirely interest-free loan. A ticket cost 10 shillings: much in excess of what an ordinary citizen could afford. While estimates of modern value are vague, it equated probably to well in excess of £100. As a result people could buy shares in a single ticket.

In addition to the monetary prizes was something that would now be considered highly unusual if not inappropriate. Ticket-holders were granted freedom from arrest, apart from for serious crimes: murder, felonies, piracy or treason.

The concept of a lottery had been tried in France but not previously in England. It would be used again, early the following century, to raise funds for the Virginia Company, which would establish a colony in the New World. Of course in recent years lotteries have become a routine part of modern life.

12 January

At the end of March 1895 a donation was made by Mrs Fanny Talbot – a 'motherly, bright, black-eyed woman' – of 4.5 acres of Welsh clifftop land overlooking Cardigan Bay to a new organisation, which became known as the National Trust.

Those 4.5 acres were called Dinas Oleu: 'Citadel of Light'. The art critic and historian John Ruskin, who had become a personal friend of Mrs Talbot, described her as 'curious beyond any magpie that ever was'. Though, he noted, she kept 'giving her spoons away instead of stealing them'. Both Talbot and Ruskin were keen on playing chess and carried on their games by communicating the moves of the pieces by letter.

Fanny Talbot had wanted for a long time, she said, to secure Dinas Oleu for the public for ever, and as such 'your association has been born in the nick of time'. This was the first bequest made to an organisation that had been founded on 12 January that year, in response to the change and encroachment wrought by the Industrial Revolution upon rural Britain.

Three people are considered to have founded this institution to own and care for places 'of Historic Interest or Natural Beauty': Octavia Hill, Sir Robert Hunter, and a Lake District clergyman called Hardwicke Rawnsley, who had encouraged the young Beatrix Potter to write and draw her first book, *The Tale of Peter Rabbit*, and who lived in a house in Grasmere once inhabited by William Wordsworth (which was later left to the Trust).

The National Trust is the largest membership organisation in the United Kingdom. Its extraordinary growth – and its impact on contemporary life – is a twentieth-century phenomenon. Today it is one of the country's largest landowners, looking after more than 600,000 acres, and owns hundreds of properties. Once protected by the Trust, it would take a specific Act of Parliament to sell, demolish or develop them.

13 January

Afghanistan is where empires go to die. Or, at the very least, take a terrible beating. Today in 1842 Britain, a global super-power, was humiliated, as its soldiers were slaughtered by Afghan tribesmen.

Britain had invaded Afghanistan to prevent the Russians from using it as a base from which to threaten India. Occupying it was the easy part. Once the British were in Kabul local resentment flared into open rebellion in late 1841. The British decided to retreat to Jalalabad nearly a hundred miles away, through snow-covered mountains in the heart of winter.

There were 700 British and 4,000 Indian troops under British command, and around 9,000 civilians. Sir William Elphinstone was the 59-year-old commander, a man of perfect breeding and manners, but ill and utterly indecisive. Tricked by assurances of a safe passage, he led a slow retreat that allowed the Afghans to prepare their ambush. As they entered the Kabul–Jalalabad pass they were assailed on either side. Elphinstone became withdrawn, sitting in silence before being captured by Afghans posing as good faith negotiators.

The British suffered thousands of casualties. Survivors froze to death or took their own lives. After six days the force had disintegrated. By the 13th the largest coherent group was about sixty-five British officers and men of the 44th Regiment of Foot. At the village of Gandamak they made a final stand. Invited to surrender, a sergeant roared, 'Not bloody likely!' When the ammunition ran out they fought with steel and fists before being overrun. One captain wrapped the regimental colours around himself and thanks to this attire was taken into captivity. The rest were massacred.

The following day only one person made it to Jalalabad – army surgeon William Brydon. Some prisoners were later returned, and a few Indian troops survived after a terrible ordeal in the mountains. The British Empire was not invincible.

14 January

Young people travelled from all over America for what was advertised as 'a Gathering of the Tribes'. Today in 1967 an event took place in San Francisco's Golden Gate Park, which with hindsight marked the outset of what has become known as the Summer of Love: the epitome of the 1960s counterculture which fundamentally affected attitudes throughout the Western world. It was punningly called the Human Be-In.

The Haight-Ashbury district of San Francisco had already become notorious as a centre of 1960s hippie counterculture. Late in 1966 the drug LSD was banned by the California legislature, instantly criminalising a large part of the district.

A small rally then intended, as its organisers proclaimed, to celebrate 'transcendental consciousness. The beauty of the universe, the beauty of being' – with (among other things) flowers, flutes, feathers, chimes, gongs, beads and incense – was followed by the much larger 'Human Be-In' early the following year.

A few thousand attendees gave way to some thirty thousand. Enduring themes included personal empowerment, ecology, communal living, higher consciousness (the attainment of which was much assisted by the ready availability of psychedelic drugs) and the rejection of what – in the phrasing of 'gurus' like poet Allen Ginsberg – was denounced as a stifling 'middle-class morality'.

Media attention was caught by this hippie, psychedelic event or 'happening'. Countless other similar gatherings followed, many with 'in' in their title. Authority was questioned, but real differences – direct political engagement over issues like the Vietnam War, on the one hand, and the vaguer, non-political peaceful protest favoured by the hippies – were submerged.

15 January

The new queen knew the power of pageantry. Every aspect of her coronation, today in 1559, was meticulously planned to proclaim peace, unity, stability and grandeur. Elizabeth I's coronation was joyful, celebrated by the English people, who lined the streets to watch her process to Westminster. Sick of the bloody rule of Mary Tudor, this reign promised hope and perhaps even the restoration of the Protestant faith.

Elizabeth's childhood was troubled. Her mother was famously beheaded, her father declared her illegitimate, and her own sister had her imprisoned in the Tower of London, where, for a time, she lived uncertain whether she would share the same terrible fate as her mother, Anne.

On Thursday 13 January, Elizabeth was rowed down the Thames in the royal barge as part of the great spectacle of her coronation, described by an onlooker as like the 'mystic marriage of Venice with the sea'. By Saturday, the streets were heaving with people gathered to watch the princess travel from the Tower, the great emblem of London, to Westminster, the heart of monarchy. From Fenchurch Street to Cheapside regalia adorned windows and doors; banners streamed from the tops of houses.

Elizabeth stepped through the great doors of Westminster Abbey, and on towards the chair of state, her train delicately carried by her cousin, the Countess of Lennox. She was seated, crowned and consecrated, in a manner described to have 'exceeded the bounds of gravity and decorum'. It was the last formal Latin service in England.

Although not averse to spying and torture, she endeavoured to win the hearts of her people and would later reminisce: 'When I received this ring I solemnly bound myself in marriage to the realm.' Her reign began on a snowy January day, and lasted for forty-four years. A steady presence in turbulent times.

16 January

An old soldier died in Tokyo today in 2014. He was ninety-one, and like millions of others he had been thrown into the maelstrom of the Second World War; unlike them, however, his service in the war lasted not for a few years but for decades.

Hiroo Onoda had joined the Imperial Japanese Army at age eighteen in 1940. He was descended from a long line of samurai warriors. Service to the emperor ran through his core. His father was killed fighting in China in 1943, and Onoda ended up being stationed on Lubang Island in the Philippines as the war reached its climax in late 1944. Bereft of hope, the Japanese troops were ordered to do what they could to resist American attacks, and never, under any circumstances, to surrender.

So he didn't.

The American military machine swept ashore weeks later. Onoda's unit was wiped out. He took to the hills and fought a lonely guerrilla campaign for the next twenty-nine years, refusing to believe that the war was over. He burned rice stores and exchanged fire with the police. Only when the Japanese government sent his former commanding officer Major Yoshimi Taniguchi to order him to surrender did Onoda do so. He turned over his sword, his rifle, ammunition and the ceremonial dagger, given to him by his mother for killing himself to avoid capture.

He arrived back in Japan to a hero's welcome. The living embodiment of the unswerving samurai ideals of Bushido, which had made the Japanese Empire such a resolute adversary.

17 January

As Captain Robert Falcon Scott arrived at the South Pole today in 1912, he found a Norwegian flag flying there already, planted by Roald Amundsen one month earlier. It was a bitter moment for Scott and his party.

Soon after Scott's expedition had anchored in an icy bay – the largest, best-equipped attempt ever to reach the South Pole – a party went on an exploratory mission. They were shocked to find other European ships: Amundsen's. The race for the pole was on.

Scott's ponies and mechanical sledges caused major problems in the cold and thick snow. Not familiar with using dogs, his men had to pull the sledges. Amundsen left first in a smaller group, using dogs and wearing light furs like the Eskimo, favouring speed (eating their dogs as the sledges became lighter) and protected from scurvy by the fresh meat. They were soon further south than any human had been. It seemed impossible for the British to beat them. 'And yet,' Amundsen wrote, 'and yet . . .'

Amundsen need not have worried. At the Pole was the vast, snow-covered plain he had imagined. The Norwegian flag was planted and they quickly set off back to their ship, the going 'splendid' – very different to Scott as his men struggled in deteriorating conditions. When they did reach the Pole the Norwegian flag was flying. 'Great God!' Scott wrote, 'this is an awful place'.

The return journey was worse. Temperatures plummeted. Supplies dwindled. Frostbite and scurvy struck. One man left the tent to die – a colleague described it as 'the act of a brave man and an English gentleman' – but the sacrifice failed to save his companions. 'It seems a pity,' scrawled Scott in his diary, 'but I do not think I can write more.'

While Scott became an archetype – of heroic failure – it was Amundsen ('free from all ostentation and egotism', as Ernest Shackleton admitted) who triumphed.

18 January

It was the birth of Germany. Long a geographical expression, never a state, the German Empire was officially proclaimed today in 1871 (after Prussia had decisively defeated France in the Franco-Prussian War). In an excruciating insult to their French adversaries, the ceremony took place at the Palace of Versailles near Paris. There King Wilhelm I of Prussia was proclaimed kaiser of the new empire; 18 January, the chosen date, had been the date on which Duke Frederick of Prussia had crowned himself king, and now it would also be the day that his descendant turned that kingdom into an empire.

The real force behind the birth of Germany was the 'Iron Chancellor' Otto von Bismarck. He used the threat of a resurgent France to terrify the patchwork of German states, and unite them behind Prussian leadership. It was not a difficult task. Once again a Bonaparte sat on the French throne (Napoleon I's nephew) and once again France was seeking to expand its borders, absorbing Nice and Savoy and hugely increasing the size of its overseas empire. Bismarck exploited a dynastic squabble, and goaded the French to declare war against Prussia. The French Army was utterly routed. Napoleon fled into exile. Just six months later the Prussians used the Palace of Versailles as the backdrop to one of history's greatest pieces of political theatre.

A religious altar was placed in the Hall of Mirrors, a stage was built opposite where Louis XIV, the Sun King, would have sat on his throne. Hundreds of senior German officers and members of German royal families crowded into the magnificent room, a Te Deum was sung, and Bismarck in full uniform read out a proclamation that was greeted with loud 'hurrahs'. Bismarck's empire was born beneath the paintings of King Louis routing German armies on the Rhine. Yet far from being the end of Franco-German rivalry this was just another way point in an intense and destructive conflict that would see further bloody confrontation, humiliation, occupation and regime change.

19 January

When humans master a new dimension, it's only a matter of time before it becomes militarised. Underground, sea, air, space and ether, the excitement of discovery is quickly tarnished by its use by warriors.

Aircraft had an immediate and obvious military benefit; they could fly over defences, look at the enemy's dispositions and perhaps even interrupt them. Less than a decade after the Wright brothers' first flight, an Italian dropped bombs on Libya. In the opening months of the First World War bombs were dropped in a haphazard fashion on Liege in Belgium and Paris, accompanied by a note demanding that France surrender.

As the Western Front stabilised and it became clear that this was a war that could not just be won on the battlefield but by breaking the will of a society, German planners developed the idea of strategic bombing. It would be a sustained assault on the enemy population to terminate their willingness to fight on. The kaiser agreed, but forbade bombing London in case any of his royal relatives were hurt. Today in 1915 an initial raid was launched. Two Zeppelin airships crossed the North Sea to attack Humberside. Strong winds pushed them off course, which meant that the first victims of the first proper campaign of strategic bombing in history were the sleepy seaside towns of King's Lynn, Sheringham and Great Yarmouth in Norfolk.

The bombs were dropped absolutely indiscriminately. Samuel Alfred Smith, a 53-year-old cobbler, became the first Briton to be killed by aerial bombardment. No target of military significance was hit, but the spectre of aerial assault on the civilian world was now a reality, no longer was fighting restricted to warriors in the front line. That first raid may have had elements of farce, but it was the birth of a new era that would see bombs kill millions and change the course of history.

20 January

At about eleven o'clock at night on 20 January 1936, King George V lay in a coma at Sandringham Castle. His doctor then administered two injections – of morphine and of cocaine – which he knew would hasten what he had described as the king's life 'moving peacefully towards its close'.

Much better, it was felt, that what seemed an inevitable announcement should break in the morning's *Times* than in a 'less appropriate' evening tabloid. 'A Peaceful Ending at Midnight' was the prepared headline that ran the following day.

Not until King George's doctor, Lord Dawson, and his wife, had died themselves was any mention made of the euthanasia (or the premeditated murder, depending upon your point of view) – the 'mission of mercy' as Lord Dawson had put it – which had actually taken place.

The heir to the throne, who would succeed as Edward VIII until he abdicated, had made clear that he did not want the king's life prolonged if the illness was certainly fatal. The fact that relations between him and his father were far from cordial has added to unease, though he could scarcely be said (in the light of subsequent events) to have yearned for the throne. The fact is, though, that it was a question not of *not prolonging* the king's life, so much as deliberately terminating it.

Meanwhile Dawson's own position was made clear during a subsequent discussion in the House of Lords. 'One should make the act of dying more gentle', he said, 'even if it does involve curtailment of the length of life' – 'if we cannot cure for heaven's sake let us do our best to lighten the pain'.

The amusing tale of George's last words – that on being told he would soon be recuperating at Bognor Regis he said, 'Bugger Bognor!' – may in fact be a fiction, invented to cover a problem for which British society has still not found a satisfactory solution.

21 January

At the close, traders looked at their screens in disbelief. The London Stock Exchange had experienced 'a bloodbath'. Today in 2008, in response to a financial crisis in the United States, the Financial Times Stock Exchange 100 Index (or FTSE100) collapsed. Its fall of 323.5 points was the biggest one-day points fall in its history, wiping £77 billion off the values of Britain's biggest companies. The Great Recession, of which the crash was an opening salvo, has had an enormous impact. The war in Syria, Trump, Brexit, resurgent nationalism and even *Love Island* have all been linked to the economic hardship inflicted by the upheavals of 2008.

Historians were not hugely surprised. The world's first stock market emerged in the seventeenth-century Dutch Republic. Shares in the Dutch East India Company could be bought and sold, which made them attractive to investors. If they needed to withdraw their money, they could, via the stock exchange. Companies were happy because it meant it was easier to raise money from the selling of stock to investors. The problem emerged almost immediately; humans do not make rational long-term decisions. We are passionate lunatics who get greedy, take fright quickly and stampede with the herd.

Giant spikes and vertiginous drops have shaped the history of stock markets. When times are good, people mortgage their houses to put into stocks; at the whiff of trouble they sell everything and precipitate exactly the crash that they feared. The first book on the stock market was *Confusion of Confusions*, written in 1688 by the wealthy Dutch merchant Joseph de la Vega. In it he warns would-be speculators, 'Profit in the share market is goblin treasure: at one moment, it is carbuncles, the next it is coal; one moment diamonds, and the next pebbles . . . He who wishes to become rich from this game must have both money and patience.' Throughout history crashes have been caused by those of us who lack both.

22 January

There were kings of France who refused to go into battle without them. Curiously, they were just as sought after in the armies of German and Italian princes. In the fourteenth and fifteenth centuries the most feared infantrymen in Europe were the Swiss. Young men, bred in mountainous communities with limited economic opportunities, developed over several generations a martial culture that made them Europe's shock troops, units who fought not for their country, but for the highest bidder.

Today in 1506, under their veteran commander Kaspar von Silenen, a contingent of Swiss soldiers arrived in Rome. They were there to protect the 'Mother of Christianity' from 'any tyrant, avid for wealth' according to one preacher, and the Pope, Julius II, granted them the title 'Defenders of the Church's Freedom'. It was the start of a period of service to the papacy that lasts until today, making the Pontifical Swiss Guard one of the world's oldest active military units still in existence.

For all the lofty claims made of them, they chose to fight for the Pope as their countrymen chose to fight for anyone else, because he was paying them hard cash. Time and again they proved the wisdom of the investment. Their columns of armour-clad pikemen won victory after victory, helping to build an unbeatable reputation that became central to their brand.

They were willing to die for their clients. Von Silenen and his men were hacked to pieces in a surprise attack by the Duke of Urbino a decade later, but the cantons of Switzerland yielded new recruits and another decade after that the Swiss Guard famously made a heroic stand against the rampaging forces of Emperor Charles V as they sacked Rome. Heavily outnumbered, the Swiss Guard were annihilated, almost to a man, but they bought time for Pope Clement VII to escape. No wonder his successors have continued to regard the Swiss Guard as great value for money.

23 January

Nearly one million died. It was the worst natural disaster in recorded history. This morning in 1556 Chinese sources described an 'earthquake catastrophe' in Shaanxi. An unprecedented wave of destruction destroyed most of the province's buildings and caused damage as far away as Beijing, Chengdu and even Shanghai, 800 miles away.

A 500-mile wide area was destroyed. In some counties it was reported that well over half of the population were killed. Many of the casualties lived in *yaodongs*, or caves, hollowed out of the silty soil of the Loess Plateau. Blown onto the plateau from the Gobi Desert by thousands of years of steady westerly winds, the soft rock seemed to be a natural gift to the people who burrowed into it for shelter. The earthquake turned these boltholes into death traps. Caves collapsed or their terrified occupants were swamped by landslides.

A chronicler recorded that 'mountains and rivers changed places and roads were destroyed'. In some places, 'the ground suddenly rose up and formed new hills, or it sank abruptly and became new valleys'. Great canyons were torn in the earth, streams and springs appeared out of nowhere and 'huts, official houses, temples and city walls' suddenly and dramatically collapsed. The shock waves shattered a large number of the ancient collection of steles, or carved stone slabs, for which Xi'an, the provincial capital, was famous.

People cast around for meaning in the face of an overwhelming natural disaster. The first European to hear of it, a Franciscan friar who visited in 1556, predictably ascribed it to divine punishment for people's sins. One Chinese scholar was less interested in cause and instead wished to learn its lessons. His advice prefigured modern practice by 500 years. Do not rush outside immediately, he warned, many had died in the open. Instead 'crouch down and wait. Even if the nest has collapsed, some eggs may remain intact.'

24 January

The corpses that lay thick on the ground spoke of the humbling of a superpower. Today in 1900, the British were badly defeated by the Boers at Spion Kop – kop being the Boer word for 'hill' and finding its way into English descriptions of steep football terraces, like the 'Kop' at Liverpool Football Club's Anfield ground.

Accounts of the battle are notable for what seems in hindsight almost comical incompetence. A British advance was slowed by the fact that their unwieldy baggage train included General Sir Charles Warren's cast-iron bath. Having climbed the hill in the darkness, shrouded also in mist, the British seized what they thought was the summit, only to realise, once dawn broke, that in fact the Boers continued to occupy higher ground.

With a thin soil quickly giving way to rock, 'trenches' dug were less than half a metre deep. British artillery, further down the hill, while relatively powerful, was more hindrance than help, one soldier remarking that 'our gunners, by the inaccuracy of their fire did far more damage to our front line of infantry than to the Boers!'

It seems appropriate for a battle more notable for its trivia connections than for the events themselves that two men present would come to number among the twentieth century's most famous individuals (and would become, of course, bitter rivals): Winston Churchill and Mahatma Gandhi.

Churchill was a journalist stationed in South Africa, describing the shallow trenches 'choked with dead and wounded'. Gandhi, meanwhile – working as a lawyer in Natal – founded a volunteer Ambulance Corps, tending, and evacuating, those very wounded, and was awarded a medal in the aftermath for his bravery.

Warfare, of course, was changing fast, and it seems appropriate for this pointer to the future that such eminent individuals were there as young men.

25 January

Al (Alphonse) Capone was so notorious that his name and the term 'mobster' are almost synonymous, just as his look (slicked hair, pinstriped suit, pocket handkerchief, fedora hat) came to define the way a racketeer of this period would present himself.

But today in 1947 he died aged forty-eight after a long decline in his mental faculties. Untreated syphilis had caused his brain to degenerate. He lived out his final years, after the Second World War, in his Florida mansion, before a stroke and cardiac arrest led to his death. One of his old cronies who visited him in Florida had reported him as being 'nuttier than a fruitcake'. And a psychiatrist who analysed him late in life concluded that he had the mental age of a twelve year old.

He was born in New York City to Italian immigrants and later moved into the world of organised crime. It has been suggested that he was responsible for over thirty deaths. Capone's rise as a gangster in the United States coincided with the era of Prohibition, in which alcoholic liquor was forbidden by law but 'bootleggers' brewed alcohol secretly to meet a persistent demand, with vast profits being made by violent gangs. (The term 'bootlegger' dated back to Georgian England, when smugglers liked to conceal packages in their large boots.) In 1931 he was convicted for income tax evasion and then at the age of thirty-three sent to the penitentiary in Atlanta, Georgia.

When it was clear Capone had contracted syphilis, the condition could have been treated with an injection of penicillin. But this was something that Capone, who had a terror of medical needles – trypanophobia, to give it its fancy name – refused to contemplate. It seems grimly ironic that a man so associated with violence and criminality died young because he was unwilling to undergo a simple injection.

26 January

Today is both Australia Day and Republic Day in India. The former celebrates the British arriving in Australia, the latter, the British finally leaving India. The fact that both are still marked indicates a serious divergence in the way that British colonialism began, was managed, and came to an end – as well as divergence in the way in which it is remembered.

The fundamental difference between Australia and India (both, of course, became unified regions in the manner that they did as a result of British intervention) was that while Australia was what became known as a 'settler' colony, India was not. Substantial numbers of British people relocated – or in many cases were forcefully transported as a means of punishment for various crimes – to Australia, while in India the British always constituted a tiny, albeit dominant, ruling minority.

In India, the existing indigenous population was much larger, had more advanced governmental traditions, *and* – since it inhabited the Eurasian mainland – had had long exposure to European pathogens. So while diseases like measles, smallpox and tuberculosis wreaked devastation among the indigenous people in Australia (as they had done in the Americas) it was more likely to be the European population that had health problems and succumbed to disease in the subcontinent.

In the wake of decolonisation, India declared itself a republic while Australia of course has not, though the London Declaration of 1949 did enable the former to continue to accept the British monarch as Head of the Commonwealth.

So while Australia Day commemorates the British flag being raised at Sydney Cove in 1788, India's Republic Day in 1950 naturally recognises the birth of a republic and at the same time its independence.

27 January

One nation's naval hero is another nation's blood-slaked pirate. Henry Morgan was the scourge of the Spanish Main, hated and feared by Spaniards who scared their children into obedience with tales of his monstrous crimes. Yet the English government knighted him, appointed him Lieutenant Governor of Jamaica and gave him a full state funeral upon his death.

Morgan was particularly active during the second half of the seventeenth century against the Spanish Empire in the Americas and the Caribbean, and it was today – on 27 January 1671 – that he and his soldiers arrived at Panama City. Setting out on the mission he had led thirty-six ships and some 2,000 'buccaneers' – an astonishing number which clearly suggests that his raids enjoyed official support.

Having seized the Atlantic port of Chagres, the party ascended the Chagres River – at times by canoe – before wading through swamp and hacking their way through thick rainforest. The Spanish governor knew of the group's approach and sent men to confront them, but Morgan was able to repel the attacks.

Outside the city it was obvious that they were significantly outnumbered. They were not, however, unnerved and the Spanish assumption that they were retreating was a disastrous misapprehension: cavalry rushing out to confront them met with a barrage of disciplined and devastating fire. In the ensuing battle the Spanish lost almost 500 men while Morgan lost only around 15.

Determined not to surrender the city, the Spanish governor ordered barrels of explosives detonated next to largely wooden buildings, and the resulting conflagration lasted for a full day. When Morgan's men did capture the city, the place they ransacked was already a charred ruin which required fundamental rebuilding.

Nevertheless, it was the end of a successful expedition by Morgan, a pirate whose violence and rapacity aligned him neatly with English foreign policy.

28 January

It was the end of one of the most famous, as well as most infamous, reigns in English history – today in 1547 Henry VIII died.

Historians have argued, though are unlikely to agree, about the cause of his death at the age of fifty-five. He was vastly overweight (with a 54-inch waist) and was tormented by pus-filled boils that covered his body. Was this the result of a jousting accident a decade earlier, which also caused severe mood swings and a personality shift? Perhaps.

Henry is best known for his six marriages, and his efforts to have his first marriage to Catherine of Aragon annulled. His disagreement with the Pope over the annulment led him to initiate the English Reformation. Henry's alleged final words – 'Monks! Monks! Monks!' – sound, as perhaps they are meant to sound, like those of one who was tormented by his action in evicting them during the Dissolution of the Monasteries.

Having been embalmed, his body first lay in state and was then moved to Windsor and buried in a vault next to Jane Seymour. A century later the decapitated body of Charles I would be lain with him.

For all the harm, and the cruelty he inflicted, there is no doubt regarding the great changes in England's status wrought by and during his reign. The land he inherited was a peripheral Catholic kingdom – small and rather backward. It could not compete with a rising global empire like that of Spain.

By the time he died, while the monarchical succession was disputed, the first shoots were beginning to emerge of a country that yearned to look outwards, to take its place in the world: transfixed (even if Henry largely ignored it himself) by the 'great ocean sea' to the west and by the unknown lands on the other side of it.

29 January

It was a new kind of war, and for the first time ever civilians back home were receiving regular reports from the battlefield. So today in 1856, the UK's highest medal for gallantry, the Victoria Cross, was born, to honour acts of conspicuous courage during the Crimean War. The metal from which the medals have been cast has traditionally derived from cannons then captured from the Russians.

For the first time the Crimean War saw the presence of journalists at the battlefront and so there was immediate reporting of incidents of bravery. As a result popular feeling grew in Britain that these acts should be recognised, regardless of class background or length of service.

In the first ceremony, held on 26 June 1857 in London's Hyde Park, the Queen invested 62 of the 111 Crimean recipients. One jewellery company – Hancocks of London – has manufactured every Victoria Cross since the medal's inception.

Eight medals were awarded, then forfeited, up until 1908, when George V's heartfelt opposition put a stop to the practice. 'Even were a VC to be sentenced to be hanged for murder,' the king wrote, 'he should be allowed to wear his VC on the scaffold.'

The medal has thus far been awarded 1,358 times to 1,355 recipients. Three people have won the award twice – have won, what is called, 'the VC and Bar', recognition that is, as George VI remarked, 'very unusual indeed'.

Arthur Martin-Leake, of the Royal Army Medical Corps, won his first during the Boer War and a second early in the First World War. Noel Chavasse, also of the Royal Army Medical Corps, did so twice during the First World War, dying of his injuries (his gravestone bearing the unique engraving of the two medals). The New Zealand soldier Charles Upham won two Victoria Crosses during the Second World War – 'an inspiration to the Battalion', as his first citation declared.

30 January

On a bitterly cold January day in 1649, Charles I, anointed king of England, addressed the crowd who had gathered at Whitehall with what would be his last words before he was decapitated, by order of Oliver Cromwell.

Charles's execution was the result of the first war crimes trial of a sitting head of state, and subsequently the first regicide in history. After six years of bloody war, and the loss of 7 per cent of the English population, Cromwell and Parliament had successfully overthrown the monarchy.

That morning, following a sad last meal of claret and a piece of bread, Charles walked through St James's with his pet dog. At his execution, he wore two heavy shirts in order to protect his body from the chill, and to not appear to shake with fear. He gingerly tucked his hair beneath a cap; 'Is my hair well?' he asked the executioner, before encouraging him to make the blow strong and accurate.

At 2 p.m. he laid his head on the block, and after a short pause the executioner did as he was bid. The axe fell heavily and severed his head from his body in one blow. A witness recalled that his death was met with 'such a groan as I have never heard before, and desire I may never hear again'. People had eagerly gathered below the scaffold to await the blood that would inevitably make its way through the cracks in the wood. They dabbed at it with handkerchiefs, to covet as a sacred relic or trophy.

After Charles's execution Cromwell made himself Lord Protector of the Commonwealth, inflicting a rigid Puritanism upon the country.

In 1661, twelve years later, Charles II ordered the body of Oliver Cromwell to be exhumed and posthumously beheaded in revenge for his father's execution. Cromwell's corpse was dragged on a sledge through London, so people could witness the deteriorating body. It was hung on the gallows before his head was severed and skewered on a pole above Westminster Hall, where it remained on grisly display until the late 1680s.

31 January

As global temperatures increase, Arctic ice melts and sea levels rise, the past provides a vision of our future. Today in 1953 Britain and its North Sea neighbours were hit by a catastrophic flood. It was one of the worst natural disasters in recorded British history. Climate scientists warn that it may be a harbinger.

In late January 1953 a deep low-pressure system developed off the coast of Denmark. North-easterly winds drove a mass of water into the British coast and the narrows of the Channel. This surge was exacerbated by a low atmospheric pressure, which provided less resistance to mounting water levels and a very high spring tide. The combination wrought havoc.

Seawater poured over sea defences and raced inland. One thousand miles of the east coast was damaged. Tens of thousands of homes and buildings were damaged and around 35,000 people had to be evacuated. The village of Crovie on the Moray Firth was almost entirely swept into the sea, and the community suffered lasting damage as many inhabitants never returned. Around Skegness the flooding reached three miles inland. Elderly people were carried to safety on makeshift rafts through fast-moving flood waters more than a metre deep. Over 50 people died on Canvey Island in Essex. Even east London saw hundreds made temporarily homeless. The damage has been estimated at over £1 billion in today's money.

Flood defences were rebuilt and strengthened following the disaster. The UK moved to defend its capital by launching the Thames Barrier project. This was an ambitious attempt to protect the entire London area flood plain from a repeat disaster. The Barrier was opened in 1984. At first it closed around once a year. In the winter of 2017/18 it closed three times to protect the city from tidal surges. Experts are now calling for an even more extensive barrier to make sure London can be protected from the storms of the future.

FEBRUARY

1 February

One of the greatest strategic mistakes in history was made today in 1917 by the Imperial German government.

The First World War was going badly. The terrible and bloody offensive at Verdun had failed to break the will of the French on the Western Front even though their losses were huge. Britain had unleashed the vast Somme offensive, with enormous casualties on both sides, but costing the lives of hundreds of thousands of experienced German troops. The battleships of the German navy were penned in their bases by a superior British fleet. The allies had more men, more munitions and more access to global raw materials.

In desperation the German admiralty advocated sending its fleet of U-boats into the Atlantic to sink any and every ship arriving in Britain. Germany could starve the UK into making peace. The problem, as German Chancellor Bethmann-Hollweg pointed out, was that many of those ships belonged to neutral America; sinking them would bring the United States, the world's largest economy, into the war on the allied side.

The kaiser's naval advisers promised their volatile emperor that the Americans were 'undisciplined' and even if they did send troops the U-boats would ensure that 'not one American will land on the Continent'. The kaiser agreed and taking a terrible gamble he signed the order for 'unrestricted U-boat warfare'.

The chancellor said simply, 'Germany is finished.'

The United States did enter the war in April 1917, and mobilised a vast army that at its peak saw 2 million 'Doughboys' in France, disembarking at a rate of up to 10,000 in a single day. Not one troopship was sunk by German U-boats, nor did they manage to knock Britain out of the war. Germany now faced insurmountable odds.

2 February

It was an extraordinary gathering of European royalty. Only the funeral of Queen Victoria, today in 1901, could have drawn such a number of mourners. Kaiser Wilhelm of Germany had come to Windsor Castle, along with the kings of Greece, Norway, Belgium and even Archduke Franz Ferdinand of Austria. Not for nothing had she been called the 'grandmother of Europe'.

In Britain (and in its empire) it was the end of an era. No monarch had been buried in this country for sixty-four years. With life expectancy only creeping into the forties, plenty of Britons had come into the world and died in the interim.

Ways of carrying out royal funerals had to be significantly changed for a new century. Having insisted upon a military funeral, as the daughter of a soldier, Victoria's coffin was mounted upon a gun carriage, a custom which has endured.

An innovation that has not endured was her instruction that mourners were to be dressed in white. Her own body and her coffin were also draped in white. Having died at Osborne House, on the Isle of Wight, mourners could witness the rare sight of a state funeral cortège travelling by ship.

In her coffin, at Victoria's side, was placed one of Prince Albert's dressing gowns, along with a plaster cast of his hand. Less openly, a lock of her late Scottish attendant John Brown's hair, and his photograph, were secreted in her left hand, concealed from her family by an artfully positioned bunch of flowers.

3 February

It was just after midnight when the plane took off. The stiff breeze sent the snow horizontally across the airstrip. The owner of the aircraft charter company watched as it turned to the north-west, and then saw the tail light slowly descending until it was out of sight. Fearing the worst and unable to raise the pilot on the radio, he took off in another plane as soon as it was light and followed the route. Within minutes he spotted its wreckage only five miles north of the airport. There were no survivors. Three of America's greatest rock 'n' roll stars and their pilot had all been killed. The loss of Buddy Holly, Ritchie Valens and the Big Bopper today in 1959 has been mourned ever since. According to Don McLean 3 February was 'The day the music died.'

Buddy Holly had been sick of the long coach journeys across the freezing Midwest in the grip of winter. After a gig in Clear Lake, Iowa he had chartered a plane to take him to Minnesota. The Big Bopper had the flu so he had been given a seat by Holly's bassist, while Ritchie Valens won his seat in a coin toss against Holly's other guitarist.

The official inquiry found that the pilot was insufficiently qualified for the night flight in very poor visibility, and unfamiliar with instruments like the gyroscope which should have told him he was descending rather than climbing. Whatever the cause, the plane smashed into the ground nose first at nearly 200 mph. The three musicians were thrown through the torn fuselage into the field beyond, all sustaining 'gross trauma to the brain'.

Buddy Holly had pioneered a new era in music. His death was a catastrophe to a generation of fans who had embraced revolutionary rock 'n' roll culture. But even the death of one of its founders could not staunch its unstoppable advance. Holly continued to exercise a powerful influence over artists like The Beatles, Elton John, Bob Dylan, Eric Clapton and the Rolling Stones, which ensured that contrary to McLean's pessimistic assessment the music most certainly survived.

4 February

The warlords had come to divide up the world. Today in 1945 was the first day of a famous conference held in Yalta, in the Crimea, between Franklin Roosevelt, Joseph Stalin and Winston Churchill: the leaders of the Allied nations of the United States, the USSR and the United Kingdom. Stalin, who was afraid of flying, had refused to travel further.

The Second World War, of course, had not yet ended, but with the Red Army rampaging across central Europe it was only a matter of time. The defeat of Nazi Germany in particular had seemed inevitable at least since the previous autumn, though it was not until 30 April that Adolf Hitler committed suicide.

With the division and occupation of Germany already agreed, much of the decision making at Yalta involved the likely balance of power between the democratic and the Communist worlds. Broadly speaking, Stalin's promises were believed: that there would be free elections, for instance, across occupied eastern Europe: in Poland, Czechoslovakia, Hungary, Romania and Bulgaria.

It was assumed (wrongly as it transpired) that Russia's assistance would be needed in the defeat of Japan: a strong incentive for accepting Stalin's assurances. The USSR's entry into this eastern conflict was guaranteed within two to three months of the German surrender, though by the later conference held in Potsdam in late July Japan's 'prompt and utter destruction' also seemed a matter of time. The two atomic bombs were dropped on Hiroshima and Nagasaki early in August, guaranteeing Japanese surrender without the land invasion previously envisaged.

Since the USSR occupied eastern Europe at the time, both the United States and UK assumed that there was little they could do to affect Stalin's actions. As one member of the American team put it, 'it was not a question of what we would *let* the Russians do, but what we could *get* the Russians to do'.

5 February

Today in 1885 King Leopold of Belgium gained international recognition for his personal rule over the Congo basin, through an entity he would name the Congo Free State (now called the Democratic Republic of the Congo). It was one of the most remarkable individual land grabs in history, and was the prelude to enslavement and genocide on an appalling scale. This terrible history helps to explain why even today the Congo, a country with vast natural wealth, remains one of the world's poorest and most misgoverned countries.

Belgium was a small, neutral kingdom, hemmed in on all sides, with no room to expand. As other European powers absorbed vast tracts of land in the nineteenth century, King Leopold of Belgium raged at his country's confinement. He dreamed of buying a province of Argentina, renting Asian colonies from the Spanish or seizing bits of Africa, but the Belgian government refused to allow it. So as a private citizen he decided to lead efforts to secure the Congo basin for philanthropic and charitable reasons, protecting the locals from instability and slave traders from the east.

It suited the world's powers to have Congo as a neutral buffer, and they agreed. Within months 1 million square miles of territory along the Congo River had become Leopold's personal possession. The charitable front was quickly dropped and Leopold unleashed appalling atrocities as he forced the Congolese to collect ivory and then to harvest and process rubber. Several million Africans were murdered, a huge number were mutilated.

Leopold, who never visited his personal fiefdom, stuffed millions of pounds into a secret bank account and died in his bed in 1909, and many of his Belgian subjects remembered him fondly as the 'Builder King'.

6 February

It was a long time coming. Today, on 6 February in 1918, a significant slice of British women finally got the vote. Practically all property qualifications for men were abolished and they were able to vote from the age of twenty-one. Women over thirty could vote provided that they satisfied minimum property qualifications. Full gender equality had to wait until the Representation of the People (Equal Franchise) Act of 1928.

Later in 1918, in November, the Parliament (Qualification of Women) Act permitted women to stand for election, though the only woman then elected represented Sinn Féin and refused to take up her seat. Not until Nancy Astor was elected a year later did a woman actually sit in the House of Commons.

At least as important, then, as the desire to increase the female vote – given both the suffragist and suffragette campaigns as well as the contribution women had made to the war effort – was the feeling that returning soldiers could not be denied a vote. The changes saw the size of the electorate jump from under 8 million to over 21 million – a tripling of those entitled to vote, the largest increase ever and a fundamental change to the political system in this country. Among other changes was the adoption of voting on a single day.

One significant reason for the failure to establish complete gender equality in 1918 was the fear that, with so many men killed during the war, to have done so would have ensured that women comprised a clear majority of the electorate: a dangerous departure from precedent!

After a sizeable majority in the House of Commons, Lord Curzon, president of the National League for Opposing Woman Suffrage, abstained in the upper house, other opponents also lost heart, and the bill passed by 134 votes to 71.

7 February

No one in the Americas was expecting the Spanish Inquisition. But that's what they got today in 1569. On the orders of King Philip II of Spain, tribunals of the infamous body known as 'the Spanish Inquisition' opened across the Atlantic in South America – in the modern countries of Mexico and Peru, where its practices were particularly grim.

For centuries, as the Christian kingdoms in Spain unified and fought to expel Muslim rivals, religious unity had been an abiding preoccupation. In 1492, the same year America was discovered, the 'Reconquista' was completed, and Jews were expelled. Such things were due to the Spanish monarchs' conviction that they held a divine, *Christian* mission to impose correct faith and doctrine throughout Spain and – as its empire grew – throughout the world.

An 'inquisitor general' was appointed within Spain, an equivalent for the colonies soon followed. A top target were secret 'Judaizers'. Don Luis de Carvajal was from a Portuguese-Jewish family. In the New World he was able to build a life and a fortune as a businessman and soldier. In the 1580s he was dragged before the Inquisition and admitted practising his Jewish faith in secret. Nine of his family were tortured and burned at the stake in the heart of Mexico City; one of them, a nephew, had tried unsuccessfully to avoid this fate by committing suicide. He jumped out of a window but survived and was killed with his family.

Other victims include men like Nicolás de Aguilar, a colonial administrator who tried to protect the Indians from the attentions of the Franciscan priests or men rumoured to be homosexual. Dozens of people are believed to have been burned in Spanish America alone, but the institution also owes its appalling reputation to vitriolic Protestant propaganda during the Reformation, which painted it (unreliably) as the archetype of Catholic illiberalism and brutality.

8 February

There was a bold Japanese plan to press their claim as a regional power. Destroyers were sent using darkness to disguise their approach, and carry out a surprise attack on their greatest adversary in the Pacific. But this was February 1904, not December 1941. The base they were approaching was not Pearl Harbor but Port Arthur in Manchuria, and the enemy was not the Americans but the Russians.

Admiral Tōgō Heihachirō had studied naval warfare in Britain. His fellow cadets at Dartmouth Naval College had called him 'Johnny Chinaman', but he had thrived in the bosom of the world's best navy and had returned to Japan to command a British-built ship and play a central role in turning the Japanese navy into a modern, industrial fighting force.

As China grew weaker, her predatory neighbours circled. Russia wanted Manchuria, Japan eyed Korea. Russian officials, blinded by European domination of the globe, refused to take the Japanese seriously and laughed at the idea of war with Japan.

The attack was Tōgō's idea. His fleet of fast, torpedo-carrying destroyers would swoop down on the Russians, without the niceties of a declaration of war, and sink them in their own base. The Russian fleet had its lights on while its officers attended a splendid party.

In the early hours the Japanese attacked. Russia's most powerful ship, *Tsesarevich*, was struck by a torpedo. Another was set on fire and a third was holed by the bow. While not a decisive victory, the weakened Russians were blockaded in their base while Japan overran Korea. The following year Admiral Tōgō annihilated a reinforcing Russian fleet and Russia collapsed, seething with revolution.

Japan was the first Asian power to win a war against the Europeans since the start of the modern era. The British officers who had once bullied Tōgō now referred to him as the 'Nelson of the East'.

9 February

Lord Darnley, the 'lusty and well proportioned' husband of Mary Queen of Scots, was brutally murdered on this day in 1567, at his home, Kirk o' Field House, in Edinburgh.

Prior to his death, Darnley had been recovering at home, from either smallpox or syphilis; the latter attributed to reckless and debauched behaviour. Unknown to him, in the weeks before his death the cellars of the house were being packed with gunpowder, enough to ensure the building would be obliterated. At around 2 a.m. the silence of the night was broken as a huge explosion tore through Kirk o' Field, reducing it to rubble. Instead of being incinerated in his sleep, Lord Darnley escaped the inferno, but was intercepted before he could flee for his life. Later in the day, he was discovered, partially clad, dressed only in his nightshirt, beside a pear tree in the orchard. He had been strangled to death.

As royal protocol dictates, Mary observed official mourning for forty days after the death of Darnley and their short-lived, turbulent marriage. Nevertheless suspicion fell immediately upon Mary and the Earl of Bothwell, who she married only three months after Lord Darnley's murder.

Mary had ventured into matrimony with the notorious Darnley against the advice of her cousin, Queen Elizabeth I, and subsequently suffered his philandering and violent outbursts. In a fit of jealousy only the year before, Darnley murdered the queen's secretary and confidant David Rizzio. Rizzio was dragged from the Scottish queen's table and stabbed fifty-six times. However, Mary did appear to forgive Darnley and there is no evidence that she orchestrated his assassination.

Mary never had a successful marriage. She lived until 1587, spending twenty years under house arrest before her execution. She was described by Sir Walter Scott as in 'every sense one of the most unhappy Princesses that ever lived'. The murder of Lord Darnley was never solved.

10 February

The students were complaining about beer in an Oxford pub. Hardly newsworthy, but this dispute got wildly out of hand and the hangover lasted for centuries.

Today in 1355, the landlord of the Swindlestock Tavern, John Croidon, responded to student criticism of the quality of his beer, with what was called 'stubborn & saucie language'. The two drinkers, Walter Spryngeheuse and Roger de Chesterfield – who no doubt were inebriated already – were enraged. They hurled their drinks in Croidon's face, and then assaulted him. Already there was pronounced tension between 'town and gown' in Oxford and clearly this was the fuse that ignited a highly explosive situation. A request for the mayor, John de Bereford, to arrest the two students involved was ignored.

Bells at both the city and the university churches were rung to summon people to the fray. Locals came from the surrounding countryside as well as from the town. Some two hundred students became involved, and participants urged each other to 'give gode knocks!' This they certainly did. Far from being a case of overexuberant violence which could be slept off, in the riots that resulted and which lasted for two days almost one hundred people were killed, more than half of them scholars at the university.

It was subsequently decided that it was the town rather than the university that was at fault, and annually on 10 February, for the next 470 years – almost half a millennium – the city's mayor and councillors were obliged to walk, bare-headed, through the city in penance, attend Mass and pay the university the fine of one penny for every scholar killed. The relationship between 'town' and 'gown' in Oxford was not enhanced by this humiliating charade, and even now remains sensitive even after the ceremony was ended in 1825. An attempt at conciliation came today in 1955 when the mayor was finally awarded an honorary degree.

11 February

He was the world's most famous prisoner. Found guilty of attempting to overthrow the government, he had been sent to prison for life in 1964. Yet incarcerating him only seemed to make him more powerful. Nothing happened in the prison without his acquiescence and little happened in the internal politics or external relations of South Africa without reference to him. He was one of the most well-known men despite the fact that no new picture of him had been published in two decades. Today in 1990 the whole world would see his face. Nelson Mandela walked out of the gates of Victor Verster Prison hand in hand with his wife and the world's media beamed his hitherto banned image all over the globe.

Nearly three decades of confinement by an authoritarian, racist government had taken its toll. The hair was grey, the face lined. But his defiant resistance to minority rule in South Africa, where under a system known as 'apartheid' civil and political liberties were denied to those with dark skins, seemed undimmed. Coming to a stop on his walk to freedom, he raised a clenched fist, the symbol of struggle. He then rode a cavalcade of cars into Cape Town, along roads lined with supporters. There, he told a large crowd that, 'Now is the time to intensify the struggle on all fronts.' His attempt to overthrow the government had been a 'defensive action against the violence of apartheid'.

But he was magnanimous as well. He praised South Africa's white president, F. W. De Klerk, for going further than any of his predecessors in searching for a solution, and he opened his address by saying, 'I greet you all in the name of peace, democracy and freedom for all.'

Mandela defeated his former gaolers. He dismantled apartheid, won the presidency and became *Madiba*, 'Father of the Nation': a title used by black South Africans who he had led to power, and white South Africans, grateful that he used his office to reconcile, not to punish.

12 February

Known as the 'nine-day queen', Lady Jane Grey was proclaimed Queen of England on 10 July. Nine days later she was imprisoned in the Tower of London. It was not until this day in 1554 that she received her sentence, death by beheading, for committing high treason.

Jane had been a pawn in a larger political game, played out to decide who would take the throne of England after the death of Edward VI. The reason was a desperate attempt to prevent the country going back to Catholicism, which was inevitable under the queenship of Mary Tudor. Following overwhelming support for Princess Mary, the Privy Council switched their allegiance to support Mary as Catholic queen and Lady Jane Grey was accused of treason, her guilt made evident by a document which she signed 'Jane the Queene'.

The moment of Lady Jane Grey's untimely death has been dramatised in the iconic 1833 painting by Paul Delaroche. He depicts a pale, blindfolded girl in white, tentatively grappling for the executioner's block, aided by John Brydges, Baron Chandos, who draws it close to her fingertips. The painting has shaped historical memory but was in fact drawn from a source who claimed to have witnessed her final moments. The execution took place on Tower Green, inside the Tower of London, with a more private audience. Jane admitted her guilt and knelt before the block, requesting that the executioner 'dispatch her quickly'. As Delaroche so articulately presents, Jane allegedly lost her way and cried: 'What shall I do? Where is it?' before she was assisted and subsequently met her end.

In an iconic piece of political propaganda, produced 300 years after the event, Delaroche created a eulogy of Jane which has cemented the popular perception of her death: dramatic, melancholy; the first Protestant martyr of a bloody campaign to restore England to Popery.

13 February

The aircrew remember how strange it was to feel the heat from the burning city even at 8,000 feet. They realised, even from high above, that the fury of the fire was unprecedented.

Tonight in 1945 British and American bombers began their aerial bombardment of the German city of Dresden, a raid so destructive that it has come to symbolise the suffering of the German people at the hands of the Allies and remains at the centre of the heated debate about whether the Allied strategic bombing campaign was worth the appalling casualties it inflicted on the civilian population.

Dresden was known as the 'Jewel Box'. The seat of the Kings of Saxony, it was festooned with baroque buildings. Its reputation for art, music and learning was as glittering as its palaces and churches. By early 1945 it was teeming with refugees who were fleeing from the Soviet offensives in the east. At Russian urging, the British decided to launch massive raids against Dresden to paralyse communications, slow the flow of German troops heading to the Eastern Front, and 'show the Russians . . . what Bomber Command can do'.

Just before 10 p.m. the sirens sounded in the city. Over 700 bombers, in two waves to frustrate firefighters and rescue teams, carpeted the city initially with 500 tons of high explosives and nearly 200,000 incendiary bombs, which were designed to start a firestorm, then three hours later another 1,800 tons of bombs were dropped.

Five-hundred American bombers hit the burning city again over the next two days. The firestorm on the ground destroyed around 2.5 square miles (6.5 square kilometres) of the city. The survivors' accounts are appalling. Glass melted, people were sucked into the flames by howling winds caused by the fire, or were boiled alive as they sought shelter in pools of water. Around 25,000 men, women and children are thought to have been killed. The Allies maintained that Dresden was an important industrial and military target. Survivors have called it a terrible crime against humanity.

14 February

Britain's love affair with its favourite sailor was ignited today in 1797. Horatio Nelson shot to fame amid the smoke and fury of a clash between battleships near Cape St Vincent in Portugal.

Spain had declared war against Britain in late 1796 and the newly combined Franco-Spanish fleet forced the outnumbered Royal Navy out of the Mediterranean. Led by Sir John Jervis, a man who had run away to sea at thirteen and served as a common sailor 'before the mast' before being made an officer, the British lay in wait in the Atlantic hoping to pounce on a detachment of Spanish ships.

The day before, in thick fog, Jervis received a report from a thrusting 38-year-old commodore, Horatio Nelson, that he had just slipped unseen through the Spanish fleet. The enemy were at sea. In the thin dawn light Jervis was horrified to see that the Spanish outnumbered him by two to one. 'Enough, sir,' he snapped at an aide who kept updating him on each new enemy ship that he spotted, 'no more of that; the die is cast, and if there are fifty sail I will go through them.' He hoisted a signal in the rigging of his flagship, HMS *Victory* – 'Engage the enemy'.

Nelson needed no more encouragement. Seeing an opportunity, he broke formation, and hurled his vessel straight into a group of enemy ships. His rigging and steering were shot away, and with no other option he rammed the *San Nicolás*, roared 'Westminster Abbey or Glorious Victory!' and led his men onto the enemy deck. In the swirling melee of ships Nelson realised that he could leap aboard another ship, the *San Josef*, and captured that too.

It was an unprecedented feat. Nelson was knighted, became an admiral and Georgian Britain's biggest celebrity. The Spanish retreated to Cadiz, cut off from their South American empire by the wooden walls of the Royal Navy's ships.

15 February

It was the largest-ever surrender of British troops. Winston Churchill described it as the worst disaster in British military history. Today in 1942, Singapore, the lynchpin of Britain's empire in the east, surrendered to the Japanese.

While the Imperial Japanese Navy attacked Pearl Harbor in Hawaii, thousands of miles away the Japanese Army launched a simultaneous assault across east Asia. From December 1941 the Japanese stormed into Hong Kong, the Philippines, Malaya and shortly after, Indonesia. The advance down the Malayan peninsula was particularly rapid. The Japanese enjoyed air superiority, sinking British battleships off the coast and sowing terror among defenders on land. By the end of January the British had retreated to Singapore island, blowing up the causeway to the mainland behind them.

The British had 85,000 men. There were also Australian, Indian and local troops. They outnumbered their attackers; the Japanese only had 30,000 men. But many of the defenders were ill-equipped and inexperienced. Japanese bombing disrupted defensive plans and morale. Contrary to the popular myth Singapore's big guns, designed to protect against a threat from the sea, could be swung around to fire at the Japanese but they did not have enough of the right ammunition to make a decisive difference.

When the Japanese landed on Singapore there was intense fighting. By 14 February the British had been forced back into a small perimeter, and were concerned about the supply of water, fuel and ammunition. After a heated discussion about whether to counter-attack or surrender, the British decided to give in the following day.

The Japanese could not believe their luck. Their commander later said the attack on Singapore was 'a bluff'. He had been 'very frightened' that the British would fight on and he was at the end of his supplies. The 'Gibraltar of the East' had fallen. Thousands of troops marched into a terrible captivity. It was the beginning of the end of Britain's empire in Asia.

16 February

Towards the end of 1922 an archaeologist called Howard Carter, who was leading digs in the Valley of the Kings in Egypt, found some ancient stone steps descending to what he hoped was the tomb of a pharaoh named Tutankhamun. He'd been told he had one year of funding left and must find something good in that time. This, he hoped, might be it.

With a chisel given to him by his grandmother he made enough of a hole to peer into the musty gloom with a candle. Famously, he was asked impatiently whether he could see anything. 'Yes,' he replied, 'wonderful things!' Heralded as the best-preserved pharaonic tomb yet found, it caused a frenzy in the world's media.

Beyond the antechamber lay another sealed doorway, between guarding statues. Not until 16 February the following year was this second door formally opened and the sarcophagus of Tutankhamun seen – his mummy nestling within three separate coffins, the innermost one of pure gold.

In the *Daily Express* the following day H. V. Morton reported that this inner chamber had been entered for the first time in three thousand years, and that when it was, 'every expectation was surpassed': glorious paintings covered the walls while priceless treasures lay within the vault.

Only nineteen years old when he died unexpectedly, it is thought that Tutankhamun was buried in a small, makeshift chamber more likely to escape the attention of robbers. Though not distinguished among the many pharaohs, his fame since has exceeded all of them.

Mysterious deaths of a few members of Carter's team gave rise to the idea of a curse. Lord Carnarvon, the financial backer of the project, died six weeks after the tomb was opened. Yet a study showed that of the fifty-eight people who were present when the tomb and sarcophagus were opened only eight died within twelve years. 'King Tut's Curse' was nonsense but stoked the world's obsession with history's greatest archeological discovery.

17 February

On this day in 1863 five men from Geneva set up the International Committee for Relief to the Wounded, later to become known as the Red Cross.

In 1859 a young Swiss man named Henry Dunant witnessed a bloody battle in Solferino, Italy, as part of the Italian War of Independence. On the battlefield 40,000 men lay dead or dying, desperate for medical attention where there was none. Appalled, Dunant set about helping the wounded. He organised a group of local volunteers and directed them to dress the soldiers' wounds, to feed and comfort them.

Dunant then turned his attention to creating 'relief societies whose object would be to have the wounded cared for in time of war by enthusiastic, devoted volunteers, fully qualified for the task'.

In 1863 the emblem of a red cross on a white background, the inverse of the Swiss flag, became the formal symbol of the Red Cross. A year later, twelve governments adopted the Geneva Convention, which meant looking after those wounded in combat. People administering care were regarded as 'neutral' on the battlefield, not to be targeted by the opposition.

The charity became indispensable in times of conflict, and provided essential humanitarian aid in the First World War. Due to the intervention of the Red Cross, about 200,000 prisoners were exchanged between the warring parties, released from captivity and returned to their home country. The organisation's card index accumulated about 7 million records from 1914 to 1923, each card representing an individual prisoner or missing person.

Careful not to take sides in conflicts, the Red Cross has built a nonpartisan reputation which allows it entry into countries, prisons and camps denied to any other ostensibly 'Western' organisation. On occasion it has broken its silence. It denounced the Rwandan genocide in 1994 and has accused the military government in Myanmar of 'major human rights abuses'. Strict neutrality has not always been possible, or desirable.

18 February

It is never easy being the ambitious younger brother of a king, and today in 1478 one royal duke was sentenced to an infamous death after one betrayal too many. The 'false, fleeting, perjured Clarence' was condemned by his brother King Edward IV for his persistent involvement in several major conspiracies.

Clarence was taken to the Tower of London and executed in the Bowyer Tower. Legend has it that he was permitted to choose the method of his execution, allowing him to select the unconventional method of drowning, not in water, but in a barrel of his personal favourite drink, Malmsey wine.

George, Duke of Clarence wavered during the Wars of the Roses. Initially he supported his brother, and the house of York, but over time became resentful of the power Edward had as king, and found himself deeply involved in a plot to overthrow him; a plan initiated by his father-in-law, Richard Neville, Earl of Warwick. After its failure, Clarence returned to court and was pardoned. Before long he began to scheme again and became connected to yet another conspiracy. He was eventually arrested for high treason in January 1478 and a Bill of Attainder was passed that declared he was guilty of 'unnatural, loath treasons', and the death sentence was passed.

The story of execution has never been proven, but it has endured, prompting Shakespeare's interpretation and subsequent infamy. There is little evidence to support this version of Clarence's bizarre death, however a portrait of George's daughter, Margaret Pole, Countess of Salisbury, shows her wearing a bracelet featuring a wine barrel charm, which lends some credibility to the tale. Speculation has since been aided by the later exhumation of what were believed to be his remains. The male corpse was found to be fully intact, when ordinarily, an executed royal would be headless, with beheading being the swiftest and most genteel method of execution, one reserved for high-status victims. It seems Clarence, did meet an unusual end.

19 February

The harbour was packed with ships. Warships and merchantmen packed in, anchored close together, providing the perfect target from the air. On shore there were just sixteen anti-aircraft guns, whose crews had very limited training thanks to a shortage of ammunition. There was no radar, only a handful of aircraft, and the pilots lacked experience. It was inadequate protection for one of the most important outposts of the British Empire, but then again few could imagine that the war would come to the sleepy city of Darwin, Australia.

Japanese advances in the Pacific had made Darwin a lot less remote. They had seized Borneo, Celebes (now called Sulawesi) and other islands in Indonesia. Java was next and the Japanese wanted to forestall any Allied interference by striking the nearest important base. The war was about to come to Darwin.

At 8.45 a.m. on 19 February 1942 Commander Mitsuo Fuchida, leader of the Pearl Harbor strike, flew his Nakajima B5N bomber off the deck of the aircraft carrier *Akagi* and led 152 bombers and 36 fighters towards the Australian coast. They arrived over Darwin before the air-raid sirens even sounded. For thirty minutes the Japanese pilots bombed and strafed the mass of shipping. Plumes of smoke towered into the sky as they sank 3 warships and 6 merchant vessels, and damaging 10 more.

Around midday a second raid arrived, 54 aircraft, aiming for the Royal Australian Air Force base in the city. They bombed it at their leisure. Defective fuses meant the shells fired by the few anti-aircraft guns there were failing to make any impact.

There was chaos on the ground. Troops panicked, civilians fled, property was looted. The Japanese had dropped more bombs than they had on Pearl Harbor, killing around 250 people and succeeding in halting the resupply of Allied units in Indonesia. Although further raids followed, there was no invasion, and this first attack of the Second World War remains the largest-ever foreign assault on Australia.

20 February

Today, on 20 February 1472, the islands of Orkney and Shetland passed formally from the King of Denmark and Norway to the King of Scotland, in lieu of a dowry payment, and have remained Scottish ever since.

By the Treaty of Copenhagen, Margaret of Denmark – daughter of the King of Denmark and Norway – was promised in marriage to King James III of Scotland. The agreed dowry (60,000 Rhenish florins) proved quite beyond her impoverished father's ability to pay. In desperation, instead of the money he offered two groups of islands in his control: first the Orkneys and then the Shetlands.

Margaret – shipped off to Scotland at the marriageable age of twelve – is considered to have been rather better than her husband at governing their realm. But given that James conspicuously lacked political ability (mocked at the time for preferring effete things like music to manly activities like fighting, horse-riding or hunting) this was perhaps not saying much.

Orkney and Shetland had been under Norwegian rule ever since the eighth and ninth centuries when they first came under Viking influence (and when large numbers of settlers came from Norway). Formally annexed in 875, they were then passed to descendants with cheery names like Thorfinn Skull-Splitter.

In practice, relations between Scotland and Denmark-Norway became increasingly intertwined over the centuries. From around 1100 the Norse *jarls* – the word gives us our own *earls* – owed allegiance both to Norway for Orkney and to the Scottish crown for the lands they held as Earls of Caithness. Only from Margaret's arrival did the modern assumption develop that these were Scottish islands.

Margaret died in 1486, but her gift to first Scotland and then Britain proved extraordinarily valuable. Orkney was the crux of Britain's maritime defence in both World Wars and, more recently, Britain's claim to North Sea oil rests largely on these two fortuitously placed little archipelagos.

21 February

It was a sensation. Today in 1765 saw the first public performance in London's Haymarket of a symphony by a child. Wolfgang Amadeus Mozart's First Symphony was written while the precocious composer was just eight years old. The previous summer, he had composed the piece living in Ebury Street, while being shown off in salons around Europe and while his father recovered from a serious throat infection.

Tales of the young Mozart's astonishing musical gifts abound. The second son of a composer and violinist called Leopold, he was experimenting with thirds at the age of three. At four he learned to play the harpsichord. His father – who recognised his own musical gifts as trifling when compared with those of his son – travelled with him around the courts and salons of Europe where he would improvise 'as long as may be desired and in any key'. In London, it is said, he astonished the British royal family, accompanying Queen Charlotte, wife of King George III, in a song.

To Grimm – renowned now for his fairy-tales – Mozart as a boy was 'so extraordinary a phenomenon that one finds it difficult to believe unless one has seen him with one's own eyes and heard him with one's own ears'. In Vienna, Francis I called him 'a little master-wizard'. The great writer Goethe later recalled of his performance in Frankfurt: 'I was only fourteen years old, but I see it, as if I were still there, the little man with his child's sword and his curly hair ... A rare phenomenon like that of Mozart remains a truly inexplicable thing'.

Since those days little has changed regarding appreciation of his music. His genius remains, in the twenty-first century, as treasured as it is – just as Goethe said – inexplicable.

22 February

Under cover of darkness the French troops splashed ashore through the surf. At least one boat capsized, the gunpowder it carried transformed instantly into unusable sludge. As soon as they were ashore, many of the men deserted and crept off to loot whatever unsuspecting settlements they could find. It was not the ideal start to the last invasion of Britain.

Tonight in 1797 French soldiers, sent by the Revolutionary government, landed on the coast of Pembrokeshire in Wales. The French had planned a three-pronged attack on Britain in support of the Society of United Irishmen. Two forces would land in Britain while the main body would land in Ireland. Adverse weather and ill discipline halted two of the forces but the landing in Wales consisting of 1,000 men went ahead. Even so, it collapsed as soon as the reluctant French soldiers arrived on British soil. The Welsh were uninspired by the gospel of revolution, and instead flocked to join the local militia. Some French troops got hold of a shipment of wine and drunken comatose Frenchmen littered the surrounding area within hours. The legendary Jemima Nicholas, a local woman armed only with a pitchfork, is said to have rounded up a dozen of them and locked them in a church.

However, news that the French were ashore sent London into a panic. There was a run on the Bank of England. The bank suspended the payment of gold in return for paper money, and that precedent, that banknotes could not be redeemed for the value they represented, has been the guiding principle for modern banknotes ever since.

While Londoners lost their nerve, the men and women of Pembrokeshire held theirs. Only thirty-six hours after the French landed, it was all over. The French surrendered in the Royal Oak pub in Fishguard, which still serves ale to indomitable locals and invading tourists alike.

Never again would an enemy force land on British shores.

23 February

Mexican troops raised a blood-red flag as they entered the town and surrounded the small fortress. It meant 'No Quarter'; the band of rebels within could surrender now or face certain death. They chose the latter. Today in 1836 Mexican forces began the siege of the Alamo, a fortified former Catholic mission in southern Texas in which just over 150 separatists were defying the Mexican government.

In late 1835, Texas, a Mexican province, had rebelled against the government over its attempt to replace a loose federalism with tighter central control. Texas had seen a mass of immigration from the United States and these settlers felt no loyalty towards the government in Mexico City for a range of cultural, linguistic and religious reasons. That government responded in early 1836 with a military expedition to bring the rebellious province to heel.

One army marched up the coast, sweeping aside opposition. Another, led by the president himself, Antonio López de Santa Anna, marched inland aiming for San Antonio de Béxar (now San Antonio, Texas) where the rebels had taken refuge in the Alamo. When Santa Anna arrived he described it as an 'irregular fortification hardly worthy of the name'.

The rebels rushed to cobble together enough food and ammunition for a siege. They dismantled a blacksmith's forge and rebuilt it inside, herded in cattle and looted food from nearby houses. Some brought their families. By late afternoon the Mexican force, ten times larger than the rebels, had surrounded the fort and a bugler sounded the request for a parley. William Travis, a rebel commander who had moved from Alabama to Texas only five years earlier, ordered a cannon to be fired in response. There would be no talking.

The siege that followed lasted a fortnight and ended with the capture of the fort and the massacre of its defenders; but the siege became a thing of legend. Today, the building is a site of almost religious devotion, and the garrison's unflinching defiance remains the wellspring of Texan pride.

24 February

The British Parliament likes to think of itself as one of the world's oldest institutions. The summoning of important figures to advise the king dates back to the thirteenth century. In a long and deeply eccentric history there have been duels, dictatorship and debauchery. Parliament has been frequented by larcenists, lunatics, dilettantes and drunks; terrorists and traitors. But until today in 1919 there had never been a speech by a Member of Parliament who was a woman.

Some women in the United Kingdom were finally given the vote in 1918. Female MPs quickly followed. Constance Markievicz won a Dublin constituency in late 1918 but she was in prison and, like the rest of Sinn Féin, refused to attend Westminster. In late 1919 another woman won a seat, this time in Plymouth. She too had a somewhat unusual story. She was an American, born Nancy Langhorne in Virginia, but she was also, thanks to marriage into the Astor family, a viscountess.

When Nancy Astor's father-in-law died in October, Nancy's MP husband inherited his title and was sent to the House of Lords. This triggered a by-election for his seat in the Commons. She entered the race and won with 52 per cent of the vote having impressed the voters with a straight-talking American attitude to policy and hecklers alike.

In the first words ever spoken by a female member, she recognised that 'it was very difficult for some honourable Members to receive the first lady MP into the House'. This was greeted by a polite collective drawl of 'Not at all!' She then praised the voters of Plymouth who she said had shown the same disregard for risk that its famous residents like Drake had done in the past, before launching into a passionate appeal for restrictions on alcohol.

Over the course of a long parliamentary career she advanced causes that most male members had neglected, like recruiting women for the civil service, juvenile victims of crime and primary education, demonstrating that Parliament's evolving composition would change the character of its legislation.

25 February

Captain Lord George Paulet, aboard HMS *Carysfort*, sailed into the port of Honolulu, the capital of Hawaii, to investigate an allegation of unfair treatment towards the British on the island, after a series of land disputes between traders and locals. His solution, today in 1843, was to proclaim himself head of a provisional government, to hoist the Union Jack and exert British authority.

Britain and the Hawaiian Islands had been allies since the late eighteenth century, as Britain's reach extended to every part of the globe. Hawaiian rulers had hoped Britain might protect their independence from other circling colonising powers, like the French or Americans, hence they adopted a national flag with the Union Jack in one corner. (It remains on the Hawaii state flag to this day.) But Captain Paulet pushed too hard. He presented the king, Kamehameha III with an ultimatum, which Kamehameha conceded to in an attempt to avoid bloodshed. The Hawaiian flag was removed, and Kamehameha was effectively overthrown. Captain Paulet dominated island politics, vastly overstepping his authority. He appointed himself and three others to a commission to be the new government and insisted on direct control of all land transactions. However, his rule was short-lived as almost six months later a more senior British figure arrived in Honolulu.

Admiral Richard Thomas commanded the Royal Navy in the Pacific and was appalled by Paulet's actions; they catastrophically undermined Britain's image as a benevolent protector. Paulet was stripped of power and the Hawaiian kingdom was restored. By November 1843, France and Britain formally recognised Hawaii as an independent nation. Ultimately though Hawaii would be absorbed by a predatory empire: the Americans in 1898. Britain, despite its past interest and flag sharing did not wish to fight the United States over the fate of a distant archipelago in the Pacific Ocean.

26 February

The fulsomely moustachioed John Harvey Kellogg – whose birthday was on 26 February 1852 – was brought up and remained a committed Christian revivalist. He became a member of the Seventh-day Adventist Church, though it was a fissiparous group and, during one serious schism (in which his views raised doubts among other worshippers) he was 'disfellowshipped' – to use the catchy contemporary term. He trained also as a doctor, anxious always to uphold what he called 'the harmony of science and the Bible'.

In Michigan he set up and ran what he called a 'Sanitarium' – an enduring term – which operated at Battle Creek on the basis of Church principles. From his family he had absorbed a firm belief that the Second Coming of Christ was imminent, and as part of his strict mindset he advocated abstinence from alcohol, abstinence from meat-eating, abstinence from smoking and abstinence from sex, including masturbation – all of which forms of denial were vigorously promoted at Battle Creek. He also espoused a regimen of exercise (and colonic irrigation) making much of his reform menu sound quite modern.

There is little doubt about the invention for which he is best known, or his biggest contribution to the modern diet. His brother Will left some dough out overnight then ground it, calling it 'Granola' until forced for legal reasons to alter the name to 'Corn Flakes'. Kellogg believed that bland foods, such as this indubitably was, would decrease sexual excitement and so reduce arousal and masturbation.

Such foods were perfect, in other words, and he backed them wholeheartedly, attaching his name to the manufacture of breakfast cereals. He refused adamantly to profit, hoping only 'to propagate the ideas of health and biological living' as part of what he called his 'general philanthropic work'.

In a world where the poor began the day with porridge or gruel (grains boiled in water), while the wealthy ate eggs and ham, the breakfast cornflake had a transformative appeal.

27 February

Keir Hardie was never put off by the prospect of failure. His childhood had been a desperate struggle. Not yet a teenager, his meagre earnings in the workshops and coalmines of Lanarkshire supported his family. A brother died and his mother struggled to keep the rest of the family alive. He experienced the fragility of employment in a non-unionised world when he was instantly fired for being late. All this only steeled his resolve. He attended night classes, learned the art of oratory through his chapel and began to agitate for better wages and conditions. By the 1880s he was standing in elections. And losing badly. He never gave up. In 1892 he ran as Independent Labour candidate and narrowly won a parliamentary seat in West Ham. He flouted Westminster's dress code, wearing a tweed suit rather than frock coat, was widely lambasted and he lost his seat three years later as Independent Labour were crushed across the UK.

Undeterred, he sought to unite the disparate left-wing groups. Today in 1900, after years of wrangling, a conference at the Congregational Memorial Hall on Farringdon Street of 129 delegates drawn from trade unions, and a spectrum of other left-wing organisations, passed a motion to establish 'a distinct Labour group in Parliament'. The UK Labour Party was born.

The next election was too soon. The poll in October 1900 saw Labour only able to raise £33 and they won just over 1 per cent of votes nationwide, although Hardie managed to win one of two seats. It was a start.

Britain was changing and the franchise was widening to include ever more working-class voters. Labour offered these men a more radical alternative than the existing progressive, but patrician, Liberal Party. Just twenty-four years after the conference in Farringdon, a vastly expanded electorate, now including some women, swept Labour to office. A former child labourer from the pits of Lanarkshire had precipitated a peaceful revolution.

28 February

The men of the Somerset Light Infantry were the last to board ship. Today in 1948 the last British troops left India, marched through the monumental Gateway of India in Bombay (now Mumbai) and embarked on the long journey home. There was a range of emotions as they left Britain's prize imperial possession. Some were appalled; they had repelled a Japanese invasion only four years earlier, they had won the Second World War and now they were skulking off like a defeated foe. Others felt guilty that the end of British rule had been accompanied by terrible violence.

India had been considered the 'jewel' of Britain's empire. Prior to the arrival of the English it had known economically dynamic, hugely sophisticated societies. Unlike North America, Australia, New Zealand or parts of Africa when they were colonised, British rule never eclipsed local tradition and religion or fundamentally altered the demographics.

Rule by distant British politicians over such a large region had long been contested. By the end of the nineteenth century Indians were frustrated by the glass ceiling that prevented them from occupying the top jobs. The First World War magnified calls for independence. India had provided much money and many troops, but after victory in 1918 Britain appeared to renege on promises of greater autonomy. The killing of peaceful protesters by British led troops at Amritsar in 1919 caused outrage both in Britain and throughout India.

During the Second World War, when India provided substantial assistance once again, an offer of 'Dominion status' was refused. A great global struggle against the imperial ambitions of the Axis powers made it almost impossible to justify the maintenance of Britain's own imperial project in south Asia. When Attlee's Labour government won the general election in 1945, Indian independence was assured. The mishandling of that process led to ethnic cleansing, murder, rape and chaos on a gigantic scale, which the British garrison, now departing, had done little to halt.

29 February

It was an astonishing mismatch. A nation of 3.5 million pitted against an empire stretching across eleven time zones, incorporating 170 million people. Against extraordinary odds, the winter of 1939/40 saw the Finns humiliate the Soviet war machine. Stalin was furious and ordered the Red Army to do whatever it took to break Finnish resistance. Today in 1940 that pressure became intolerable and the Finnish government had no choice but to open peace negotiations.

Finnish–Soviet hostility was born in the chaos unleashed by the First World War. Finland had broken away from Russia during the Russian Revolution. Stalin was determined, at the very least, to reoccupy some of the lost provinces. In 1939 he had partitioned Poland with Hitler, and also forced the Baltic States to accept large garrisons of Red Army troops. He ordered Finland to cede territory. It refused.

In late November Stalin sent 500,000 troops into Finland. He expected Helsinki's fall within weeks. Instead white-caped, ski-mounted Finns inflicted appalling losses on the Red Army. Columns of tanks were cut off and annihilated in ambushes in near impenetrable forests. Soviet troops lacking snowsuits froze to death as the temperature plunged to minus 30. The Finns successfully fought one of history's most notable David and Goliath contests.

By February a furious Stalin flooded the southern front with reinforcements. Now around 600,000 men attacked 150,000 Finns. Tanks and infantry were thrown into battle with little regard for casualties. By the end of February Finland faced inevitable defeat and the negotiations that began today ended with the ceding of 11 per cent of Finland's landmass and about a third of its economic assets to the USSR.

Stalin's victory proved pyrrhic. Hitler was so struck by the Red Army's feeble performance that he determined to launch his great eastern assault as soon as possible. By advertising his army's impotence, Stalin had invited a titanic fascist assault that would come close to destroying his regime.

MARCH

1 March

Three women, Sarah Goode, Sarah Osborne, and a slave named Tituba were arrested today in 1692 in the small town of Salem, Massachusetts. They would be tried for the crime of witchcraft.

The trials were carried out between February 1692 and May 1693, and resulted in the executions of twenty people, mostly by hanging, and most of those executed were women. Allegations spun out of control after eleven-year-old Abigail Williams, niece of Samuel Parris the Puritan minister of Salem, accused the family slave Tituba of witchcraft. Tituba was questioned alongside Sarah Osborne and Sarah Goode, and although there was very little to condemn the women, they were found guilty. As part of an overall contrived fantasy, they were accused of meeting in a witches' sabbath, or coven, and of having sexual relations with the Devil.

Inside a hot, noisy and packed courtroom, the proceedings were difficult to hear. The confused and scared women stood before the jury and pledged their innocence and good Christian faith before a staunchly puritanical audience. As a desperate strategy, Tituba admitted everything and begged for forgiveness. Her tactics remarkably worked and she narrowly escaped the noose, remaining in jail until Samuel Parris sold her in order to pay for her jail fee.

Tituba's confession and subsequent release provoked other women to plead guilty to witchcraft and name others as active witches, in the desperate hope that in doing so, they would be also be spared. Yet things spun out of control. Through the whole process of confession, fear and excitement, a web of stories and allegations grew and those who pleaded innocent were charged anyway and executed.

The horrors of the Salem Witch Trials have been immortalised through theatre, re-enacted on stage in *The Crucible* by playwright Arthur Miller. In history, they remain one of the most famous examples of stunning injustice, superstition and misogyny.

2 March

Its first pilot nicknamed it 'big bird'. Its two front windows and movable nose did indeed give it an avian appearance. And today in 1969, for the very first time, it flew like a bird. Taking off from Toulouse, Concorde, cheered by anxious spectators, flew for almost half an hour.

It flew then at a sedate pace, rather than the supersonic speeds – double the speed of sound – for which it was designed. Its first supersonic flight took place later that year. It was a symbol, as its name implies, of cooperation between Britain and France, with companies from both countries having worked together on its design and construction.

As released government papers have revealed, though, significant doubts existed regarding the project's commercial viability, with fears that it might prove only an embarrassing and colossal expense – a white elephant rather than a white bird. Its fuel consumption was huge. And at the time of its development, an oil crisis – making fuel very expensive – prevented it from entering the lucrative market for planes crossing the Pacific.

The loud sonic 'boom' which took place when the sound barrier was passed was banned over land, meaning that supersonic flight could only be trans-oceanic. Development costs were vastly higher than anticipated, only the absorption of these by the British and French governments – and high ticket prices – allowed its operation to be viable. A mere twenty aircraft were built and only seven were flown by each country.

In spite of everything, though, Concorde would become a much-loved and much-admired institution. It still holds the record for the fastest transatlantic passenger flight of just 2 hours 52 minutes and 59 seconds set in 1996 with a roaring tailwind. But high oil prices and a crash in Paris in 2000 forced its retirement from service in 2003.

3 March

It was a crusade, America's War on Obscenity. On 3 March in 1873 the US Congress approved what became known as the Comstock Law, after Anthony Comstock, a mail-worker, politician and fervent Christian moralist who styled himself a 'weeder in God's garden'.

Comstock campaigned against what he considered the fostering of immorality, of 'every filthy book, pamphlet, picture, paper, letter, writing, print, or other publication', and persuaded lawmakers to forbid the delivery of this 'obscene, lewd, or lascivious material' – notoriously difficult to define, of course, as the prohibition of medical textbooks demonstrated – as well as any information relating to the prevention either of conception or of venereal disease. His campaigns destroyed 15 tons of books, 284,000 pounds of plates for printing 'objectionable' books, and nearly 4 million pictures. He boasted that he was responsible for 4,000 arrests and claimed he drove fifteen people to suicide in his 'fight for the young'.

'Comstockery', as the censorship was termed, aroused considerable hatred and contempt. He made numerous enemies, one condemning him as the leader of America's 'moral eunuchs', and it was a physical assault that led, eventually, to his death. George Bernard Shaw – another denounced by Comstock, this time as an 'Irish smut dealer' – called this moralising tendency 'the world's standing joke at the expense of the United States' which confirmed that it was 'a provincial place'.

Of course, this was a wider social phenomenon and scarcely the work of one man. Abortion continues to arouse fervent resistance in America to this day, and the strong opposition to perceived immorality was seen too in the prohibition of alcohol that followed the First World War – after Comstock's death.

Perhaps the ultimate criticism, though, may be left to the judgement of history. As a result of what are known as the 'Comstock Laws' the United States was the only allied army during the First World War not to be provided with condoms. Around 400,000 of its soldiers contracted VD.

4 March

Heavenly portents were said to have foretold the arrival of the foreigners who would destroy the Aztecs; though these tales were probably made up later by Mexicans to explain the eclipse of their world. Either way, that process of destruction started today in 1519 as the keels of longboats carrying Hernán Cortés and his men crunched into the sand of the Yucatán beaches. The Spanish had come to Mexico.

Cortés was distantly related to Francisco Pizarro, conqueror of the Incas, and the two men are among the most famous of the Spanish conquistadors whose reputation for brutality and oppression – the horrors of the Spanish conquest appalled many contemporary observers as well as our own anti-colonial age – tarnishes their memory.

In early life Cortés had been called 'ruthless, haughty, and mischievous' and little in his later career throws this verdict into question. He had been in the Indies for some fifteen years when he ventured to the mainland, becoming a man of substance on the island of Cuba. Though official support for his Mexican venture was revoked, Cortés went anyway, confident that success would be welcomed and recognised higher up within the Spanish state.

Strong-minded and decisive, Cortés scuttled the seven or so ships that he had sailed from Cuba to Mexico, making retreat an impossibility. Aztec gifts of gold did nothing to placate either him or his companions, and everything to fuel their greed and ambition. He faced down threats to his position (and to his life) both from the Aztecs and from Spanish rivals.

When the Aztec capital, Tenochtitlán, was finally captured by the Spanish in 1521, it was renamed Mexico City. Aztec temples were destroyed and construction began on the ruins of what was soon (and has remained) one of the most populated and important cities in the Americas.

5 March

Today in 1936 an engine roared and an icon took to the sky for the first time.

Early in the morning Captain Joseph Summers, known to his friends as 'Mutt', a test pilot who flew nearly four hundred prototypes in his career, pushed the throttle forward and surged down the runway at Eastleigh Aerodrome, now Southampton Airport. For eight minutes he soared above the airfield in the Type 300 aircraft powered by a Rolls-Royce PV-XII V-12. It was the first flight of a world-changing combination, better known by their later names, the Spitfire, and its Rolls-Royce Merlin engine. When Mutt landed he was beaming from ear to ear and barked at the ground crew, 'Don't touch anything.'

The chairman of the Vickers-Armstrong aircraft company named the plane after his young daughter, Anna, who he said was a 'right little spitfire'. The genius responsible for the plane, Reginald Mitchell, grumbled, 'It's the sort of bloody silly name they would give it.'

There was nothing bloody silly about its performance. The Rolls-Royce Merlin engine provided raw power, while the airframe design, including its famous elliptical wing, transmitted this power into speed and agility.

The Spitfire arrived just in time to take on Hitler's Luftwaffe over northern France, at Dunkirk and then Britain itself as Germany sought to knock the country out of the war in 1940. It was a superbly balanced, high-performance aircraft that even fairly inexperienced pilots could fly. During the Battle of Britain it gave the RAF a decisive advantage.

Germans came to fear the unmistakable silhouette. When their commander, Hermann Goering, was midway through a morale-boosting speech and asked rhetorically if there was anything his pilots needed, they shouted back, '*Ja*, Spitfires!'

6 March

It was one of Europe's most powerful castles. Built in just two years by Richard the Lionheart to bind Normandy in perpetuity to the English crown, Chateau Gaillard was a masterpiece of defensive architecture. It towers over the Seine on a rocky outcrop. Its concentric defences included three successive rings of walls with a keep in the middle. This was a military stronghold, and a statement of royal power. Yet, today in 1204, only five years after it was completed, it fell.

King Richard had left powerful castles but a weak successor. The King of France, Philip II, immediately moved to conquer Normandy as soon as John had replaced his brother Richard on the throne. By summer 1203 he was ready to lay siege to Gaillard. Trenches were excavated around the castle and then covered with roofs so the besieging army could work their way ever closer to the walls. It was a grinding subterranean battle of inches. Miners tried to undermine the walls. Tunnellers from the castle attempted to intercept them. Vicious, claustrophobic battles flared up as miners broke into an enemy passage.

King John made a few attempts at relief but abandoned the garrison to its fate by Christmas 1204. The defenders expelled the old, very young or unwarlike from the castle but the French king refused to let them through his lines. The refugees were forced to squat in no-man's-land. Their distress was in plain view of their family members and friends in the garrison.

In early March the French stormed the castle, and bloody fighting saw them seize a foothold on the walls forcing the garrison to retreat to the inner bailey. French knights climbed up a sewage chute and emerged through a toilet to capture this next obstacle. The survivors fled to the keep but finally bowed to the inevitable and surrendered.

Once Gaillard was in French hands, Normandy followed. By August 1204 King John had lost the duchy of his ancestors, which in turn weakened his grip on the English throne.

7 March

Ellen Turner climbed into a carriage at her school gates. The fifteen-year-old thought she was being collected to see her mother who had been taken ill. Instead, today in 1826, she was transported to the Albion Hotel in Manchester, where she was kept against her consent until she agreed to marry a man twice her age – Edward Gibbon Wakefield. They were legally married in Gretna Green by a blacksmith, before journeying to France. Through the union with Ellen Turner, Edward Gibbon Wakefield hoped to gain a large marriage settlement and inherit her future fortune.

The forced elopement was not Wakefield's first marriage. His method of acquiring a fortune through matrimony had worked before with Eliza Pattle. In 1820, Wakefield had eloped with the heiress; her family begrudgingly accepted the marriage and paid a sum of £70,000 to avoid a scandal. When Eliza died four years later, Wakefield hatched a plan to marry the heiress of Shrigley Hall in Cheshire.

On marrying Ellen Turner, he had a letter delivered to her father, the landowner and miller William Turner. Wakefield expected the Turners to fall into line as the Pattles had done and pay him a substantial dowry. However, William Turner did not take the union lying down.

Turner approached the Foreign Secretary, who had the couple tracked down to Calais. When it became apparent that Ellen Turner had no emotional attachment to Wakefield, she was taken back to England and Wakefield was arrested. He was brought to trial in a case known as the Shrigley abduction and sentenced to three years' imprisonment in Newgate Prison. The marriage was annulled by Parliament. Two years later, at the age of seventeen, Ellen Turner was legally married to a wealthy neighbour. Her case remained at the centre of much public debate, as it raised the issue of the rights, or lack thereof, of women and girls in a deeply patriarchal society.

8 March

It is too little known that the Russian Revolution in 1917 was heralded by women, not men, taking to the streets.

That day – 8 March – was International Women's Day. In the socialist calendar it had been a significant day since inaugurated, less than a decade before, in 1909. In 1917 a substantial march took place in what then was the Russian capital of St Petersburg. By midday tens of thousands had gathered along Nevsky Prospekt, the main street, most of them women. Many waved banners that called for change, if primarily for better supplies of food: 'Feed the children of the defenders of the motherland'.

The First World War was placing huge strain on a weak economy and a crippling famine seemed imminent. In the febrile and unstable environment of early twentieth-century Russia, one led to the other: calls for bread gave rise to calls of 'down with the Tsar'.

The city governor noted that the crowd consisted of 'ladies from society, lots more peasant women, student girls and, compared with earlier demonstrations, not many workers'. Before long, though, numerous men had also joined and revolutionaries capitalised on the unrest. Most experienced soldiers were away on the front lines, and troops mustered to quell the disturbances had little sympathy with the authorities. The troops were also discontented at the poor state of the army. Many joined the protesters, while entire units began to mutiny. Police stations and courts were attacked while military arsenals were commandeered. Unrest spread to other cities, and just a week later the tsar was persuaded to abdicate.

A provisional government granted women equal voting rights, though its inability to deal with food shortages or the economic crisis led to another revolution – the Bolshevik Revolution – later that year.

9 March

In sixteenth-century Europe a second, deadly round of plague was spreading like wildfire and city officials across Europe desperately sought methods of prevention against the fearsome epidemic. In Naples it was believed that one way to battle against the spread of the disease was to ban kissing in public. On this day in 1562, the ban was imposed. Authorities took the new law so seriously that philandering couples caught stealing kisses could be punished by death.

It was not the first time that a city had enforced such a strict law on public displays of affection. In 1439, Henry VI banned kissing in England in another attempt to prevent infection from spreading. People refused to accept the ban and it was subsequently lifted. Bans of this nature were also imposed during more modern times. In 1910, kissing was banned at railway stations in France, in the belief that lovers, family and friends saying their goodbyes caused delays to the train service. In 1982, kissing for 'pleasure' was outlawed in Iran, and similarly in 1992 students at Qingdao Binhai University in China were prevented from openly displaying any form of affection, including holding hands or sharing earphones. Most recently in 2003, to the horror of the general public, a law was passed in Moscow enforcing a ban on kissing in public, imposed on all members of society. This was intended to raise levels of public morality. People of Moscow defied the ban by kissing complete strangers and the proposed law was eventually abandoned.

Thankfully, these retrograde laws have been outliers. Since 1562, kissing in public has been generally accepted and even endorsed, with 6 July being marked as International Kissing Day; a way of openly celebrating the act between loved ones.

10 March

The French tricolour fluttered all night from the flagpole on the banks of the Mississippi river before being finally pulled down this morning in 1804. In its place, another red, white and blue flag was hoisted, the Star Spangled Banner of the United States with its fifteen white stars.

Onlookers had just witnessed one of history's most important handovers. A giant transfer of territory gained not by violence, but by cash. Emperor of France Napoleon Bonaparte, who is famous for attempting to redraw the map of Europe, should perhaps be remembered for his enduring American legacy. The French despot, frustrated in his attempts to sustain France's colonies in the western hemisphere, and fixated on his wars within Europe, sold a vast swathe of territory to the United States. As the flag fluttered up the St Louis flagpole 828,000 square miles became American. This 'Louisiana Territory' had been part of France's empire along the Mississippi, from modern Louisiana, Arkansas and parts of Texas up to Montana and into what is now Canada.

The United States government scrambled to come to terms with their new territory. US Army Captain Meriwether Lewis and William Clark were told to explore the terrain, get to the Pacific and establish a presence to dissuade other European nations from staking a claim. They returned after more than two years with tales of natural abundance, giant rivers, and endless virgin land.

The whole deal cost President Thomas Jefferson $15 million, or 3 cents an acre. For that he doubled the size of the United States. What had been a collection of states on the east coast was now a continental power. It was certainly one of history's greatest bargains.

11 March

Tonight in 1864 disaster struck Victorian Britain.

A strong south-westerly gale lashed the surface of the Dale Dyke Reservoir outside Sheffield. Great waves crashed against the dam that had only just been completed. The nervous engineer, John Gunson, stayed up to check whether his dam would hold, and what he saw sent a chill through him.

A large crack was opening in the face of the dam. Water was gushing through. He ran to open the emergency valves, which would take the pressure off but it was not enough and the dam catastrophically ruptured. Some 3.1 billion litres of water crashed down the Loxley Valley, smashing farms and hamlets on the way.

Sheffield, a rapidly expanding industrial hub whose population had grown 400 per cent in sixty years, lay in its path. The wall of water was a 'sudden and overwhelming rush', wrote one eyewitness. Water rushed down the valley at 20 mph and within forty-five minutes the reservoir was empty.

People were asleep in bed as the deluge hit. Bodies were found washed miles from their homes. Survivors said the ruined buildings looked as if they had been battered by artillery. Just under 250 people and 700 animals were drowned, 15 bridges swept away and hundreds of buildings destroyed or damaged. It was Victorian Britain's worst (non-maritime) civilian loss of life.

Naturally it became a huge tourist attraction. Visitors flocked to see the aftermath and a few contributed to a relief fund. Over £42,000 was raised. Even Queen Victoria sent a cheque for £200.

The dam's failure led to reforms in engineering practice, setting standards that needed to be met when constructing such large-scale structures. The dam was rebuilt on a smaller scale in 1875, using a different contractor.

12 March

It was a significant milestone. Today in 1881, Andrew Watson became the first black football player to play in, and to captain, an international football team.

He led Scotland to a comprehensive 5–1 win over their southern neighbours – a margin of victory not then unusual, dominant as the Scottish team was. There is little sign that the colour of his skin was much noticed. Observers were more intrigued at times by the brown (as opposed to black) hue of his boots.

Watson was descended from a sugar-planter who had had a relationship with a British Guianese woman called Hannah Rose. The family moved back to Britain, probably without their mother, and though the father then died young, he left the children amply provided for.

Andrew lived in the south, attending school in Wimbledon, then went to university in Glasgow, where he studied natural philosophy, mathematics and engineering. What he excelled at most, though, were sporting activities, particularly football, as a left or centre back.

As an adult, his work as a maritime engineer took him between London and Liverpool and Glasgow. Sport then was largely amateur, certainly not a career in its own right. After his first wife died, he married a second time, sharing four children between the two relationships. Wherever he went he played football, and his ability was much admired. When the *Scottish Football Association Annual* for 1880–1 was published it lauded: 'Watson, Andrew: One of the very best backs we have'.

By the time of the 1911 census, in which he described himself as a retired seagoing chief engineer, he was living again in Liverpool. When he died in his early sixties he was in Kew, in West London. He had been a pioneer, little aware of it, and little remembered.

13 March

William – Wilhelm – Herschel was a maverick. He was a Jew from Germany who immigrated to Britain as a penniless young adult and lived in Bath. While working as a music teacher, in his spare time he followed his passion for astronomy and built telescopes in order to observe the stars.

He worked alone (or almost alone, his also brilliant younger sister, Caroline, was a constant companion; it not always being obvious, as William himself remarked, which of them was the planet and which the moon). Today, in 1781, he realised that a body he had been observing was not in fact a star, or a comet, as many presumed, but a planet orbiting our Sun. This was the first time since the days of ancient Greece that a new planet had been discovered.

The very idea of a 'solar system' was of course not old. The standard view – until Copernicus – had always been that the earth was stationary and the heavens revolved around it. At the same time it began to be realised that the planets were imperfect: full of craters, and mountains, and storms. One of Herschel's early papers discussed what he thought were forests as well as craters on the Moon ('lunacy' as the obsession was labelled).

Gradually, through the spring and summer of 1781, growing numbers of astronomers came to agree that 'Uranus', as the new entity was called, was indeed a planet circling the Sun in a massive ellipse approximately twice as large as that of Saturn – doubling the size of the solar system.

Having brilliantly transformed our understanding of space and the universe, Herschel was rewarded with being the first President of the Royal Astronomical Society and a post as the king's official astronomer. Now well funded and celebrated, he made further important discoveries including the moons of Saturn and Uranus and infrared radiation. His sister continued to work after his death and observed several comets, bringing the total number of astronomical objects discovered by the sibling team to 2,400.

14 March

It was a grim day on the Solent. A gale was blowing today in 1757 as the fifty-year-old Admiral John Byng – a career naval officer who had followed his successful father to sea at thirteen and risen to vice admiral by his early forties – boarded a ship for the last time in Portsmouth Harbour. A coffin already engraved with the words 'The Hon. John Byng, Esqr. Died March 14th 1757' had preceded him.

It was 7 a.m. At midday, with a 'composed countenance', he re-emerged onto deck to face a firing squad. The event was made famous (or infamous) by the French writer Voltaire who wrote that 'in this country [Britain], it is good to kill an admiral from time to time, in order to encourage the others': '*pour encourager les autres*'.

During the early exchanges of the Seven Years' War against France, Byng had been made responsible for preventing the French from seizing a British fort on the island of Menorca. Finding that a large French force had landed already and was laying siege to the fort, Byng decided against landing his own troops to confront them, explaining in a letter to the Admiralty that doing so would not have stopped the French.

To many in the Admiralty, though, Byng's failure to fight sounded simply cowardly and King George II himself raged: 'This man will not fight!' After an encounter a few months later from which the French fleet sailed away unharmed, Byng was ordered home and charged by a court martial with 'failing to do his utmost'.

At a time of war fever the case aroused popular hysteria, was widely reported, and crowds chanted 'swing, swing Admiral Byng'. Pandering to the popular mood a court ignored recommendations for mercy and opted to impose the death penalty. There is little doubt that Voltaire was right, and that Byng was the victim of an unusually harsh decision intended to instil fighting spirit in others.

15 March

Julius Caesar had been tempted to skip the meeting of the Senate on the Ides of March, today in 44 BC. His wife, Calpurnia, had been wracked with nightmares, and begged him not to attend; his friends had heard disturbing, swirling rumours, but with the encouragement of his old friend Marcus Brutus, he brushed their concerns aside.

The Ides of March was an important religious festival when Romans would sacrifice and, in particular, settle debts. In the heart of the bustling forum, the theatre built by his old adversary, Pompey the Great, a series of gladiatorial clashes was being hosted. A group of Roman senators steered Caesar into the theatre while another senator intercepted Caesar's loyal friend Mark Antony with pressing news that just could not wait.

The men who were now near Caesar were those who had the most to lose from his dictatorship. No longer would senators rotate through the most senior and lucrative offices in the Roman state now that Caesar, with his string of remarkable victories and backed by loyal legions, had assumed the title *dictator perpetuus* or dictator for life. Their wealth, status and prospects were all diminished by an all-powerful Caesar, and they were determined to act.

The conspirators thronged around him, all pushing petitions and requests. Then Tillius Cimber tore at Caesar's toga. Servilius Casca lunged at his neck, and that sparked a frenzy of stabbing from those around him. The dictator had no chance, he died beneath a hail of blows. Sadly his infamous 'Et tu, Brute?', dripping with betrayal, was an invention of Shakespeare.

The man who had first taken Roman arms across the Rhine and the English Channel lay dead in the theatre of his nemesis Pompey. His body was quickly examined in history's first recorded post mortem, but the aftermath of his death was protracted. Thirteen years of civil war followed, the Roman elite and the Republic itself were destroyed. In their place Augustus, Caesar's great-nephew, would fashion an empire that would endure for centuries.

16 March

When the constitutional amendment abolishing slavery in the United States of America squeaked through the House of Representatives, 119 to 56, just four votes over the required two-thirds majority, there was jubilation in the chamber. Some representatives wept and black onlookers in the gallery, who had only been allowed access the previous year, cheered themselves hoarse. This most enlightened piece of legislation had required bribes, threats and promises of patronage to get ratified, but Lincoln had bludgeoned it through Congress and signed it the following day, on 1 February 1865, weeks before his assassination.

Constitutional amendment requires not only Congress and the president but also three-quarters of state legislatures. States signed up through the rest of the year, until in the first week of December, North Carolina and Georgia confirmed it and it was enshrined as part of the constitution. Mississippi however held out. The state wanted reimbursement. Britain had compensated slaveholders for taking their 'property' when Westminster abolished slavery in 1833, and Mississippi wanted a similar deal. The federal government refused and Mississippi refused to ratify the amendment for another 130 years. It was only today in 1995 that Mississippi finally ratified it and an administrative oversight meant that the ratification was not formally submitted to Washington, DC until 2013 when a local doctor, inspired by the film *Lincoln*, campaigned to complete the process.

Mississippi's hold-out was not accidental. Of all the slave-holding states, it had a reputation for the most enthusiastic embrace of the barbaric custom and from 1865 had pioneered the so-called Black Codes which allowed white-controlled state governments to perpetuate the subjugation of African Americans through the criminal justice system. Black people could be sentenced to long periods of forced labour for crimes such as obscene language, petty theft or even selling cotton after sunset. Slavery endured, *de facto* and *de jure*, until long after the passage of Lincoln's signature piece of legislation.

17 March

He was from a privileged imperial family but he was abducted and enslaved. It was the start of an adventure that would see him become one of history's most celebrated missionaries. Patrick, the patron saint of Ireland, who died today in AD 461, was not Irish. He was Romano-British but was taken to Ireland by slave traders. He was put to work as a herdsman in the hills of what is now County Antrim, but while he tended to sheep and pigs he clung to his faith, using daily prayer as an escape from his miserable solitude.

Legend has it that Patrick escaped Ireland after hearing the voice of God. He fled from his master and boarded a ship bound for Britannia. After disembarking in what he described as a wilderness, he walked for twenty-eight days with other travellers, famished and exhausted. He prayed for food and his hungry party came across a wild boar, which filled their bellies and renewed their belief in God, and convinced Patrick that he had performed a miracle.

Patrick took up life as a priest but was compelled to return to Ireland, inspired by a holy vision. He travelled back as a missionary, intending to convert the Irish people to Christianity. After thirty years in Ireland, he was appointed as a bishop and founded monasteries, schools and churches all over the country. Before his death he wrote the *Confessio*, a remarkable account of his life. Missing from this autobiography is his celebrated use of the shamrock. The story goes that he used a three-leaved clover to explain the doctrine of the Holy Trinity. This story, probably fabricated, appeared in the eighteenth century but nonetheless has become a symbol of Ireland.

The seventeenth of March is now St Patrick's Day, a day of wild celebration not just in Ireland but all over the world. Ireland is everybody's second favourite country and in an impressive example of 'soft power' Irish bars are packed in cities around the world as people channel their inner 'Irishness' for a day of drunken companionship and song.

18 March

It is one of the most important machines in history. Developed by one of the most gifted scientists. Today in 1940 Alan Turing watched as his code-breaking machine, the 'Bombe', was installed in Hut 1 at the top-secret UK Government Code and Cypher School at Bletchley Park. It was a vital step towards breaking the German Enigma codes.

The Germans believed that their Enigma encryption machines were unbreakable. They could be set up 158,962,555,217,826,360,000 different ways, and even if by chance the enemy guessed the set-up, it was changed daily.

To defeat this machine, Turing, the father of computer science, realised he needed another machine. Building on the work of Polish mathematicians, his Bombe mimiced several Enigma machines, which tried a vast array of combinations in a short amount of time to guess the German daily setting.

Code-named 'Victory', the Bombe was two metres tall and weighed a ton. It had nearly 100,000 parts and 12 miles of wiring. It certainly did not deliver victory straight away. A long slow process of learning and improvement ensued.

By 1941 some German codes were being reliably broken. Two hundred more Bombes were built and stationed across the country to protect them from German bombing raids. By 1943 Bletchley Park was spewing out decrypted German signals, allowing the navy to destroy German submarines in the Atlantic or redirect convoys. By the time of D-Day in 1944 Allied leaders discovered that the intercepted German messages from the front line reached their desks faster, and were more useful, than reports from their own troops.

So secret was the whole operation that all mention of the Bombe was forbidden for decades, and this ancestor of today's computers, a machine that helped to win the war, was unknown to all apart from those who had witnessed the clunk and whir of its daily grind through millions of different combinations.

19 March

It was one of the largest mass suicides ever recorded. Today in 1644 at least two hundred, and perhaps many more, members of the Peking (now Beijing) royal family killed themselves out of loyalty to the Chongzhen emperor – the last emperor of the famous Ming dynasty – who had committed suicide himself as the world around him collapsed.

First established in 1368, from the outset of the sixteenth century the Ming dynasty had been weakened by corruption. China closed in on itself, the emperor banning Chinese ships from sailing beyond coastal waters while Europeans were doing the opposite – arriving in China by sea from 1517.

Factionalism weakened the ruling elite. Rising taxation made Ming rule widely unpopular. Climatic problems – effects of the 'Little Ice Age' which produced droughts and famines – fostered unrest. Rebellion began during the 1630s. By 1641 rebels had taken over parts of China, and by 1644 they had reached the capital. Defending garrisons were unpaid and poorly prepared.

With military defeat inevitable, the Chongzhen emperor gathered the imperial household together (with the exception of his sons) and attacked them with his sword, killing some, injuring others, before hanging himself – declaring himself in a suicide note, some say, unable to face his ancestors, 'dejected and ashamed'. Hundreds of others followed his example and killed themselves.

Manchus from the north (from where Manchuria derives its name) were waiting to capitalise, and they moved swiftly south, crushing rivals and setting up in Peking their own alternative Qing dynasty. They brought with them the Chinese pigtail – a Manchu hairstyle – familiar now from images and films, which was imposed on the Han Chinese. A symbol of their subordination to a new regime.

20 March

At the end of the nineteenth century a new, disturbing device emerged to threaten Britain's dominance of the world's oceans. Britannia might rule the waves, but humans were now taking to vessels that could dive beneath them. Rear Admiral Arthur Wilson VC, controller of the Royal Navy, called these new submarines 'underhand, unfair, and damned un-English'. But he was not stupid enough to reject this new technology outright. While expressing outrage in public, the navy began testing submarines in private, and today in 1902, *Holland 1*, the navy's first submarine, dived for the first time.

Bizarrely, much of the research and development for submarines was paid for by the Irish Fenians. These Irish freedom fighters rightly believed that the only way to defeat Britain's awesome fleet of battleships was to find entirely new technology that would make them obsolete. They supported engineer John Holland as he attempted to marry a standard internal combustion engine with an electric propulsion system, a bit like a modern hybrid car, but which could run above and below water. Holland was not fussy about his backers; when the Fenian money ran out he turned to their arch-enemy the Royal Navy.

Holland 1 was built in great secrecy in Barrow-in-Furness. Parts were labelled 'pontoon no. 1'. On 20 March 1902 she was cautiously submerged in a basin which could be drained if necessary. The submarine successfully dived and resurfaced. With growing confidence, sea trials were scheduled for April. By the end of the year, now HMS *Holland 1*, she was a commissioned vessel in Portsmouth.

It was the start of a new era in war at sea. In time submarines and aircraft would make battleships obsolete, and Britannia would have to fight above and below the waves if Britons were to avoid becoming slaves.

21 March

The young woman was buried in Gravesend, on the banks of the muddy Thames, thousands of miles from the inlets of the Chesapeake where she had played as a child. She died when she was barely in her twenties. Today in 1617 the woman known as Pocahontas – a pet name that meant something like 'little wanton' – was laid to rest. Her formal name was Matoaka.

As a girl, Pocahontas paid regular visits to the English settlements near Jamestown in Virginia, showing off her ability to do cartwheels and impressing the English colonists with her 'wit and spirit'. That did not save her from being caught up in their brutal exploitation. She was kidnapped to provide a bargaining tool. Her captors hoped that her people would give them information about the location of deposits of mythical gold and silver.

It was while held as a hostage that she met an Englishman named John Rolfe, in a new settlement called Henrico, upriver of Jamestown. They fell in love. Rolfe was deeply religious and asked her to take the Christian name Rebecca, evoking the beautiful Old Testament foreign servant girl whose arrival signified God's blessing. In the spring of 1614 John and 'Rebecca' duly married.

Rolfe was famous for his experiments with tobacco and it was to advertise the wonderful properties of the plant that the pair visited England two years later. She caused a sensation, and their son Thomas was hailed as the physical embodiment of the possibility of peace and fraternity between the English and local Indian tribes.

She boarded a ship to take her back to Virginia, but only made it as far as Gravesend, when she became gravely ill – from what is unknown – and was taken ashore where she died. In life, she had been a symbol of hope that coexistence might be possible; her premature death was a grim portent of her people's fate.

22 March

It was the Great Escape of the seventeenth century. Today in 1621, the scholar Hugo de Grotius escaped his prison where he had been incarcerated for two years. He was smuggled out, hidden inside a bookcase.

Hugo de Grotius was imprisoned for getting involved in the frenetic religious disputes of the Dutch Republic, when he publicly advocated for greater religious toleration, which was against the popular but fanatical Calvinist approach. Grotius believed that only the basic idea of the existence of God should be enforced, other ideologies should be private. In a time of religious fanaticism, these claims landed him in Loevestein Castle to serve a life sentence. His wife, Maria, devoted to her husband, elected to join him in his imprisonment.

During his time in prison, Grotius was permitted to read and books were delivered to his cell inside a bookcase, very similar to a large trunk. Initially, as the bookcase was delivered into the cell, and as it came and went, it was carefully inspected. As time went on, the guards became more relaxed, and saw the coming and going of the bookcase as an unimportant event.

With help from his wife, Grotius climbed inside the chest, amid the books that had granted him the only freedom possible over the last two years. The case was collected and carried openly, through the castle, and into the outside world. The couple fled to Paris where he remained in exile and produced some of his most famous work, pioneering the idea that there should be a society of states governed by legally enforceable international agreements. He laid the foundations for modern international relations and the intellectual blossoming of the Enlightenment.

The bookcase that Grotius used for his escape still survives to this day, and is on display at the Rijksmuseum in Amsterdam.

23 March

It was an authoritarian response to a terrorist attack. Today in 1933, following an arson attack on the Parliament building, the Reichstag, Adolf Hitler passed a law turning Germany into a dictatorship. With hindsight it was a deeply significant moment.

On 27 February the Reichstag building had been deliberately set on fire. It remains (and no doubt will always remain) unclear whether this was by the Communists, or by the Nazis trying to make it look like the work of the Communists. Since then Parliament had gathered not in the Reichstag building, as was customary, but inside the Kroll Opera House opposite.

That day Hitler arrived, dressed, as was customary, in brown military uniform with the swastika symbol wrapped around his upper left arm. A vast swastika hung behind the speaker's lectern. Communist Party members had been denied admittance.

Having failed in the election to achieve an absolute majority, unfettered control required what was officially called the 'Law to Remedy the Distress of People and Reich', known more commonly as the 'Enabling Act'. Critically, this would allow the Reich's Nazi government to enact laws without the approval of Parliament, which was being asked, effectively, to vote itself into irrelevance.

Hitler needed a two-thirds majority. But after he had spoken – working himself up into his accustomed frenzy – the act passed with 441 votes to 94. Only the Social Democrats voted against, their leader Otto Wels having bravely insisted that 'one can take away our freedom and livelihoods – but not our honour'.

No sooner had the law passed than the Reichstag – all trace of democratic government in Germany – was effectively abolished, and the Nazi leader Adolf Hitler had become a dictator. Otto Wels ironically lasted longer than many of the lickspittles who had facilitated Hitler's rise. He went into exile in Paris and died in his bed in 1939.

24 March

Robert Carey had served on enough diplomatic delegations to recognise an opportunity. In March 1603 he visited the court of Queen Elizabeth I and saw that her death was a matter of days away. He lurked until the morning of 24 March, when whispers of the queen's death reached him, and then bolted. The court was in lockdown, travel was banned, fortresses alerted and London reinforced. But Carey managed to dodge the restrictions and galloped north.

Elizabeth left no children to inherit her crown. She had executed her cousin, Mary Queen of Scots, like her a grand-daughter of Henry VII, which left Mary's son James VI of Scotland as the heir. His relationship with his cousin Elizabeth, his mother's killer, was distant but proper. The crown of England was a prize not worth endangering for the sake of retribution. He bided his time. Elizabeth never promised him the throne but her senior courtiers assured him that it would fall to him upon her death.

These courtiers were now trying to transition from a Virgin Queen to a Scottish King and Carey was determined to gain from it. A mere two days later, exhausted and saddle sore, he burst into Holyrood Palace to bring James the news of Elizabeth's death and his accession as James I of England. He was instantly rewarded with a senior position in James's court.

James was determined to rule England and Scotland as one united kingdom. 'I am the husband,' he told Parliament, 'and the whole isle is my lawful wife . . .' But despite his best efforts, England and Scotland remained autonomous states with fiercely independent political elites. They were only finally united a century later in 1707, during the reign of his great-granddaughter, another ageing, childless queen, Anne.

25 March

It was simply the Great Escape. A massive breakout of Allied prisoners of war from Stalag Luft III, in present-day Poland, in the early hours of this morning in 1944.

Prisoners of war were duty-bound to make life difficult for their gaolers. No one took this more seriously than RAF Squadron Leader Roger Bushell, a champion skier and fluent German speaker. He had been shot down in 1940 during the Battle of France but did not regard his war as being over.

His ambitious plan was that three tunnels would be carved into the sandy soil, which once completed would enable a staggering 200 prisoners to break out. Nothing on this scale had ever been attempted before.

Six hundred prisoners played their part. The tunnels were deep, nine metres below the surface and they were code-named Tom, Dick and Harry. Bushell threatened anyone who even said the word 'tunnel' with dire consequences. Around 4,000 bed-boards and 52 large tables were stolen to shore up the tunnels. Despite the secrecy, the Germans found Tom and blew it up. Dick had to be abandoned, but Harry was completed by March 1944. Bushell and a group of thirty men who spoke German and had the best chance would lead the way. After them were seventy more men, who had worked the hardest on the tunnel. Another hundred were chosen by lot.

On the evening of 24 March they squeezed through the narrow, 102-metre long tunnel, opened the hatch on the far side of the barbed wire and one by one slipped into the woods. At 1 a.m. on the 25th there was a minor collapse that needed repairing. Seventy-seven men managed to get out until at 4.55 a.m. the guards spotted Henry Trent VC heading into the woods and sounded the alarm.

The tunnel was found and filled with sewage and debris. As for the escapers, only three made it out of Hitler's empire. The rest were rounded up and fifty were executed in contravention of the Geneva Convention, including the ringleader, Roger Bushell.

26 March

The words were inscribed on gold plates. The lettering was unique, described as 'reformed Egyptian' by the lucky seventeen-year-old who had discovered this remarkable buried stash. He had been led to the spot in upstate New York by an angel, Moroni, who had told him to translate the plates and restore the true faith. The chosen man, Joseph Smith, eagerly obeyed, helped by magical spectacles provided by Moroni. Smith's translation was published today in 1830 under the title *The Book of Mormon*.

The most striking claim in Smith's book was that Jesus Christ had appeared in North America shortly after his resurrection. He joined an existing community of exiles from the Holy Land who had gone to America in 600 BC, and with their cooperation established a peace-loving society, governed with just and wise laws that endured until it collapsed into internecine violence.

The book was greeted with derision. Scholars pointed out that no archaeological evidence whatsoever existed for the absurd proposition of a pre-Columbian wave of migration from the ancient Near East; moreover it was riddled with anachronisms, describing sheep, goats, elephants, steel, iron, chariots and horses, all of which were brought to the Americas by European settlers after 1492. Modern critics have strengthened the critique by establishing that absolutely no DNA evidence exists that links any indigenous American group with Smith's ancient band of settlers.

The publication marked the founding moment of a religious movement. The scorn of elites only legitimised Smith in the eyes of his believers. Mormonism is now adhered to by over 15 million people, with the book translated into eighty-three languages. To the rest of us, Mormonism appears absurd because we know a huge amount about its genesis. It is possible that our reverence for Muhammad, Buddha or Peter and Paul would not be as profound if they had founded their faiths in the fierce glare of modern scholarship and forensic cross-examination.

27 March

It is one of history's lesser-known riots. The violence occurring in Basingstoke today in 1881 was a very British battle as locals clashed with temperance campaigners over the right to booze. When the Salvation Army hit the streets they were met by a crowd of angry locals, workers at the many breweries in the town, publicans and others who had a definite interest in the industry's prosperity.

In fact it was the location not for one riot but for many. The unrest continued for three years. Basingstoke is not, perhaps, notable for much. It was, though, a focus for the nineteenth-century brewing industry, which was why the Salvation Army chose it as a site for its protest.

Basingstoke's mayor was a brewer. It had no fewer than fifty public houses – many of them brewery-owned – which now seems a remarkable number for a place of that size. As the Salvation Army tried to spread the 'word of God', and tried to 'cure' the town's many regular drinkers, people were intolerant of this do-goodery and some responded by throwing stones.

On this day in 1881 it was a Sunday – the usual day for the Salvation Army's weekly meetings. With trouble on the 20th, police were recruited for a week later though not enough to ease fears that 3,000-odd protesters would disturb the peace. The mayor had literally to read the Riot Act, and the convenient fact that the Royal Horse Artillery were visiting meant that they were summoned to clear the crowds.

In the feverish, violent and no doubt drink-fuelled atmosphere, assaults took place, while temperance campaigners were ducked in the canal. Windows were smashed. Of the additional special constables, some refused in disgust to defend those they called these 'damned hypocrites'. At least twenty people subsequently appeared in court and ten rioters were imprisoned. Basingstoke did not go dry.

28 March

Russian ambitions were making the British government nervous. The tsar was expanding Russian influence in eastern Europe and the Middle East. Today in 1854 Britain declared war, plunging the country into its first European military entanglement since the defeat of Napoleon. There was fighting in the Baltic, Far East and the Caucasus but the war became known by the theatre that saw the worst of the violence, the Crimea.

The international order abhors a vacuum, and the once dominant Ottoman Empire was in danger of becoming one. The sprawling domains of the sultan spread from the Balkans, through the Middle East to the Red Sea, rich territories that invited the interest of circling rival empires. Russia had long sought warm-water ports to base its navy, while its rulers dreamed of 'liberating' their Slavic cousins from Ottoman rule, and perhaps even occupying Constantinople, the wellspring of their Eastern Orthodox faith.

Britain and France wished to prop up the ailing Ottoman regime. It suited them to have a harmless hegemony ruling over this region with its complicated patchwork of religions and ethnicities. An expeditionary force was sent to besiege the key Russian military base, Sevastopol in the Crimea. Turkish, French and British troops endured appalling conditions exacerbated by inadequate supplies and medical facilities as they spent a year beneath the walls of the fortress.

Almost for the first time, the battlefields were photographed. Newspaper correspondents were present on both sides: one a young writer named Leo Tolstoy. One nurse, Florence Nightingale, became a celebrated national figure and battlefield medicine was transformed. A telegraph cable was sunk to allow updates within hours; politicians found themselves reacting to a hostile press enflamed by stories of shortages or incompetence. War had begun to assume its modern character.

29 March

It is probably Britain's bloodiest battle. Yet it was not in the fields of Flanders, or the D-Day beachhead. It was not even in the twentieth century. The men were not killed with high explosives or machine-gun bullets, but with cold steel. For this was a battle fought today in 1461, a clash of Englishmen, on a field in Yorkshire.

The Battle of Towton was the culmination of a brutal war between the descendants of Edward III as to who would wear the crown. The War of the Roses tore the country apart as the weak, ill king, Henry VI of the House of Lancaster, struggled to protect his throne against his cousins the dukes of York.

Edward of York was physically impressive. He was eighteen years old, well over six feet tall and fought alongside his men. Henry VI was the opposite. Deeply infirm, he left the fighting to others. Edward's outnumbered army positioned themselves with the wind behind them so their arrows showered down on their enemy. By contrast the forces of Lancaster saw their arrows labouring into a headwind and falling short. Unable to stand the punishment they surged forward, forced to fight on Edward's terms. A brutal, long, hand-to-hand melee ensued. Young Edward steadied his flank in the face of sustained attacks by providing visible and inspirational leadership. A snowstorm blinded the men, breaking the battle down into pockets of desperate butchery, close-range arrows piercing mail shirts and the wounded lying shrieking in the churned-up mud.

When reinforcements arrived for Edward, the Lancastrian army broke and ran. Now a mass of terrified individuals, they were slaughtered. Rivers barred their flight. The desperate men trampled each other, drowning their comrades in their heavy armour. The water ran red with blood for days afterwards.

Edward of York made himself King Edward IV on that terrible battlefield. Perhaps 28,000 men died, more than on the first day of the Battle of the Somme. But like the Somme, the fighting would continue, many more young men would die before the Wars of the Roses would come to an end.

30 March

It was a transparent act of desperation, but it let the genie out of the lamp. Today in 1815, Joachim Murat, King of Naples, a man who had fought on every side in the great war that had raged across Europe for a generation, attempted to reinvent himself as a champion for Italian liberation and unification. His release of the Rimini Proclamation was a clarion call for Italians to rise up against their foreign, Austrian overlords and seize their independence. 'Italians!' it roared. 'The hour has come to engage in your highest destiny.'

It was pretty rich coming from him. Murat had been born the son of an innkeeper in France. His life was transformed by the Revolution. Handsome, arrogant and dashing, Murat was sensible enough to hitch his star to that of a young Napoleon Bonaparte, sourcing the cannon that the ambitious general blasted his enemies with from the streets of Paris and himself to the pinnacle of power.

Murat's battlefield bravery saw him heaped with honours, including the wonderful title 'First Horseman of Europe' while a canny marriage to Bonaparte's younger sister brought him a royal crown as King of Naples. It was his attempt to cling on to his kingdom after Napoleon's series of defeats in eastern and central Europe that saw Murat first switch his allegiance to Austria and then finally portray himself as an Italian patriot. It failed. He was an unconvincing agent of Italian patriotism. He was captured and shot.

The proclamation however did help to awaken a powerful impulse for self-determination in Italy. Over the following decades, Italian nationalism became one of the nineteenth century's most disruptive forces. Patriots, poets, mercenaries, utopians and fraudsters were drawn to the peninsula, partitioned and occupied by foreigners since the fall of Rome, in a nationalist struggle that sent shock waves far beyond its own borders.

31 March

It is the most popular tourist attraction on earth, and one the most recognisable structures, yet when the Eiffel Tower opened today in 1889 it was not an instant hit.

France was determined to mark the 100th anniversary of the start of the French Revolution with a giant party that would showcase the extraordinary scientific and engineering advances of the intervening century. The Exposition Universelle was a giant festival, bursting with the swaggering self-confidence born from this remarkable age of progress and European domination of the globe. The centrepiece of the festival, through which the public would enter the site, was a tower built by Gustave Eiffel. In a city famous for its genteel eighteenth- and nineteenth-century boulevards, this was to be a total contrast. A monster made of wrought iron, anchored in concrete. It would celebrate, Eiffel said, 'not only the art of the modern engineer, but also the century of Industry and Science in which we are living'.

Inevitably many artists went ballistic. They protested 'with all our strength' the erection of this 'useless and monstrous' tower. 'Our humiliated monuments will disappear in this ghastly dream. And for twenty years . . . we shall see stretching like a blot of ink the hateful shadow of the hateful column of bolted sheet metal.'

Eiffel was unmoved. It was built in just two years and today in 1889 he led a party to the top of what was then the tallest building on earth, by stairs as the lifts were not quite working yet. It took an hour, many of the politicians opted to go no further than the first stage, but Eiffel went to the top and unfurled a giant Tricolour at 2.35 p.m.

It was supposed to be a temporary structure but it soon became an indispensable symbol of France, a focus for national pride, emblem of fortitude in the face of the German invasion of 1914 and implacable resistance during the Nazi occupation during the Second World War. It is also an enduring reminder that sometimes cherished national monuments begin life as 'hateful columns'.

APRIL

1 April

It was a short, punchy novel from a man who was not known for brevity; a scathing critique of an unequal society. Today in 1854, Charles Dickens's *Hard Times* began to be serialised in the magazine *Household Words*. It appeared in weekly instalments (as many of his novels did) between April and August that year.

For some years Dickens had been a literary giant, ever since the extraordinary success of his novel *The Pickwick Papers*, late in the 1830s. Any editor would have jumped at the chance to serialise a new novel. In this case, though, the editor – the 'conductor' as he was called – was in an unusual position, since he (it was a he) was Dickens himself: forty-two years old and in his prime.

Dickens was all too conscious that humanity in Britain stood on an important threshold. In editorials he welcomed readers 'faithful in the progress of mankind' and 'thankful for the privilege of living in this summer-dawn of time'. But he was under no illusion that civilisation had a way to go as this novel, with its revealing title, all too plainly showed.

Hard Times is the only one of Dickens's novels based away from London, in a fictional northern mill-town; it also deals with a new class of people: an industrial 'working class', treated by owners as mere commodities – 'hands' – rather than as people, educated in useful 'facts' at the expense of the imagination. With his character Gradgrind, Dickens satirised those utilitarians who saw what he described as 'figures and averages, and nothing else'.

Dickens's enormous popularity meant that the journal's circulation doubled, a 'fact' that made him both frustrated and delighted (he was 'three-parts mad, and the fourth delirious', he noted, 'with perpetual rushing at *Hard Times*'). The novel has never lost its relevance. We are still having the debate on how we soften the impact of revolutionary technological change on those whose lives it destroys.

2 April

In the eighteenth century Venice was infamous as the pleasure capital of Europe, the star attraction on the Grand Tour, tempting young men with its wild parties. It is only appropriate, therefore, that the most famous womaniser in the world, Giacomo Casanova, was born here on this day in 1725.

Born to bohemian parents, Casanova was the eldest of six children. With his father dead and his mother working as an itinerant actress, he found himself in the care of a tutor, Abbe Gozzi. Aged only eleven, Casanova was subject to a sexual advance by Gozzi's sister, Bettina. He fondly remembers her in his memoirs as the instigator of his adoration of the opposite sex: 'It was she who little by little kindled in my heart the first sparks of a feeling which later became my ruling passion.'

Casanova developed a quick wit, a passion for gambling and a curiosity for women that quickly led him into debt, and growing unpopularity. His diary is a refreshingly honest account of a remarkable life. 'I have always liked highly seasoned food,' he wrote. 'As for women, I have always found that the one I was in love with smelled good, and the more copious her sweat the sweeter I found it.'

He refers to over 120 sexual encounters in his diary, with references to male lovers as well as female. His behaviour got him arrested in 1755 for affront to religion and common decency. He escaped solitary confinement, and continued 'cultivating whatever gave pleasure to my senses'. Casanova recorded his methods for seducing women, suggesting women could be conquered by a 'dint of gratitude'. It was the publication of his diary in English in the late nineteenth century that saw his name turned into a noun to describe anyone with multiple notches on the bedpost. He died aged seventy-three, with a face scarred from smallpox, and on his deathbed he looked back at his adventures, duels, imprisonment, escapes and plots and said simply: 'I can say that I have lived.'

3 April

The Templars had grown too rich, and too powerful. Today in 1312 the Pope sided with their enemies and issued a papal bull that abolished the order. The bull was called '*Vox in excelso*', a 'voice from on high', and decreed that many of the brothers of the Knights Templar had lapsed into 'the sin of wicked apostasy, the crime of detestable idolatry, and the execrable outrage of the Sodomite'.

The Order of the Poor Knights of the Temple of Solomon was founded in Jerusalem in 1119, charged with the protection of pilgrims at Christian sites of worship in the subsequent years after the First Crusade had seized the Holy Land from Muslim rule. Over the course of 200 years they became an elite force of highly skilled warrior knights, holy brothers and even great landowners; they were successful, tough and vastly wealthy.

The fortunes of the Templars began to falter when the Muslims recaptured Jerusalem, and finally after the fall of Acre in 1291 they were forced to flee to Cyprus. Heavily in debt to the Templars, King Philip IV of France seized the opportunity to attack the organisation by rounding up Templars and torturing them, beginning one of the bloodiest political persecutions in French history.

Philip compiled a dossier of accusations such as Templar brothers spitting on images of Christ, icon worship and illicit homosexual ceremonies. The reputation of the Templars had been irreparably damaged and under pressure from Philip, Pope Clement V had the order formally disbanded. Templar lands and assets were given to the Order of the Hospital of St John and by 1314 any remaining Templar leaders were executed, many being burned alive at the stake.

The Knights Templar retain a formidable reputation. Their entirely mythical association with secret treasure, the Holy Grail and King Arthur ensures that they are prominent in the popular perception of the Middle Ages.

4 April

No politician has monopolised the pinnacle of British power for as long as the man who was made First Lord of the Treasury today in 1721. So great was his influence, so complete was his grip on affairs of state that his enemies coined a new term for him – 'prime minister'. His name was Robert Walpole and he forged the role of prime minister, cementing it at the heart of the British constitution.

Walpole was from a gentry family in Norfolk. He was bright. After Eton and Cambridge he managed his family's lands efficiently and entered Parliament. He never lost his ability to talk to the sort of country gentry that filled the benches of the House of Commons and his skill at marrying their interests to those of London's trading and financial classes allowed him to dominate the political scene for decades.

There was one other source of his power, the crown. This was a time when the relationship between monarch and Parliament was ill defined and ever-changing. Who, ultimately, was in charge? Walpole always kept the confidence of the crown, partly through the important women in the king's life, in the case of George I, his mistress, of George II, his wife. But also through his management of the potentially volatile Parliament. He delivered a secure throne for the new dynasty of German kings, a steady revenue and a quiet life, and Parliament was listened to, with low taxation and sensible economic management.

He became an indispensable bridge between the crown and Parliament, maintaining the confidence of both executive and legislature in a balancing act requiring consummate skill. George II was so grateful to his minister that he gave him a gift, a house, 10, Downing Street. Walpole accepted but on the condition that it belong not to him but to First Lords of the Treasury in perpetuity. At the end of his twenty-year tenure, Walpole had ensured that his successors would inherit the house with the job of prime minister.

5 April

He was the undoubted giant of British twentieth-century history. Winston Churchill, the great war leader, was also prime minister from 1951 until today in 1955 when he reluctantly retired. He continued to be an MP, though did not speak again in Parliament.

During the summer of 1949, on holiday in the south of France, he had suffered a mild stroke and already at the end of 1951 George VI considered asking him to retire (though the king's own death the following spring may have prevented him from doing so).

The early 1950s was a time in Britain both of radical social change and of international retreat, phenomena with which Churchill was uneasy and for which he was certainly unsuited. 'I did not become Prime Minister,' he had declared in 1941, 'to preside over a dismemberment of the British Empire.' But this of course was precisely what did occur. Churchill's own decline, and that of Britain, continued side by side – and he tried to deny them both.

June 1953 saw the coronation of a new queen – the beginning of a new era – and for Churchill a second, much more damaging stroke. The medical notes were 'doctored,' to mask details of what had happened and, somewhat to his own surprise, Churchill was able for a time to continue working. But, not surprisingly, he was old and inflexible, set in his ways, as President Eisenhower privately remarked.

At international conferences his refusal to wear a hearing aid necessitated the unseemly raising of voices. He believed still in the centrality of the British Empire and the 'special relationship' that he had forged with Franklin Roosevelt, long after both had lost much basis in reality. He survived for another ten years. At his death he had been a Member of Parliament for five different constituencies for an almost continuous sixty-four years.

6 April

The fighting had lasted a generation. King Edward I of England had used a succession crisis in Scotland to press his own claim to be overlord of Britain. He invaded Scotland in 1296, refusing to recognise Robert the Bruce as king, or Scotland as a country independent of English authority. The Scots had resisted and the fortunes of war had swung violently from side to side. Today in 1320, long after Edward's death, the Scots declared independence. It was in the form of an appeal to Pope John XXII urging him to recognise an independent Scotland, with Robert the Bruce as king. Written and sealed by eight earls and around forty barons, it became known as the Declaration of Arbroath.

It is a patriotic declaration of Scotland's autonomy, 'As long as but a hundred of us remain alive, never will we on any conditions be brought under English rule. It is in truth not for glory, nor riches, nor honours, that we are fighting, but for freedom – for that alone, which no honest man gives up but with life itself.'

The trouble had begun almost thirty years earlier and in the middle of a storm. King Alexander III of Scotland had spent the evening at Edinburgh Castle feasting, and merrily toasting his new marriage and the prospect of an heir. Drunk and lusty, he was determined to visit the queen and would not be persuaded to wait until morning. He set out on horseback to Fife and in terrible weather, but became separated from his party. The next morning Alexander was found at the foot of a cliff with his neck broken. Perhaps his horse had stumbled.

The Declaration asserted that Scotland had always been independent, and had been unjustly attacked by Edward I. The Pope accepted the Declaration, but it was not until 1328 that the English grudgingly recognised Scotland's independence and not until 1357 was there a lasting peace with a border that remains to this day.

7 April

He was a 'violent, dangerous rogue' whose reputation is probably better than he deserves. Today in 1739, the famous highwayman and brigand Dick Turpin – Richard Turpin, to give him his baptismal name of 1705 – was executed for horse-stealing.

In fact Turpin's first-known crimes were for the stealing of deer not horses, an activity he slipped into after marrying Betty Millington and setting up as a respectable butcher in Essex. His gang then turned to robbing houses. But most of them were caught and dealt with harshly: pilloried, transported, or executed, if they had not first died in prison.

Posters offered rewards for the capture of Dick: 'a fresh coloured man, very much marked with the small pox, about five feet nine inches high' wearing 'a blue grey coat and a light coloured wig'. While this description was hardly likely, at the time, to mark him out, it was later enhanced – to portray a man 'of a brown complexion . . . his cheek bones broad, his face thinner towards the bottom'.

Only subsequently did Turpin turn to the stealing of race-horses, 'rustling' – to use a later term for animal theft – one called Whitestockings from a stable in Whitechapel. Already he was acquiring notoriety, one newspaper (plainly relishing the scandal which sold papers then as it does now) relating among the 'great and wonderful news from London' a 'hue and cry after the Great Turpin'.

Imprisoned in Yorkshire under a pseudonym, he was executed in York. Only later were his exploits glamorised in plays, comics, books, prints and advertising – stories that included a fictional gallop up the length of England from London to York on his trusty steed, Black Bess. The popularity of his myth demonstrates that even the supposedly law-abiding Brits love a rebellious, flawed, charismatic anti-hero.

8 April

It was the defining sound of early mornings in suburbs across Britain and further afield. The whirr of the float, the clink of the empties, the rattle of crates of bottles. Today in 1879 the British were able to buy milk in glass bottles for the first time.

The 1870s saw improvements in bottle manufacture. By the early years of the twentieth century they could be mass-produced by machines that meant it was now possible to produce huge numbers of bottles, and transport vast amounts of fluid over large distances. It was part of a revolution that included canning, preservation and cold storage, bringing about a revolution in how human beings sourced, transported and consumed foods. No longer did people have to take earthenware jugs to fill with milk. Now they could buy glass bottles, or the milkman could go around neighbourhoods, first with a horse and cart, and from the 1930s with electric milk floats, dispensing milk and collecting the empties. Milk could also now flow into cities to nourish the urban poor.

The sound of the milkman on his rounds is often remembered with affection by people of a certain age, yet, far from being obsolete, the home delivery of healthy produce, often straight from the dairy, in recyclable containers, in electric vehicles feels rather progressive. The age of the milkman may have passed but the spirit is very much alive. Perhaps it is the once mighty supermarket that we should be feeling nostalgic for . . .

9 April

It was the bloodiest war in American history. More people were killed than in all the other American wars *combined*. Eventually the carnage came to an end; the US Civil War effectively finished today in 1865 when General Robert E. Lee surrendered the main field army of the secessionist Confederate States of America to Ulysses S. Grant of the US Army. It happened in a nondescript house, in an unremarkable village in rural Virginia where the ebb and flow of fighting had finally and arbitrarily ended. It was a seismic moment, but it was also one of history's most bizarre coincidences.

It was mid-afternoon when General Grant hurried into the house. Lee was dressed immaculately. Grant was mud-splattered and shabby. The two masters of the battlefield spoke warmly and agreed a generous ceasefire arrangement. Lee's men would be fed and free to leave with horses and baggage, and the officers would keep their swords. They would not be imprisoned or prosecuted. When it was over, Grant forbade cheering. The work of healing had already begun.

For the owner of the house, a grocer called Wilmer McLean, it was an extraordinary moment for several reasons. First he was a witness to history, second, as soon as the ceremony was over bystanders ransacked his house for souvenirs; everything portable was carried away. But nothing was as strange as the coincidence that had brought the two sides to his house.

Four years before, McLean had been a farmer 120 miles away in Manassas, Northern Virginia. In July 1861 the first battle of the Civil War was fought on his farm. His house had been bombarded, his kitchen was damaged by Union shells. Wanting to protect his family, he had moved out of harm's way to Appomattox County. There, they had indeed managed to escape the clutches of the war until that fateful day when the generals needed a venue for the surrender ceremony.

Wilmer McLean was absolutely right when he told people, 'The war began in my front yard and ended in my front parlor.'

10 April

It was the largest eruption in recorded history. Today in 1815 at Mount Tambora in Indonesia tremors and smaller explosions gave way to one that was catastrophic. Columns of flame rose up and the whole mountain was turned into a mass of 'liquid fire', reduced, in the aftermath, to only two-thirds of its previous height.

The column of smoke and sulphur dioxide that followed the flames reached some 43 kilometres into the air. Although estimates vary widely, some 10,000 people were killed in the immediate vicinity, and perhaps another 80,000 died from delayed effects such as the loss of agriculture.

The presence of atmospheric particles created long and colourful sunsets all over the globe and caused more serious short-term climate change. The curious, unusually wet weather experienced in Europe (which mired the battlefield of Waterloo in thick mud, preventing Napoleon from using his cannon and cavalry as he would have liked, and thus perhaps making a critical difference to the outcome) may have been the result of this eruption.

The following year experienced significant cooling. With harvest failures widespread, it became known as the 'Year Without Summer'. Western Europe and North America witnessed unseasonal snowfalls during June and July. There were severe typhus epidemics in the following years in south-east Europe and the eastern Mediterranean that may have been made worse by the eruption. Large numbers of livestock died in New England during the winter of 1816/17, while cool temperatures and heavy rains led to failed harvests in the British Isles. There was famine in Ireland following the failure of wheat, oat and potato harvests. Food prices rose sharply in Germany and demonstrations at grain markets followed by riots, arson and looting took place in many European cities. It was the worst famine of the nineteenth century, and one which brought political turmoil in its wake.

11 April

The only joint husband and wife team in British history were crowned today in 1689. A compromise solution to a perilous situation that could easily have spiralled into armed conflict, nearly forty years after Britain had been torn apart by the Civil Wars. It was a success.

William, leader of the Netherlands, and Mary his wife were first cousins. It was an arranged, yet happy, dynastic marriage. Remarkably the marital bliss survived William's decision to invade England and eject his father-in-law, and uncle, James II from the throne. Mary supported the removal of her father who, unlike her, had become a Catholic, and was far too close to the French 'Sun King' Louis XIV, a man William described as his 'mortal enemy' and who they feared was amassing a universal empire covering western Europe.

Mary had been James II's heir, but suddenly in 1688 her 54-year-old father was blessed with a baby son with his second wife. The infant was baptised a Catholic, his godfather was the Pope himself. English Protestants begged William to intervene, he invaded and James II fled. Chaos ensued. William wanted to be king, Parliament preferred to make Mary the sovereign. In the end the unique formula of joint rule was accepted by both sides. The Bishop of London crowned them both in Westminster Abbey; William did not enjoy the ceremony, which to a man used to the Spartan habits of Calvinism reeked of Catholicism. Unusually the Archbishop of Canterbury refused to crown both of them because James II, for all his faults, was God's anointed. To him, William and Mary could never be the legitimate monarchs.

Mary died of smallpox five years later. William had slept by her sickbed and was devastated by her death. He ruled alone for another eight years; his regime far less popular now that his partner was gone. The ousting of his father-in-law triggered seventy-five years of intrigue and rebellion resulted in the following as the supporters of James, known as Jacobites, who dreamed of putting his line back on the throne.

12 April

It may well be one of the worst business decisions in history. Today on 12 April 1976 Ronald Wayne, one of the three founders of Apple Computers, sold his 10 per cent holding in the company – for $800. Had he held on to it, it would now be worth over $90 billion. Even the document that he signed he later sold for a few hundred dollars: the same document that would fetch over $1.5 million. He has often said that he is a much better engineer than businessman.

While Wayne was only at the company for a couple of weeks in the very early days, he played, as Steve Wozniak admitted, a 'huge role'. Among numerous other contributions, he designed the Apple logo, one of the most famous symbols in the world.

Of course it is easy with hindsight to mock his decision to leave Apple. But Wayne denies feeling regret, insisting that he made the 'best decision with the information available to me at the time'. Unlike Jobs or Wozniak, he felt old and cautious. Working with them, he has said, was like holding a tiger by the tail. He functioned as the 'adult supervision'. Having experienced start-up businesses that failed, as most do, he had no desire to be left picking up the pieces.

Apple put personal computers into people's homes, then a portable super-computer into their pockets. In 2018 it became the first US company to be valued at over $1 trillion and there are over 1 billion Apple products in use today. None of them belong to Ronald Wayne, who lives in a remote settlement in the Nevada desert. Instead his small bungalow, surrounded by cactus plants, is full of gadgets that he repairs and makes himself.

13 April

If you are going to tell a lie, make it a giant lie. That is the lesson of one of the greatest confidence tricks in history, which started today in 1821. Gregor MacGregor, a Scottish soldier and adventurer in the British Army (he had served in the Peninsular War), returned to London from South America, declaring himself the 'Cazique [prince or chief] of Poyais'.

He declared that his intention was to attend King George IV's coronation, and he invited migrants and investments in his faraway country. Conditions in Latin America were ever-shifting and little understood, which made it seem quite plausible that there could be an unknown country called Poyais with a decorated general as its leader.

To the sophisticated people in the salons and ballrooms of the British capital, MacGregor – the 'Cazique' – was a sought-after embellishment to any event. The many social invitations that he received included one from the Lord Mayor of London.

He opened a legation and a land office, and sold commissions in a 'Poyaisian' military. The country's capital of St Josephs he described as having a cathedral, a bank and magnificent public buildings. Many stumped up funds, or even travelled (and many died), before they realised that it was all a complete invention. When exposed in London MacGregor simply moved to Paris, where he continued to sell land and issue advice in high society.

When the fraud was revealed in Paris he returned to Venezuela, where earlier he had joined the republicans in the struggle for independence from Spain (taking, in an early sign of his fondness for the grand gesture, a large library and a personal piper). There he lived, and died, peacefully. Rarely, if ever, has 'chutzpah' been so bold.

14 April

The ship had been making record time. Every day 176 firemen shovelled over 600 tons of coal into furnaces that powered three engines, generating 46,000 horsepower as four vast smoke stacks ejected 100 tons of ash into the air.

However, at 11.40 p.m. on the night of 13 April 1912, the RMS *Titanic* hit an iceberg 375 miles from Newfoundland, and a few hours later this brand-new engineering marvel slipped beneath the icy cold, dead-still surface of the Atlantic. The collision was fatal because the iceberg ripped a gash along the side of the ship, flooding five of its watertight compartments, too many to maintain buoyancy. Within the space of three hours, the *Titanic* had broken apart, with over a thousand people still on board, including the resident band, who serenaded the terrified passengers until they perished along with the ship.

The lifeboats were allocated to women and children, and cast into the Atlantic often less than half full. Of the 2,200 passengers on board, only around 700 survived the most famous shipwreck in history.

One of the passengers achieved significant fame after the ship's sinking, due to her remarkable efforts during the disaster. The 'Unsinkable' Molly Brown was a lucky survivor, and found herself on board the rescue vessel, the *Carpathia*. She handed out food, drinks, blankets and even raised $10,000 for those who had lost their worldly possessions. In a letter to her daughter after she reached New York, Molly wrote: 'After being brined, salted, and pickled in mid ocean I am now high and dry . . . They are petitioning Congress to give me a medal . . . If I must call a specialist to examine my head it is due to the title of Heroine of the *Titanic*.'

Molly was awarded a French Legion of Honour for her efforts, and used her fame later to campaign for women's rights. In popular adaptations of the sinking of the *Titanic*, Molly Brown became a consistent and well-loved character, providing a sliver of hope in what was ultimately the most tragic commercial maritime disaster in history.

15 April

For months, as the First World War raged in Europe, Ernest Shackleton and his men on board their wrecked ship *Endurance* had camped upon the ice, endeavouring to cross the Antarctic as part of what has been called the 'heroic age' of Antarctic exploration.

They were aware, always, of movement beneath them and the possibility of a sudden split in the ice. As the ice floated they neither remained where they were nor were able to escape. When a deep chasm did suddenly rupture, allowing them to launch their three lifeboats, it was rather too close for comfort: 'right under where our tent had been'.

Now facing a choice of destinations, they fixed upon 'Elephant Island' (so-called from an early sighting there of elephant seals rather than the land mammals), and inched towards it on high seas. Eventually, on 15 April 1916, they made it, pulling the boat up onto a shingle beach.

The weather tended to be foggy, and snow was lashed into blizzards by very high winds. When the men clambered out it was the first time for 497 days that they had stood on solid ground. 'It is sublime to feel solid earth under one's feet,' wrote Frank Hurley, the expedition's official photographer, having trod 'but heaving decks and transient ice for nearly 18 months'.

While Shackleton set out on the 820-mile voyage to South Georgia in an open lifeboat, the *James Caird*, the men who remained behind built a rudimentary hut on this wild and desolate land to protect them against the elements. Over four months later Shackleton returned to rescue them.

16 April

It was the last time two armies met in a pitched battle on British soil. In the teeth of sleet and snow on a sodden moorland at the mouth of the Great Glen in the Scottish Highlands, the Battle of Culloden was fought today in 1746. An army led by Charles Edward Stuart met the Duke of Cumberland's government force of redcoats and was decisively defeated, in what was the final clash of the '45 Jacobite Uprising.

Charles Edward Stuart, nicknamed 'Bonnie Prince Charlie' by his supporters and dismissed as the 'Young Pretender' by supporters of the Hanoverian regime of King George II, decided to risk all on a battle with Cumberland's army. They were outnumbered, with 6,000 troops, largely drawn from Highland clans, against 9,000 redcoats, and the boggy moor was an unsuitable terrain for the terrifying Highland Charge. The Jacobite army was battered by superior government artillery, which forced them to lunge chaotically at government lines to get to grips with their enemy. As the sides closed, the redcoats poured volleys of musketry into the charging clansmen. Despite a hail of musket balls the Jacobites smashed into the government troops and launched a vicious melee of sword swipes and bayonet thrusts.

Despite their extraordinary bravery, the attack lost momentum, and the Jacobites broke and fled. In the rout Jacobite losses were catastrophic: 1,500 dead or injured, compared with only 300 government troops. In the weeks that followed surviving Jacobites were hunted down in a brutal pacification process. The clans had their customs, weapons and even traditional dress outlawed. The Battle of Culloden marked the end of the Stuart claim to the British throne but also the beginning of the end for the traditional clan structure and Highland way of life.

17 April

The Wehrmacht was facing the combined might of Britain and France, they were outgunned and had fewer tanks. If they were to win, they would need help. So today in 1940 the 'stimulant decree' was issued by the Nazi government. It stipulated that all soldiers of the Wehrmacht be given daily tablets, developed by a Berlin pharmaceutical company, containing a drug called Pervitin, and which is better known today as 'crystal meth'.

The drug was said to increase energy levels and confidence, to reduce depression and to boost alertness, marketed to everyone from train drivers to housewives. Tiredness could be a problem of the past! Without inhibitions – without such natural restraints as fear – soldiers fought better, or at any rate more fiercely. It was hoped that it would aid that year's invasion of France. It had not previously been realised just what nature of 'Blitzkrieg' the Allies had been facing.

What the private papers of Adolf Hitler's own personal physician, Dr Theodor Morell, reveal is the astonishing levels of drug use prevalent among the Nazi high command as well as the army in general. Hitler himself – while affecting to have unnatural levels of purity and immunity from normal, human needs or desires – was receiving almost daily injections: of amphetamines, barbiturates and opiates.

Shortly before Hitler's suicide in his bunker in Berlin the Führer was probably suffering from the symptoms of withdrawal, such medication being impossible to come by in a ruined city. This is not to say that this little-told story explains the depths of depravity and insanity to which the Third Reich descended. Much of their ideology, after all, was set before this widespread drug use began. But it does provide a new angle, and may explain why so many seemed 'drugged' by it.

18 April

It is a tiny island with a remarkable history. Heligoland, a barren rock around forty miles off the north German coast, which has been both British and German over the last 200 years, reflects the ebb and flow of national fortunes between the two powerful nations, a relationship that was carved into the rock of the island itself, culminating in one of the most monumental non-nuclear explosions of all time, today in 1947.

Heligoland was secured by the British during the Napoleonic Wars as a staging post for British trade into central Europe; it became Britain's smallest colony. A tiny piece of the British Empire in Europe, it became the focus of German nationalist poets, thinkers and artists, who visited the windswept rock, and dreamed of a united Germany.

Kaiser Wilhelm swapped it with his grandmother Queen Victoria for a swathe of East Africa and turned it into a concrete fortress, a naval base that Britain eventually reoccupied after the Second World War. The British needed to get rid of these fortifications, use up wartime munitions and deliver a crushing blow to German nationalism, and planned a vast explosion to achieve all three objectives.

Six and a half thousand tons of explosives were wired up. A very British concern for the wildlife meant that warning explosions were triggered all morning, then, when the seabirds had taken to the wing, at 13.00 hours an almighty blast went off that rattled windows on the mainland.

The British succeeded in smashing the fortifications, in fact the geography of the island was fundamentally altered, but the politics backfired. The utter destruction of the spiritual home of the Germans provoked sympathy rather than celebration. The blast that was supposed to crush the German national spirit actually helped to rekindle it. Within five years Heligoland was given back to the Germans, and the evacuated population returned to rebuild their homes on the cratered moonscape.

19 April

It was the 'shot heard around the world'. Today in 1775, at 5 a.m., a group of British redcoated troops found their route through Massachusetts barred by a colonial militia. Britain and her American colonies were engaged in a dispute about money and power, who was in charge and who paid what. Groups of volunteers were organising themselves, and they had stashed caches of powder and muskets should things turn violent. The British periodically sent troops to confiscate these hoards. This was one such dawn expedition, but this time it would be different.

The Lexington militia had planned to make a show of resisting the British and then disperse. Fired up on patriotism, but not suicidal, none of the volunteers wanted to go toe to toe with the well-drilled British infantry. A British officer ordered them to disperse, their own commander agreed. But then a shot rang out. No one knows who fired it, but it was the spark that ignited a civil war. The furious British troops scattered the militia with their bayonets and advanced. When they reached the ironically named town of Concord they found a body of militia and here too shots rang out, which quickly escalated to a hail of musketry.

The unthinkable had happened. By the end of the day the ragged, harassed British column staggered back into Boston. Some three hundred of its men were dead, wounded or missing. Boston was placed under siege. Britain and her colonies were in open conflict.

Only a decade before they had fought and died side by side fighting the French or the Ottawa, Huron, Iroquois and other tribes to bring North America under their sway; now they had turned on each other. Britain's European rivals could not believe their luck. As the American rebels stunned the British with their tenacity and organisation, first France, then the Spanish and Dutch joined in against the British. The Americans won their independence, Britain's empire was humbled and diminished, and the United States was set free to build its own vast nation and eventually replace Britain as a hegemonic power.

20 April

If a piece of meat is left for weeks in the open air, before long maggots will simply appear in it. It seemed obvious that they form from nothing.

The notion of spontaneous generation – of life forms materialising from inanimate matter – sounds now like science fiction. For millennia, though, for 'natural philosophers' seeking to understand the origins of life, the idea was a routine part of assumed knowledge: a demonstrable fact. As with the maggots, so with fungi, or other insects, or shellfish.

This was the thinking that was followed by the Greek philosopher Aristotle when he formulated a general theory. Some animals, he wrote, 'spring from parent animals according to their kind, whilst others grow spontaneously and not from kindred stock', often in 'putrefying earth or vegetable matter'.

Eventually, between the seventeenth and the nineteenth centuries, the notion was increasingly questioned. And then, on 20 April 1862, the famous scientist Louis Pasteur – the 'father' of the germ theory of modern medicine – conducted an experiment to demonstrate conclusively that it was untrue.

He took a flask with a 'swan-neck' that bent downwards, allowing the circulation of air but preventing the entry of falling particles. In it he placed a meat broth, which he then boiled to sterilise it. For a lengthy period the broth remained unclouded: free from growth. If, by contrast, the same meat broth was put in a vessel without a 'swan-neck', clouding was much faster. In other words other life did not simply appear: spores, or eggs, had somehow first to enter. It was a fundamental step towards understanding the origin of life.

21 April

He was the embodiment of the fighter ace. The first celebrity hunter-killer of war in the air. Manfred von Richthofen, aka 'the Red Baron', was killed today in 1918.

Aerial combat was virtually unknown in 1914, and both sides faced a vertiginous learning curve. The technology changed so fast that tactics had to be invented in the midst of battle. Pilots were recruited from other branches of the military. Richthofen was a frustrated cavalryman and he requested a flying job in 1915 to get into the action. Initially he struggled with flying, crashing on his maiden flight, but he was soon making a name for himself. In late 1916 he shot down his first enemy aircraft. This was followed by 79 more, the highest number of kills of any First World War aviator. By late 1917 he was known to every soldier on both sides.

He led a group of elite fighter pilots (among them his brother, Lothar) who moved like a circus to set up a temporary airfield of tents wherever the action was thickest. The constant immersion in the terror of aerial combat took its toll. Von Richthofen never fully recovered from a head wound sustained in the summer of 1917 and took to the skies again despite doctors' orders.

By the spring of 1918, combat stress, head trauma, and exhaustion may have meant that the Red Baron was vulnerable. At 11 a.m. on 21 April he pursued a novice Canadian pilot at low level above the battlefield. A single bullet tore into his right armpit and out through his breast, perhaps fired by a Canadian pilot, or perhaps an Australian on the ground below. Mortally wounded, he managed to land the plane, and as the first Australians ran up, he died. Some of them later claimed his last word was '*Kaputt*', which roughly translates as 'It's broken.'

His plane was instantly stripped by souvenir hunters; there are now fragments all over the world. His body, though, was treated with respect by his admiring enemy and buried by the RAF with full military honours.

22 April

The Royal Society – granted its second Royal Charter today, on 22 April 1663, less than a year after the first – was one of the jewels of Restoration London.

King Charles II was greatly interested in science and enjoyed conducting experiments, supervised by his French professor of chemistry, in a special laboratory in St James's Palace. It was in this second charter that the king declared himself to be Founder and Patron of the Society. Early presidents included Sir Christopher Wren (an astronomer as well as an architect), Samuel Pepys, Isaac Newton and Joseph Banks. Giants, and giants standing on the shoulders of other giants, provided a prodigious contribution to the growth of modern science.

One of the founding principles, and the motto adopted by the Royal Society, is *Nullius in verba*, which might be translated as 'Don't take anyone's word for it'. Any claim not repeatedly demonstrable is worthless. The notion – vitally important for so long – of *authority*, of believing something because someone credible said it, was cast out.

Precursors to the society are cloudy. Something called the Invisible College was pioneered, with Robert Boyle at its heart and which devoted itself to the acquisition of knowledge through experimental investigation – though aptly enough, given its name, its workings, and its early membership, are unclear. Another debate surrounds the extent of French influence – something that Charles II's own tutor might imply.

Whatever the intricacies, clearly the middle seventeenth century saw a concentration of these ideas, accelerated by like-minded men who met to discuss them, and this was the fertile world in which the famous Royal Society – the oldest national scientific institution in the world – was born.

23 April

The battle lasted from sunrise to sunset. Today in 1014 a terrible struggle took place in Clontarf, near Dublin, between Brian Boru, High King of Ireland, and a Viking-led coalition of rivals.

Brian Boru was the ambitious ruler of Munster, and by the early eleventh century he dominated Ireland as high king. From the ninth century, Scandinavian raiders had settled on the banks of the River Liffey and established the settlement which became Dublin. A hybrid city of Norse and Irish, Pagan and Christian, Dublin was a conduit for trade, making the place a desirable prize of shifting allegiance. Men from Dublin and the kingdom of Leinster formed an alliance against the powerful Boru. In April 1014 the high king brought his enemies to battle at Clontarf, described by chroniclers as loud and devastatingly bloody.

Little is known about the battle, but it appears to have been large by the standards of the time, with an estimated 6,000 Vikings being killed or drowned, out of an overall total of up to 10,000 deaths. Boru's force was eventually victorious. However, many high-profile figures lost their lives in the battle, including Brian Boru himself, as well as his son Murchad and his grandson Toirdelbach. An eleventh-century chronicler claims that Brian was struck down while praying for victory in his tent, and was subsequently eulogised as a paradigm of Christian kingship.

The Battle of Clontarf has come to be seen as a great milestone that marked the breaking of Viking power in Ireland, and in the British Isles more generally. In later centuries, as Ireland faced occupation from another foreign power – the British – Brian Boru became a figure of legend, as the king who rid Ireland of the ungodly invaders.

24 April

At 10.27 a.m. the bomb detonated with the explosive power of over a ton of TNT. It blasted a five-metre-wide crater in the road and damaged buildings as far as 500 metres away. Today in 1993, the Irish Troubles came to the City of London as a truck bomb shattered the heart of London's financial district in Bishopsgate. The fact that it was a Saturday, and that telephone warnings of a 'massive bomb' had been sent, minimised fatalities, though one person did die and almost fifty were injured.

The truck was stolen and repainted and driven – with its lethal cargo – to Bishopsgate at nine o'clock in the morning and parked outside the Hongkong and Shanghai Bank. The damage it did was severe. Before September 11, indeed, it was the most expensive terrorist attack in history.

The IRA's campaign of violence within England had begun in the early 1970s. This was a delicate, uncertain period: when peace discussions were ongoing but incomplete and controversial, certainly within nationalist circles in which a 'Provisional IRA' refused to accept the ceasefire demanded by the English government. It was only just over a year since another large truck bomb had wreaked devastation near the capital's 'Baltic Exchange', and earlier in 1993 blasts had occurred at Harrods and in the High Street of Camden Town.

Further attacks were declared inevitable: 'no one should be misled into underestimating the IRA's intention to mount future planned attacks into the political and financial heart of the British state,' warned one government source. In fact, although there were smaller incidents, this was the last large bomb attack in England, and it was in August the following year when the IRA declared a 'complete cessation of military operations'. The peace was punctuated by occasional attacks, but on the whole it has held, even as politicians still struggle with the challenges of Northern Ireland's religious divide.

25 April

It was an ancient dream. A canal joining the two great cradles of civilisation, the Mediterranean and the Indian Ocean. The Pharaohs of Egypt may have even succeeded in joining the mighty Nile to the Red Sea, and the Romans or the early Islamic conquerors of the Middle East may have been able to travel from Cairo to the sea in the east. Napoleon stumbled upon the remnants of these ancient canals during his brief campaign in Egypt and dreamed of a new route to Asia and world domination.

It was not until today in 1859, however, that work began on the Suez Canal. The French led the way; they convinced the rulers of Egypt and Sudan to excavate it and paid for it by selling shares in Europe and America. As an army of forced labourers toiled away in appalling conditions, they struggled to finance the massive project. Costs doubled. The British joked that it would never be feasible. Yet, only a decade later it was open to traffic. The first vessel through was supposed to be the French imperial yacht, but an enterprising Royal Navy skipper jumped the queue in the dead of night and had to be ushered through first to avoid gridlock.

At around the same time the transcontinental railroad opened in the United States and the world had suddenly shrunk. The transit time for goods collapsed. A new era of globalisation dawned. British aversion to the canal turned to enthusiasm as it became the central artery of empire. When an Egyptian uprising threatened the canal, the British invaded in 1882, a temporary intervention . . . that lasted until 1954.

British control of Egypt prompted in turn the infamous European 'Scramble for Africa' as the whole continent was seized by competing empires. The precious stretch of navigable water had transformed the fate of an entire continent.

26 April

Ironically it was during a safety test – when safety systems were deliberately switched off – that the infamous disaster occurred at Chernobyl nuclear power station during the early hours of 26 April 1986. On an International Nuclear Event Scale it constitutes one of only two level 7 (maximum) events, the other being at Fukushima in Japan in 2011.

A calamitous combination of a power surge, flaws in the reactor design, and mistakes in the way that the radioactive core was arranged, led to a steam explosion and graphite fire that hurled fissile material into the atmosphere. Two deaths were immediate. Of employees and the servicemen who attended the scene, 134 were hospitalised with acute radiation sickness, while 28 died during the days and months afterwards. The number of cancer deaths that might be directly attributed to the events is debated. Fifteen has been suggested.

In the aftermath of the event what remained of the No. 4 reactor building was enclosed in a large cover known colloquially as the 'sarcophagus'. This was not intended to prevent radiation leakage, but to stop the further spread of radioactive dust and debris. In part this was to protect crews who continued to work, astonishingly, at the station's other, undamaged reactors.

In the aftermath an increasing number of inhabitants of nearby towns were evacuated, often in response to political rather than radioactive fallout. One recent analysis concluded that 'relocation was unjustified for 75% of the 335,000 people relocated after Chernobyl', given that severe city air pollution, for example, could be a greater hazard to health.

Whatever prevention, or responses, should have been, the fact is that the word 'Chernobyl' has entered our consciousness as shorthand for the dangers of nuclear power, doing immense damage to the technology's credibility which – given the deaths which might be attributed, for instance, to the burning of coal – has been arguably disproportionate.

27 April

It was one of the legendary acts of war reporting, news from the front line that flew around the world. Today in 1937 a British journalist called George Steer published an eyewitness account of the destruction in the immediate aftermath of the bombing of the Basque town of Guernica during the Spanish Civil War – death and destruction wreaked by planes from Nazi Germany at Franco's behest and immortalised in Pablo Picasso's famous painting.

It was an event that has come to symbolise the atrocities of war – particularly of war in the twentieth century, civilians deliberately and murderously targeted – and one which would probably never have been plainly understood, in the face of vehement Nationalist denial, had it not been for Steer's account, including his identification of German bomb casings.

This town, greatly valued by the Basque people, Steer reported, was 'completely destroyed yesterday afternoon' by enemy aircraft – 'slowly and systematically pounded to pieces' – in spite of the fact that it lay 'far behind the lines'. The action was a crime, he said (what would later be called a 'war crime'), 'unparalleled in military history'.

Steer visited in the middle of the night. The town, he said, was 'a horrible sight, flaming from end to end'. Houses were 'crashing on either side', while all that was left of religious hospitals were 'glowing heaps of embers'. Where the heat allowed, relatives hunted desperately for loved ones. Remote farmsteads, he said – villages in the countryside round about bombed too – 'burned like little candles in the hills'.

Steer did not see the bombing itself, but having arrived soon afterwards he was able both to record its effects and to talk to survivors – though he was forced to flee west in the face of the Nationalist advance. In an era of 'fake news', and of trusted newspapers cutting back on reporters 'at the scene', no story perhaps better illustrates their value.

28 April

There was something about 1789. Revolution in France, and earlier in the year, on 28 April, another act of violent insubordination on the decks of one of His Majesty's naval ships in the Pacific.

It had recently left the island of Tahiti after a long, idle and lascivious pause. The crew had lost their appetite for naval discipline and mutinied. The captain and some of his men were set adrift but managed to sail thousands of miles in a ship's boat, while the mutineers either returned to Tahiti or met an eventual, bloody though uncertain fate on Pitcairn Island.

The ship, HMS *Bounty* was on a significant horticultural mission. It was tasked to collect perhaps 1,000 small breadfruit plants and to transport them to the West Indies, to provide food for the slave population.

In preparation for the voyage, what was usually the captain's great cabin was converted into a large greenhouse, with glazed windows, skylights and a drainage system. Space for plants meant less for officers and men, aggravating the legendary overcrowding of Georgian naval vessels.

There has been much debate about whether responsibility for the mutiny should lie more with the captain, William Bligh, or with his acting lieutenant, Fletcher Christian. The traditional view that Bligh was a bully and a monster, forcing Christian into his act of rebellion, has been challenged. In his subsequent career during the Napoleonic Wars Bligh experienced both another mutiny and a case of severe insubordination. In the latter case he was 'reprimanded' by an Admiralty court, and 'admonished' to be 'in future more correct in his language'. Plainly he was not one to calm a heated situation on an overcrowded ship, isolated on the far side of the world. He was however an astonishing sailor. His voyage in the open boat to safety is an epic of maritime history. As for the mutineers, they headed for Tahiti where many were captured by the Royal Navy, taken back to Britain, court martialled and hanged.

29 April

The British government was no stranger to war. By 1900 there were few regions of the world where British battalions or gunboats were unknown. The Mughals, Qing and Zulu had been humiliated. Britain's empire was of unprecedented size. But today in 1909 the fiery Chancellor of the Exchequer, David Lloyd George, announced that he was going to war with the toughest foe yet: poverty.

Lloyd George was brought up speaking Welsh in a cobbler's cottage in Snowdonia, he rose to power with no connections, no wealth, no military experience and no Oxbridge education. He was a new breed of politician, one that made the established elites very nervous. In a stunning, four-hour speech in the House of Commons he announced that he would 'wage implacable warfare against poverty and squalidness', in short to redistribute wealth, the first time a UK government had expressly sought to do so.

A higher rate of tax was introduced, and a supertax for incomes above £5,000. Death duties were increased, and a tax on land proposed. This extra income would pay for social welfare. It was the foundations of the welfare state. Old-age pensions and free school meals were introduced and labour exchanges were built to help people into work. National Insurance would help workers afford healthcare.

The opposition went ballistic. This was socialism. For the first time in 200 years the House of Lords, packed with Conservative land-owning peers, vetoed the budget. A constitutional crisis followed. There were two general elections in 1910; both resulted in hung parliaments. Lloyd George later wrote that Britain 'was brought to the verge of civil war'.

In the end the House of Lords blinked. It agreed to the so-called 'People's Budget' and accepted the primacy of the House of Commons. The king and his nobles stared into the abyss and opted to compromise. Their pragmatism helps to explain why Britain's recent history has been one of evolution, not revolution.

30 April

His empire was disintegrating. Enemy troops were just hundreds of metres away. The only influence he could now wield was over the nature of his own death. On 30 April 1945, Adolf Hitler, one of the most infamous men in history – responsible for more deaths and more carnage than almost any other – turned a gun on himself. He persuaded Eva Braun, the woman who had been his wife for one day, to poison herself at the same time.

Since mid-January Adolf Hitler had been holed up, his dreams of world domination collapsing around him, in his '*Führerbunker*' in Berlin. That afternoon, in accordance with his clear instructions, his remains were carried up the stairs, through the bunker's emergency exit, into the attached garden, doused in petrol and burned.

Throughout 1945 the Third Reich had been unable to resist the sustained pressure of the Allies. Now American, British and Commonwealth, Soviet and other Allied forces all advanced towards the German capital from different sides. As they did so German army groups were captured or surrendered in spite of Hitler's insistence that they fight a hopeless, suicidal battle until the end.

On 20 April – Hitler's birthday – Berlin was bombarded for the first time by Soviet artillery. The final end was clearly a matter of days away. It was on 22nd that he consulted SS physician Dr Werner Haase regarding methods of committing suicide and was recommended to combine 'pistol and poison'.

As it seemed the Red Army would storm the Chancellery in central Berlin, in the early hours of 29 April Hitler married Eva Braun in a civil ceremony within the bunker. They hosted a wedding breakfast together. Then he dictated his last will and testament. The stringing up of Mussolini and his mistress in Milan strengthened Hitler's resolve to ensure that no similar 'spectacle' could be made of him. Early the following afternoon the two entered Hitler's private study where they were alone until a loud gunshot was heard.

MAY

1 May

Traditionally in Europe today was a day of celebrations held to mark the arrival (or the return – always doubted) of spring. Late in the nineteenth century the date was appropriated by socialist movements, chosen as International Workers' Day, and May Day remains familiar as one – feared by financial, capitalist institutions – even now.

In pagan celebrations, whose origins are hazy but which were certainly marked in the ancient world, flowers were gathered, green plant growth was woven into garlands, and alcohol was drunk immoderately. The first two, at least, were considered a sign of spring. With most of the annual seeding completed, it was a convenient time for those working in agriculture to nurse headaches and have the day off.

Its association with organised labour began in 1886; the day was chosen by workers in Chicago to begin a strike for an eight-hour working day. On 4 May police opened fire on the strikers, and labour leaders were arrested. Several were then executed after sham trials. In 1889 an international congress of labour organisations, the Second International, adopted a proposal for international demonstrations on the anniversary of the start of the Chicago strike. A later congress made it 'mandatory upon the proletarian organisations of all countries to stop work on 1 May, wherever it is possible without injury to the workers'. Henceforth it would be a day to champion socialism, better working conditions for workers and international solidarity. The twenty-first century has seen May Days settle midway between its two historical poles. A day to express solidarity with progressive causes, but also to take a day off and celebrate the start of spring.

2 May

Anne Boleyn was at Whitehall watching a game of tennis when the messenger arrived. This morning in 1536 he presented her with a summons to King Henry VIII's Privy Council. The council, which included her uncle the Duke of Norfolk, informed her that she had been charged with adultery. Anne was immediately arrested, taken by barge to the Tower of London and escorted through the private Byward Tower Gate, where she was held in a luxury prison until her death.

Ten days after her arrest, four courtiers, and even Anne's brother George Boleyn, were found guilty of committing adultery with the queen, and for conspiring to bring about the king's death. Musician Mark Smeaton was the first who admitted to adultery. He never retracted his original confession, obtained under torture, which stated that he had sexual relations with the queen three times. This fuelled further allegations against Anne of 'base conversations and kisses, touchings, gifts and other infamous incitations'. Even more shockingly, she was alleged to have 'procured and incited her own natural brother . . . to violate her, alluring him with her tongue in the said George's mouth, and the said George's tongue in hers'.

Anne Boleyn professed her innocence, but after stating that the king was 'not skilful in copulating with a woman & had neither vigour nor potency', her fate had been decided. On the morning of 19 May 1536 she walked from her apartments to a private execution on Tower Green, where in one expert stroke her head was swiftly severed from her body by a specialist French swordsman. Her ladies covered her head with white cloth and her body was undressed, wrapped and stored in an old elm chest; the former queen was given no formal coffin.

Anne Boleyn was buried in an unmarked grave in the parish church inside the walls of The Tower. For the rest of Henry VIII's reign, she was effectively written out of history until her memory was resurrected by her daughter, Elizabeth I. Her coronation procession featured two life-size effigies, Anne and Henry, mother and father, side by side.

3 May

It was surely one of the most presumptuous decrees in history, a sign of Europe's newly discovered arrogance. Today in 1493 the Pope – Alexander VI – published a bull called '*Inter Caetera*', which divided the entire new world between Spain and Portugal. He was from Spain himself, but this no doubt was a coincidence. As a Borgia, his probity, after all, was legendary!

World geography then was sketchy, but plainly this grant was a very sizeable increase in the domains belonging to the two countries. A demarcation line was drawn in the Atlantic, leaving Spain exclusive right to acquire and exploit territories to its west.

It was only the previous year – the year, not coincidentally, in which Columbus first discovered America – that separate Muslim realms had finally been expelled from the Iberian Peninsula. It was still not appreciated that 'America' (the term was not yet used) was an entirely new continent rather than simply the eastern end of Asia. When John Cabot landed further north a few years later he too presumed that this was Asia – the land of the Great Khan – and it was his capital city he looked for.

It was widely assumed that the new lands being discovered held riches in profusion. Most people at the time thought that precious metals and stones, just like grains or spices, were influenced by the action of heat – that they abounded in tropical climates. As one English observer wrote, just as northern conditions fostered stones like amber, or metals like lead and tin, so the warmth further south nurtured rubies, diamonds, sapphires, gold, silver and copper.

Rights to all these lands mattered a great deal. Non-Christian, non-Catholic, non-Spanish claims were explicitly disavowed. This doctrine continued to enter legal arguments into the nineteenth century and as late as 2016 the Pope was still being urged to revoke it.

4 May

The year 1517 is popularly considered to be the start of the Reformation, with Martin Luther nailing his Ninety-five Theses to a door in Wittenburg. However, reformist views had circulated long before. In the second half of the fourteenth century, John Wycliffe, an English priest, publicly expressed his unorthodox opinions about the dominion of the Catholic Church, earning the reputation as the 'Morning Star of the Protestant Reformation'. Today in 1415, John Wycliffe was posthumously condemned as a heretic by the Catholic Church, and those influenced by his teachings were burned at the stake.

In 1374, John Wycliffe was made rector at a small parish in Lutterworth, Leicestershire. From here he began to preach that the papacy was not mandated by Scripture, and he expressed his disapproval of indulgences, church riches and clerical celibacy. 'England belongs to no pope. The pope is but a man, subject to sin, but Christ is the Lord of Lords and this kingdom is to be held directly and solely of Christ alone.'

Two years later, he wrote his 'On Civil Dominion', which stressed that the kingdom should be ruled by the monarch alone. He also oversaw the translation and production of the Scriptures in English, one of the first times in history the whole Bible had been available in the vernacular. Wycliffe's radical opinions gained popularity and were even adopted by figures within the royal family, such as John of Gaunt, who protected him against the aggressive response of the Catholic Church.

At Christmas 1384 John Wycliffe was at Mass at his parish church in Lutterworth when he suffered a fatal stroke. His views survived him, and his band of followers were given the derogatory name of 'Lollards'. In 1414 a Lollard uprising, led by Sir John Oldcastle, was suppressed and brutal repression resulted in burnings of 'heretics'. The embers of Wycliffe's teachings survived and were reignited in the sixteenth century as King Henry VIII sought legitimacy for his English Reformation.

5 May

People always ask historians which period of history they would love to have been born in or travel back to. The answer is always the same, and always disappoints: the past was pretty grim and we are extraordinarily lucky to be alive today with its painkillers, antibiotics, washing machines, dating apps and air conditioning. The story of Elizabeth of Rhuddlan, who died today in 1316, is a case in point.

Elizabeth was the youngest daughter of King Edward I and his wife, Eleanor of Castile. She was two years older than the ill-fated Edward II. Her father ruled an empire that stretched across the British Isles and into western France. He was one of Europe's wealthiest and most powerful men. His family had access to every advantage available at the time, and yet their story is one of appalling suffering and tragedy.

Edward and his wife, Eleanor, who were, unusually, very much in love, had sixteen children that we know of in just under thirty years. By the time Elizabeth was born, ten of her older siblings had died. Some were stillborn, others died as babies or children. Only three of Edward and Eleanor's children would see their fortieth birthdays. Elizabeth of Rhuddlan was not one of them. Having lost her mother when she was eight, at just fourteen she was forced to marry the Count of Holland. Luckily for her he died shortly after and she was spared a life in the Low Countries that she had been dreading. Instead she remarried and had ten children before dying in childbirth at age thirty-three.

For nearly all of human history even the richest and most powerful families in the world have had to endure pain and loss on a scale that is unimaginable in the developed world today. You're very lucky to be alive now.

6 May

'This,' proclaimed radio commentator Herbert Morrison today in 1937, 'is the worst thing I've ever witnessed.'

He was talking about the *Hindenburg* airship (it contained flammable hydrogen rather than air), which had recently burst into flames and come crashing to the ground in front of him, as he recorded the moment for a radio station in Chicago. 'Oh, the humanity!' he lamented. He apologised to listeners that he could not talk to those around him: 'Their friends are on there!'

It was in New Jersey in the United States. That year the German airship had already made one round trip from Germany to Brazil. This occasion was scheduled to be the first of ten transatlantic voyages between Germany and North America, and so there was more watching press than could normally be expected. With public faith in these huge, passenger airships shattered, their end was also hastened by the fact that aircraft could make the journey much faster, if not in the same comfort.

Given the scale of the fire (and most people have seen some of the many photographs taken of the incident), it seems remarkable that anyone on board survived. Even so they did. About a third died – thirteen of thirty-six passengers, and twenty-two of sixty-one crewmen – though others suffered severe burns. Many of those lucky enough to have been on the port side of the ship were not badly hurt.

It is by far the best-known airship disaster because of the extraordinary photographs and the commentary that exists. It was actually, though, not the worst. Only four years earlier an American airship – the USS *Akron* – had crashed into the sea causing the deaths of more than twice as many.

7 May

The attacks came in waves. The shattered defenders knew it was hopeless. But they fought on. Today in 1954 the French commander at Dien Bien Phu in the mountains of north-west Vietnam broadcast his final message, 'The Viets are everywhere . . . The combat is confused and goes on all about. I feel the end is approaching, but we will fight to the finish.' Later in the day there was one final transmission, the radio operator said simply, 'The enemy has overrun us . . . *Vive la France*!' They had been beaten by an Asian enemy that the French army had consistently despised, belittled and underestimated.

The French base at Dien Bien Phu had been supposed to lure the Vietnamese into the kind of set-piece battle that the French with their superior equipment and experience were desperate to fight. If they could make these 'terrorists' fight on French terms, they would annihilate them. Instead the opposite happened. The Vietnamese stunned the French with their mastery of the battlefield. The French artillery commander, who had boasted of what his heavy guns would do to the enemy, committed suicide when the truth dawned on him that he was unable to counter the Vietnamese.

From mid-March the French and Vietnamese fought a First World War-style battle of trenches, barbed wire, tunnelling and terrible bombardments. The French were outnumbered and surrounded. They had sprung a trap certainly, but they had caught themselves in it.

The loss of manpower, supplies and prestige at Dien Bien Phu was irreversible for the French. In the days following the defeat talks in Geneva saw the French agree to withdraw from Vietnam. There was to be a temporary partition of the country into North and South, a messy compromise which left plenty of scope for further conflict. Conflict that would draw in the new global superpower, the United States, and see Vietnam become one of the Cold War's most terrible battlefields.

8 May

Aili Jõgi and Ageeda Paavel were schoolgirls in Tallinn, Estonia. Today in 1946 they carried out one of the most audacious acts of resistance to Soviet rule anywhere in post-war Europe. They were fourteen and fifteen years old respectively and they blew a Soviet war memorial, a symbol of their oppressors, sky high.

The Baltic States suffered terribly before, during and after the Second World War. Forced to submit to Stalin in 1939, the ruling elite was imprisoned and murdered. The Nazi invasion of 1941 initially appeared as a liberation before Hitler's death squads murdered Jews and other minorities and conscripted Estonians in forced labour or military units. The Soviet reconquest in 1944 saw appalling damage inflicted on the country and its population. Estonia was reincorporated into the USSR and the Soviet authorities tore down Estonian war memorials commemorating their dead in the struggle against Bolshevik Russia in the aftermath of the First World War. In their place memorials to the Red Army dead were erected, regarded by many Estonians as monuments to their oppressors.

'We just couldn't get our heads around it,' Aili Jõgi later said. 'We decided that if such robbers are raging in Estonia, they should see how one of their memorials gets blown up. We could have just doused the wooden thing with gasoline and set fire to it, but we wanted it to go with a bang!'

Tonight in 1946 they rigged a wooden post topped with a red star in the heart of Tallinn with explosives and blew it apart. They were both arrested and sent into exile at forced labour camps deep in the heart of Russia. It was decades before they saw Estonia again. Their suicidal bravery in making a stand against the might of Stalin's Red Army at the very peak of its post-war prestige ensured that they are still celebrated in Estonia as national heroes today.

9 May

The story of the cracking of the secret German Enigma codes at Bletchley Park – making possible the reading of German messages – is well known. Much less so is a related event that preceded it, on 9 May 1941. It was then that an extraordinarily brave salvage team boarded a sinking German U-boat and seized an Enigma encryption machine.

With Europe conquered and in Nazi hands, Britain then was clinging on, dependent upon the convoys of ships that brought food and war materiel from across the Atlantic. During what is known as the 'Battle of the Atlantic', these convoys were hunted by 'wolf packs' of German submarines all too well aware of their importance.

The merchant ships were guarded by naval vessels, and HMS *Bulldog* led a group that chased and then attacked a German U-boat, dropping a depth charge which hit its target. The badly damaged U-boat surfaced and the captain of the *Bulldog* made the bold decision to risk boarding it, lest anything valuable could be removed, rather than simply to destroy it. A sublieutenant named David Balme, who was given the job of leading the boarding party, found it empty and 'abandoned in great haste'.

When one of his men saw what looked like an unusual typewriter, bolted down and 'plugged in and as though it was in actual use when abandoned', he unscrewed it, managing to carry the heavy machine out and onto HMS *Bulldog*. Such a device had never been seen before. The salvage team also took various codebooks. This little heralded moment of bravery was one of the most significant of the war, assisting in the breakthrough that is credited with shortening the war by years and saving countless lives.

So much importance was attached to preventing the Germans from realising that an Enigma machine had been captured that for months Winston Churchill did not even inform President Roosevelt, his closest ally.

10 May

At noon – Utah time – on 10 May in 1869, a final, ceremonial (golden) spike was hammered in using a silver hammer, to connect the West Coast and the East Coast by rail. The following day's *New York Times* hailed it as a 'long-looked-for moment' that made the inhabitants of the Atlantic seaboard and of the Pacific coast 'emphatically one people'.

For the first time the western states, formerly reachable only by long, dusty rides in a wagon train, had a relatively fast connection with the east. The journey time was slashed from many months to a few days. A substantial upsurge in the western population – boosted by a phenomenon like the California Gold Rush of 1849 – had created the imperative to find a way through what had seemed an impossible obstacle in the Sierra Nevada mountains.

Nevertheless, the project was dogged by difficulties. Surveying potential routes required both time and substantial funding. The significant tensions between North and South which produced the Civil War had made it difficult for Congress to agree where the line ought to begin. Labourers put up with a great deal – freezing winters, sweltering summer heat, Indian raids, brutal working conditions and the inherent dangers of the work.

Finally, though, in 1869, seven years after Congress passed the Pacific Railroad Act of 1862, the dream of a transcontinental railroad came to fruition. And once it had done, the relative accessibility of the West led to a boom there in both economic and population terms. The 'Overland route', as it became known had become a reality. Railroad technology allowed the fusion of a number of scattered settlements into a cohesive nation state of continental proportions.

11 May

Spencer Perceval would be one of our most forgettable (and forgotten) prime ministers, if it were not for the fact that on this day in 1812 he became the only UK prime minister to be assassinated. Subsequent attempts – such as the IRA bombing of Margaret Thatcher in a Brighton hotel – have not achieved their aim.

That afternoon Perceval had opted to walk to Parliament. John Bellingham was a regular attendee, unlikely for that reason to raise concerns. He was obsessed with earning redress for his treatment at the hands of the Russian authorities after a business deal had gone wrong.

Having told one Treasury official that, failing compensation, he would be forced to take justice into his own hands, the official simply replied that he should take what action seemed appropriate. Shortly afterwards Bellingham purchased two pistols and had a tailor add an inside pocket into his coat.

As Perceval entered the lobby – a man of highly conservative instincts, misleadingly mild in appearance (combining, it was said, 'the head of a country parson with the tongue of an Old Bailey lawyer') he was confronted by Bellingham, who drew a pistol and shot Perceval in the chest. Perceval staggered, shouted 'I am murdered!' then fell face down. By the time a surgeon arrived he was declared dead.

Bellingham, who made no attempt to escape, calmly insisted that he was righting an injustice, had exhausted other avenues, and felt 'sufficient justification for what I have done'. Having been told to do his worst, he said, he had done it – 'and I rejoice in the deed'. He was hastily charged and tried – too hastily, it has been argued – then imprisoned and hanged.

The public reaction to the assassination was mixed. Some rejoiced, others shed a tear, but nearly all, eventually, forgot.

12 May

It was the end of the first dangerous military stand-off of the Cold War. Escalation had been a very real threat. Today in 1949, the Soviet Union called off its blockade of Berlin – a major event that characterised the precarious and hostile relations existing for several decades between the West and the USSR, from the end of the Second World War until the fall of the Berlin Wall in 1989.

After the war Berlin was divided into American, British and French as well as Russian zones. The war-ravaged capital was also around a hundred miles within the Soviet sector of the country. The Soviet leadership – Joseph Stalin in particular – did not expect America or Britain to maintain for long either occupation or resistance to a united, Soviet-influenced Germany. He miscalculated. In spite of its practical and financial difficulty, American strategists thought remaining in Berlin was 'essential to our prestige in Germany and in Europe'. At a meeting early in March 1948, meanwhile, Stalin approved a memorandum which aimed to force the Western allies to align with the Soviet Union by 'regulating' their access to Berlin.

From 24 June attempts by the Western allies to supply their sectors of the city overland – by road, rail or canal – were blocked. Military manoeuvres were conducted by the USSR just outside the city. The supply of power was severed. In response, rather than acceding to Soviet demands that they withdraw their new currency – the new Deutsche mark – from West Berlin, the Western allies organised an ambitious attempt to supply their sectors by air, along the three permissible air corridors connecting West Germany with Berlin.

For longer than a year more than 200,000 flights were organised to supply West Berliners with fuel and food. Initial predictions had guessed the airlift might last a few weeks: in fact it continued until September 1949, through a cold and foggy winter, then after the blockade was lifted, to ensure a surplus. The USSR did not interfere with the operation for fear of provoking open conflict.

13 May

He had spoken many times in the House, from both sides, and as the holder of nearly every great office of state. But never before with so much riding on his words. Today in 1940, Winston Churchill rose to make his maiden speech as prime minister, having replaced Neville Chamberlain a few days earlier. For years he had been a divisive figure, deeply unpopular, even on his own back benches. 'I have never believed in him', wrote one MP.

Churchill was anxious that he had achieved his life's ambition only for it to be too late to make a difference. 'We are in the preliminary stages', he told the House, 'of one of the greatest battles in history.' Britain's policy would be 'to wage war, by sea, land and air, with all our might and with all the strength that God can give us; to wage war against a monstrous tyranny, never surpassed in the dark and lamentable catalogue of human crime' – its aim must be 'victory at all costs . . . however long and hard the road may be'.

German troops had invaded France days before and already France was being overwhelmed. As Churchill growled out the famous line of the speech, 'I have nothing to offer but blood, toil, tears, and sweat', General Heinz Guderian's Panzers were breaking through at Sedan making Churchill's rhetoric a reality.

The phrase was not new: it was very similar to ones that he himself had used years before, as well as to ones used by others, but Churchill's grandiloquent language and perfectly judged delivery proved ideally suited to the mood of national emergency which then prevailed, and made a vastly greater impression. His request for confidence in his government was passed unanimously.

Soon afterwards came more of his most famous speeches – in which he promised 'to fight them on the beaches', and in which he hailed the contribution of Battle of Britain pilots as 'their finest hour'. If ever a man was well suited to the moment, it was Churchill in 1940.

14 May

'My lords, it is the very truth that in this world the Marshal experienced many fine and splendid adventures. His dying was the best amongst them . . .' These are the closing lines of the *Histoire de Guillaume le Mareschal*, completed a few years after William Marshal died today in 1219. The epic piece, which runs to 19,212 lines, is the only surviving biography. It is not exactly unbiased, as it was commissioned by the Marshal's son to celebrate his father, but it gives us a useful source into the life of medieval England's most remarkable warrior and statesman.

William Marshal was the fourth son of a minor baron. By his death he was the power behind the Plantagenet throne. Even before this dramatic climax, his long career had embodied the chivalric ethos of the age, and in turn had shaped the concept of chivalry, leaving a legend that generations of young knights sought to emulate. The man who Cardinal Peter Langton eulogised as the 'best knight that ever lived' began his knight's training in Normandy at age twelve. He learned to wield weapons, ride and hunt but also an emerging code of conduct, chivalry for short, which emphasised loyalty, honour, opposition to injustice, and self-control.

His strength and skill in battle and the tilt-yard was what brought him to the attention of the court. He apparently defeated five hundred men in single combat over the course of his life. This prowess, combined with his loyalty, made him an indispensable courtier. When he pledged his allegiance, he meant it. That attribute made him a key supporter to kings Henry, Richard and John, no mean feat as each appeared to hate their predecessor. He even stayed loyal to King John when many of the nobles sided with the French, and upheld the Plantagenet claim of the child Henry III by crushing the French invaders at the Battle of Lincoln.

The myth of Marshal preceded his own death. He has become England's most perfect knight, loyally serving his lord with faithfulness, piety and a hatred of injustice.

15 May

At 7.40 p.m. the odd-looking aircraft without propellers roared down the runway at RAF Cranwell, and took to the skies for seventeen minutes. 'It flies,' one close colleague said to designer Frank Whittle, to which the reply came: 'Well, that's what it was bloody well designed to do, wasn't it?' Today in 1941 Whittle's W1 jet engine had just blasted the Gloster Pioneer, and Britain, into the jet age.

Whittle was good at maths and obsessed with model aeroplanes. He achieved his goal of flying solo, but was cautioned against over-confident flying. Thinking over the problems of aircraft design, he speculated that an engine using exhaust directly as thrust might be able to fly both faster and, at high altitude, much more efficiently. Later on he realised that replacing a piston engine with a turbine would improve its power to weight ratio.

During the 1930s, as Whittle touted the idea, he made a major impression on some, one financier and engineer declaring that 'this was genius, not talent'. In 1935 his design was given enthusiastic support in an influential report. Even so, opportunities were missed, and it was difficult to raise the funds – more difficult once the design became subject to the Official Secrets Act. In Germany a rival Heinkel design was better supported.

Whittle felt the pressure. 'The responsibility that rests on my shoulders,' he lamented, 'is very heavy indeed.' His smoking increased and he became addicted to benzedrine, sleeping at night with tranquillisers. At the end of 1940 he suffered a nervous breakdown and was off work for a month.

His mental health cannot have been helped by the nagging regret that he had not renewed his patent for the first-ever jet engine design in January 1930. It had lapsed when the RAF showed no interest and Whittle himself could not afford the renewal fee of £5.

16 May

It was an infamous secret deal, still cited by Islamic State and various other combatants in the Syrian Civil War as the root cause of the violence and instability of the modern Middle East. Today in 1916 the deal was made – secret only until the revolution in Russia caused the beans to be spilt – between Great Britain and France (with imperial Russia's assent) about dividing up the Ottoman Empire.

Under the agreement the Middle East was apportioned: a French-administered region in the north, a British-administered region in the south, and a Palestine placed – to cope with the sensitivities aroused by the Holy Places – under an international regime. The dividing line went from Acre on the Mediterranean coast to Kirkuk near the frontier of Persia (modern Iran). This example of Great Power imperialism, Britain and France drawing the boundaries of foreign, non-European states to accord with their own interests, has shaped the Middle East, and been severely criticised, ever since. Even by the standards of the time the self-interest was blatant.

In London and Paris 'expertise' had been sought from Sir Mark Sykes and François Georges-Picot – the former lacked the serious expertise that he affected and later died in the flu epidemic of 1919, the latter (his 'fluting voice' infuriating the British) was a lawyer and diplomat who served in obscure positions. Lip service (but only lip service) was paid to the promise that the British had already made to the Arabs that they would be accorded independence. The assurances made in public – that they were 'fighting not for selfish interests but, above all, to safeguard the independence of peoples, right, and humanity' – were almost comically far from the truth.

17 May

Valerios Stais was busy examining artefacts that had been uncovered from a wrecked Roman cargo ship, two years previously, off the island of Antikythera in Greece. Today in 1902 a small piece of bronze caught the archaeologist's eye. It appeared to be a small wheel, or cog. In fact Stais had just discovered what came to be known as the Antikythera mechanism, the world's first analogical computer.

This extraordinary two-thousand-year-old computer system was used by the ancient Greeks as an astronomical calculator, able to chart the planets and make predictions, such as the date of the next Olympic Games. It was able to align the lunar months with years and even display where the Sun and the Moon lay within the zodiac. The complex bronze system of gears, about the size of a shoebox, is similar to clocks made in Europe a thousand years later, as fine as anything produced even into the eighteenth century. The extraordinary device is believed to have been made on the island of Rhodes around 150 BC, and classical literature of the time does allude to mechanisms similar to this one, meaning this was unlikely to be the only one of its kind.

Although this delicate contraption is nothing like the digital computing systems we use today, it allowed an ancient civilisation to track the cycles of the solar system in a manner that would have been otherwise impossible. Well over a hundred years after its discovery, the Antikythera mechanism is still being extensively researched, in an attempt to fully unlock an ancient piece of human ingenuity.

18 May

It was the first recorded sighting of India by seafarers who had sailed direct from Europe. When Vasco da Gama's crew spotted the coast of what is now Kerala in south India on this day in 1498 it was a milestone in the formation of the modern world.

In 1450 the European diet was miserable. Potatoes, chilli peppers, vanilla, coffee, tomatoes and chocolate were unknown. Asian ingredients like cinnamon, nutmeg, ginger and pepper were hugely exotic and expensive. All the delicacies of the East were transported in small coastal craft, shouldered by porters, carried on camel trains, with every leg of the journey adding to the price. Once boat-building technology had advanced to the point when ships could travel thousands of miles on the open ocean, the first impulse of Europeans was to travel to Asia, fill up with delicious goodies and cut out the middle man.

Vasco da Gama set out from Lisbon with four ships and 170 men. They sailed far into the western Atlantic to catch the trade winds back to southern Africa, in doing so setting a record for the longest any vessel had been out of sight of land, around 6,000 miles in three months. Then they rounded the Cape of Good Hope and struck up into the Indian Ocean.

Having spotted the Indian coast on 18 May they called upon the King of Calicut, who was not impressed. He regarded the Portuguese gifts as insubstantial and told them if they wanted to trade they would have to pay in gold like everyone else. Eventually they filled their holds with cargo and set off home. It was an appalling voyage. After a year of scurvy, adverse winds and hostile shores, two of the four ships limped into Lisbon, crewed by just fifty-five weakened survivors.

For the Portuguese crown, the sacrifice was worth it. The value of the cargoes was around sixty times the cost of the expedition. The Portuguese sent fleet after fleet. By the early sixteenth century the Indian Ocean was dominated by a web of warships and forts from the distant kingdom of Portugal. The Europeans had arrived in Asia.

19 May

In the end it was his love of adventure that killed him. T. E. Lawrence – Lawrence of Arabia – had displayed a restless energy to live a life less ordinary since childhood. He had travelled across the Middle East as a student, narrowly avoiding a gruesome end on a few occasions. During the First World War he had fought in the Arab Revolt, liberating swathes of Arabia from Ottoman rule. He attempted to fill the void left by the end of the conflict with a passion for motor-bikes. 'A Skittish motor-bike with a touch of blood in it is better than all the riding animals on earth', he declared.

Today in 1935 he died from terrible head injuries sustained when, a week before, he had crashed. On a country road in Dorset he had attempted to avoid two boys on bikes, and lost control of his motorcycle.

Perhaps he was travelling too fast. Certainly he liked high speed and his machine, a Brough Superior, was capable of it. He paid a terrible price for his new passion. 'We have lost one of the greatest beings of our time', lamented Winston Churchill, while the *New York Times* called it 'a tragic waste'.

The neurosurgeon who treated him, Hugh Cairns, realised that the brain injuries Lawrence had suffered would have probably left him blind and unable to speak even if he had survived. Not long afterwards, and it could scarcely have been a coincidence, he published research entitled 'Head Injuries in Motor-cyclists – the importance of the crash helmet'.

More than a hundred motorcyclists were dying every month, many more than nowadays, on much quieter roads. It was hard, though, to point to clear statistical evidence – until, that is, the army required that its despatch riders wear helmets. After that the fall in motorcycle deaths was plain to see. Nevertheless, it was not until the 1970s that the law in the United Kingdom required civilian motorcyclists to wear helmets, and the libertarian argument – that all who undertook dangerous activities were free to choose – was lost.

20 May

It's probably the most important battle fought on British soil that you have never heard of. The Battle of Nechtansmere. In defence of all the many people who have never heard of it: it did happen a long time ago, today in 685.

In the north of what became England, the kingdom of Northumbria dominated, but its domain stretched even further, deep into what is now Scotland. By the late 670s, though, it seems as though Northumbria's southern neighbour of Mercia was becoming more powerful – having defeated the Northumbrians in a battle the previous year – and this created the conditions in which the Pictish peoples of the north decided to assert their independence.

In an attempt to wrestle back the initiative, the Northumbrian king, Ecgfrith, attacked the southern Picts under King Bridei III in 685 'with all the strength of his army'. But they were lured north into the highlands, into an ambush, and there – off their guard – were subject to a devastating attack: at a place called 'Nechtansmere', or Nechtan's Lake. As Bede put it, 'the king was drawn into the straits of inaccessible mountains, and slain with the greatest part of his forces'.

The long-term significance of this was vast. Northumbrian power in the north of Britain was drastically reduced, a large part of its army being either killed or enslaved. As the near-contemporary monk Nennius put it, 'the Saxons never again reduced the Picts so as to exact tribute from them'. Had things been different, the boundary between England and Scotland that remains to this day might never have existed.

21 May

'Her face is not so exact as to be called a beauty, though her eyes are excellent good . . . on the contrary, she hath much agreeableness in her looks altogether as ever I saw' – Charles II was pleased with his new wife, Catherine of Braganza, infanta of Portugal. He married her today in 1662.

The service was conducted in secret, a private Catholic ceremony at the damaged St Thomas's church in Portsmouth, a casualty of the Civil War. The reception of Catherine in England was largely positive. Samuel Pepys observed, 'At night, all the bells of the town rung, and bonfires made for the joy of the Queen's arrival.' The marriage between Charles II and Catherine marked another happy event for a country craving stability after war, regicide, puritanical military dictatorship and uncertainty.

On her arrival in England, Catherine brought with her, as part of her expansive belongings, a chest of expensive luxury tea, the favourite drink at the Portuguese court. Her crossing had been long, stormy and uncomfortable, and as soon as she was on dry land she requested a soothing cuppa. Her love of tea caused a stir at court, and soon it was being consumed by the wealthier classes as part of a fashionable social ritual. The beverage became such a novelty associated with the queen, a politician even composed a poem about it for her birthday: 'The Muse's friend, tea does our fancy aid, Regress those vapours which the head invade'.

Sadly the new queen gave Britain tea, but no heir. Although he was one of the most prolific womanisers in British royal history, with a slew of illegitimate children, at least twelve of which he acknowledged and heaped with wealth and titles, Charles' marriage to Catherine remained childless. The Stuart dynasty would be plunged into another crisis, but at least the nation now had tea to take the edge off the next set of upheavals.

22 May

They were a secret order, based high in mountain strongholds in what is today Iran. The grand master of this Islamic sect, Hassan-i Sabbah, called his disciples Asāsīyūn 'people who are faithful to the foundation [of the Islamic faith]'. In English they are remembered as the Assassins. Their strength lay not in the use of big battalions, but in the single lethal strike. They are renowned for the targeted murder of high-ranking opponents such as caliphs and Crusaders. Today in 1176 the most celebrated commander of the age, Saladin, Sultan of Egypt and Syria, captor of Jerusalem, only narrowly escaped their blades.

Enemies had tried before, but none came so close as the assassin who crept into his camp in May 1176. Saladin was resting in a tent when the assailant rushed in and thrust a knife at his head. It glanced off Saladin's protective cap and the sultan overpowered and killed him.

Saladin rushed to punish the sect and marched into their territory. Understandably wary, he ordered chalk spread on the ground around his tent to detect any footsteps by an assassin. Tall tales about daggers sticking out from the tent frame above Saladin's sleeping head carrying cease and desist warnings seem, sadly, not to be true. Far more likely was that Saladin, as dextrous diplomatically as he was fearsome on the battlefield, decided that the assassins were more useful as allies than enemies. He enlisted their help and turned his attention west against the Crusaders who still clung to the Mediterranean coast.

On 28 April 1192 two assassins pounced on Conrad, the crusading King of Jerusalem described by an Islamic source as 'the greatest devil of all the Franks', as he walked through the streets of Acre. Whether Saladin or a rival Crusader lord was behind the attack we do not know. His loss was a terrible blow to the beleaguered Crusader states. The blades of the assassins changed the course of history more surely than a host of warriors or a fleet of ships.

23 May

If anyone knows the long-winded term for hurling somebody, or something, out of a window, the knowledge probably derives from this event: the 'Defenestration of Prague', which happened today, just over four centuries ago, on 23 May 1618.

As the Reformation took hold across Europe, Rudolf II, the Holy Roman Emperor (among other titles) had promised in his 'Letters of Majesty' of 1609 to guarantee religious liberty. The prince of any region, it had been agreed, could define his realm's religion, free of any more central diktat. But in Bohemia – after Rudolf's death – recently built Protestant chapels were forcefully closed by officials belonging to the Roman Catholic Church.

As a direct response an assembly of Protestants was called at Prague and the two imperial regents, William Slavata and Jaroslav Martinic – hard-line Catholics – were put on trial and declared guilty of violating this promise.

'You are enemies of us and of our religion', they were told, having ignored the Letter of Majesty, '[you] horribly plagued your Protestant subjects' and 'tried to force them to adopt your religion against their wills'. They (along with their secretary, Philip Fabricius) were ejected from the third-floor windows of the council room of Prague Castle.

Extraordinarily, although injured, they survived the ordeal: Catholics quickly declaring that they had been caught by angels, while Protestants responded that their survival had been due to the fact that they had landed on a dunghill. In any case, their personal survival did not avert the onset of decades of religious struggle in central Europe: the Thirty Years' War, one of the most devastating conflicts in human history.

24 May

Today, on 24 May in 1844, Samuel (F.B.: *dot dot dash dot, dash dot dot dot*) Morse sent the first-ever telegraphic message over an experimental line strung alongside a railroad between the American capital in Washington, DC and the city of Baltimore some forty miles away.

The biblical message, which came from Numbers *23: 23* had been suggested to him by the daughter of a friend and acknowledged the massive impact of technological change upon society, of which this was only a small part – 'What Hath God Wrought?'

Morse conceived of a rapid communications system using electricity and the electro-magnet while travelling from Europe to take up a post as an arts professor in New York. It was as a result of this idea that he first developed what became known as Morse Code, a method of rendering the alphabet in a sequence of dashes and dots which allowed the sending of messages by telegraph, though his system was significantly simplified by his colleague Alfred Vail.

A decade later a project began to lay a cable on the bed of the Atlantic Ocean, to be used for telegraphic communication. After four years, in 1858, it had succeeded. Ironically it was after this – albeit not long afterwards – in 1861 that Western Union completed the first transcontinental telegraph.

Geography, and politics, were revolutionised. The old days of postal messengers on horseback were consigned to history. The course of the American Civil War was decisively influenced by this new method of rapid communication. Samuel Morse, not God, wrought a revolution.

25 May

The old man had first arrived at the monastery as a child. He had survived a plague that killed most of his brothers. He had taught and thought. Now he had reached the end of a long life. Today in 735, Bede, a monk, the father of English history, died lying on the floor of his cell. His fellow monks reported that at the end he sang, 'Glory be to the Father and to the Son and to the Holy Spirit'.

In AD 596, Augustine had led forty monks into Britain to convert the pagan Britons, known as 'Angli', to Roman Christianity. The story of those missionaries spreading God's word was recorded by Bede. His famous work, the *Ecclesiastical History of the English People*, made the Venerable Bede the first great English writer of history.

Bede went to live at the monastery of Monkwearmouth aged seven, and a few years later, moved to a twinned monastery in Jarrow, where he lived for the rest of his life surrounded by the books and manuscripts that he had dedicated himself to. He wrote around forty works in his lifetime, which covered a range of subjects from theology to history and observations on nature, and he even calculated the date for Easter. It was his *Ecclesiastical History* however, which served as the culmination of his life's work. It was translated by Alfred the Great, who was inspired by Bede's contention that England was one kingdom, a single people that could be united under a single ruler. Alfred insisted his people were 'Angelcynn', as he forged a nation out of rival states, such as Mercia and Northumbria.

Cuthbert, a disciple of Bede's, recorded Bede's last days as 'cheerful', before he died on the stone slabs of his small cell. In the eleventh century his remains were sent to Durham Cathedral. Today, pilgrims still visit a shrine to the great lover of books, and the greatest Anglo-Saxon scholar.

26 May

When production stopped, this afternoon in 1927, at the Highland Park plant in Michigan, it was the end for history's most influential car. The final Model T produced by the Ford Motor Company was the last of over 16.5 million that had hit the road in the previous two decades. Low price and ease of maintenance had ensured that nearly half the cars on America's roads were Model Ts, and it remains in the top ten bestselling cars of all time.

Henry Ford had promised to 'build a car for the great multitude. It will be large enough for the family, but small enough for the individual to run and care for.' His vision was for his factory to mass-produce a car with interchangeable parts, staffed by workers who would be paid enough to become customers themselves. He would transform motoring from a luxury for the elite to an everyday habit of the working man.

To deliver this, Ford built at Highland Park the world's first moving assembly line for automobiles. It was an innovation that brought the production time down from 728 minutes to just 93. The savings were reflected in the price. It dropped by two-thirds from nearly $900 in 1908 to $300 in the mid-1920s, equivalent to around £3000 today.

Ford invested large sums in marketing, and built plants across the world, in places like Trafford Park in Manchester, ensuring that the Model T was the first globally produced car. Year after year, sales growth was 100 per cent. The Model T established our modern dependence on the automobile while its production, pricing and marketing all created a template that all successful multinationals have adopted ever since.

27 May

The massive ship took extraordinary punishment. It had been pounded by several British ships, but eventually at 10.39 a.m. on 27 May 1941 *Bismarck* disappeared beneath the Atlantic waves. The sinking of what was recognised as 'the enemy's most powerful warship' was an event which quickly acquired legendary status in the defeat of Nazi Germany, familiar even to those little versed in naval warfare. For the British it more than compensated for the demoralising loss, not long before, of the seemingly invincible battlecruiser HMS *Hood*, which had been sunk with 1,418 crew.

After the tussle with *Hood*, the *Bismarck* made to escape to docks in occupied France in order for damage to be repaired. The British, however, wanted retribution and pursued her south-west into the Atlantic. Critically, the damage to her fuel tanks both slowed her progress and meant that she left a visible slick in the water. For a time, nevertheless, she succeeded in losing her pursuers.

Unaware that he could be traced, the German admiral sent a long radio message that was picked up, triangulated and used to locate her approximate position. An observation plane then found her, having noticed the ship's visible trail.

From the evening of 26 May to the morning of the 27th, *Bismarck* was struck first by torpedoes from aeroplanes (she was within range of the *Ark Royal* carrier but too far from land-based German air support) then attacked by ships of the British navy. When the damage seemed fatal, and sinking inevitable, the ship was then deliberately scuttled. Barely 115 survivors were rescued from the 2,200-strong crew.

In hindsight, the demise within a few days of both the *Hood* and the *Bismarck* signalled the passing of the pre-eminent battleship, and her replacement by aircraft carriers and submarines.

28 May

It was a strange place to start a global conflict. A rock-strewn patch of forest in what is now western Pennsylvania far from the nearest French or British North American settlements, let alone from the imperial capitals in Paris and London. The battle, or brief skirmish, fought there today in 1754 between less than a hundred men was the opening of what would become a world war fought over the best part of a decade with violence on five continents. It was all the fault of an over-eager, young, inexperienced man. Nothing about his decisions or leadership that day marked him out for greatness, but greatness he would eventually achieve. His name was George Washington, and on 28 May 1754 he was an enthusiastic subject of King George.

Washington had been sent to the no-man's-land of the Ohio River valley, which was claimed by the French and the British and occupied by indigenous tribes who were reluctant to be ruled by either. He had orders to tell the French to leave. The French had sent a similar expedition to tell the British to leave. When Washington heard that the French party was encamped nearby he 'advanced pretty near to them', he wrote, when 'they discovered us; whereupon I ordered my company to fire'. The battle 'only lasted a Quarter of an Hour, before the Enemy was routed'. Young Washington enjoyed the experience: 'I can with truth assure you,' he told his brother, 'I heard bullets whistle and believe me, there was something charming in the sound.'

The French, with good reason, regarded this as an unprovoked murder. They despatched a larger force out that sent Washington packing. When news reached London of fighting on the frontier, it was decided to send an expeditionary force to secure the Ohio region. It was war.

Britain and France were such fierce competitors for trade, slaves, land and influence that war had been inevitable, but that spark for global conflict had been the rash decision of a 22-year-old man out in the wilderness.

29 May

It was the end of a desperate resistance. Today in 1453 the final remnant of the Roman Empire was extinguished when the city of Constantinople, named for the Roman Emperor Constantine, was finally stormed by the forces of Islam, to remain an Islamic city ever since.

For centuries the old Byzantine or 'Eastern Roman' Empire had been in decline. But at its heart the famous city remained steadfast behind reputedly impregnable walls.

When Mehmed II became Ottoman sultan in 1451, he dreamed of its capture. He gathered a vast force that dwarfed the defenders, up to 100,000 compared to less than 10,000, bolstered by Christian volunteers from across Europe.

Only twenty-one, Mehmed II had a castle built on the Bosphorus, and a record-sized cannon. Ships were dragged overland to the 'Golden Horn' to circumvent a chain across the water. Initial attempts failed, but an all-out assault on 29 May saw the Sultan throw his Christian subjects against the walls. The weakened defenders were then hit with the elite of the Ottoman army, the Janissaries, slave soldiers removed from their family as children and forbidden to marry. The defenders broke. The Ottomans flooded into the city. In the resulting massacre, bodies, it was said, 'floated out to sea like melons along a canal'. Mehmed rode a white horse to the church of Hagia Sophia, which was converted immediately into a mosque.

The demise of Constantinople and the Byzantine Empire has traditionally represented the end of an epoch, the passing of the medieval world. Exiled Greek scholars arrived in western Europe with classical texts and an intellectual tradition which ignited the Renaissance, a crucible of art, literature and ideas that helped smelt the modern world.

30 May

National icon, saint and martyr, Joan of Arc was burned at the stake in Rouen, France, today in 1431. She was nineteen years old.

An illiterate farmer's daughter from Domrémy in rural eastern France, Joan claimed to have received a vision from God. He had given her a divine order to liberate France from the constant assaults of the English, and to restore the Dauphin Charles VII to the French throne.

Joan famously turned the tide of the Hundred Years' War by defeating the English at Orléans, leading the French army and charging into battle in full armour given to her by the dauphin, who had been convinced that she was a visionary. Further successes followed. Then she was captured by the Burgundians, allied to the English, to whom they sold her. She was placed on trial for heresy. On being sentenced to death, Joan agreed to recant, wear women's clothes and accept life in prison. But her surrender was short-lived, and after a vision from Saints Catherine and Margaret, she readopted men's clothes and reversed her recantation.

On the day of her death, dressed in a white chemise, Joan was paraded as a heretic and witch. She was tied to the stake, the flames were lit. Joan shouted prayers that were audible over the rising crackle of the flames. Remarkably, Joan of Arc is believed to have been burned three times. She was killed by smoke inhalation, then her organs were burned again, and a third burning was necessary in order to fully destroy her body, with the ashes thrown into the River Seine.

In 1920, Joan of Arc was canonised, and during the Second World War she became a national icon of resistance in the face of another brutal occupier.

31 May

In one of the worst instances of racial violence in the United States, today in 1921 a large mob of whites started attacking both residents and businesses in the affluent black community (labelled the 'Black Wall Street') of Greenwood in the city of Tulsa, Oklahoma.

Oklahoma was a latecomer as a state, and racial tensions had remained unusually high; lynchings were common and segregated housing was enforced by law. Only a few years after it appeared, the Ku Klux Klan is thought to have had over 3,000 members in the city of Tulsa, from a total population of only about 72,000.

The unrest on 31 May began when a black man was arrested and accused of raping a white lift operator: she did not press charges and there appears to be little basis for the claim. Rumour spread and ignorant hysteria escalated, a crowd of whites descended on the police station while a black crowd rushed to prevent what threatened to be (another) lynching.

That night, amid wild, feverish talk of a 'negro uprising', thousands of whites went on the rampage. They smashed and pillaged, leaving as many as ten thousand black people homeless and causing what now equates to millions of dollars' worth of damage. Plausible eyewitness accounts suggest that the white police even used aeroplanes, dropping burning balls of turpentine onto the roofs of black settlements, aiming to start fires. White rioters on the ground also threw burning rags.

For decades those affected remained silent about what had happened, and the incident was rarely mentioned in classrooms or in history books. Estimates of those killed vary widely, but all sources assume numbers in the dozens at least. No one was convicted. As late as the 1970s those seeking to publish information encountered determined silence. Only a few even then were openly penitent. One former mayor proclaimed that 'Tulsa weeps at this unspeakable crime'. But he didn't speak for the whole community then – and would he now?

JUNE

1 June

It was one of the most hotly contested sieges in Chinese history. Today in 1215 the Mongols sacked the city they knew as Zhongdu and which we know as Beijing, an event that seemed to bring to a climax the long-drawn-out struggle between the sedentary, 'civilised' Chinese and the nomadic Mongol tribes to their north.

The Jin dynasty had affected contempt. 'Our Empire is like the sea,' the Chinese leader had declared, 'yours is but a handful of sand.' The building of the Great Wall had seemingly ended any advance. But in the aftermath of what happened next, the name of the Mongol leader aroused (and continues to arouse) horror and fear across the world: Genghis Khan.

When Jin dynasty officials had sought Genghis Khan's allegiance, he had reportedly turned to the south and spat on the ground, before turning north and riding away on his horse: a response which seemed negative.

He returned with a vast army, cut off the city and began starving it into submission. The gruelling siege saw the inhabitants reach such a point of desperation that they resorted, supposedly, to using gold and silver as materials for their cannon-shot, having exhausted all other ammunition. The Mongol army succeeded in gaining entry in spite of thick, fortified walls and wreaked vengeance on the sorry, stubborn inhabitants. Virtually nothing was left standing, and months later, it is said, the ground of the city remained littered with 'white mountains' of bones, and greasy with human fat.

Over subsequent years any resistance to the Mongols was systematically rooted out. Appreciating Mongol power, many leaders transferred their allegiance. After the fall of Zhongdu, the Chinese emperor moved his capital south to Kaifeng, but this too fell to the Mongols. 'Jin' China, probably the world's most powerful and sophisticated empire, had been defeated and conquered by nomadic tribesmen who, for generations, had been held in contempt.

2 June

The Germans launched one last desperate offensive. They needed to win this conflict before their industry collapsed and their country starved from the slow but certain strangulation by Royal Navy ships, blockading their ports. Today in 1918 this German offensive ground its way towards Paris. In its path was Belleau Wood, in it some newly arrived American troops. As these 'Doughboys' made ready to stop the Germans, some retreating French officers ordered them to fall back. It was then that one US Marine – Captain Lloyd Williams – uttered the famous riposte: 'Retreat? Hell, we just got here.' It is a line that became a motto of the US Marine Corps.

Around Belleau Wood the battle continued for many days. 'Wood' in most places along the Western Front meant that there wasn't much more than mud and stumps of trees. About a week later, after suffering repeated attacks by the Marines, one German private wrote, 'we have Americans opposite us who are terribly reckless fellows'.

It took the rest of the month for US troops to secure the wood. This was one of the fiercest and most destructive battles in which Americans would be involved, and, in the aftermath, out of respect, the place was renamed 'Wood of the Marine Brigade': Bois de la Brigade de Marine. The American in charge later called it a 'shrine of great deeds'.

The battle was the largest that American forces had ever fought with a foreign adversary and 1,811 men were killed and 7,966 wounded. German losses are unknown. It marked the start of American military involvement in Europe that would expand until it would come to dominate the continent by the end of the century. Captain Williams did not survive the battle. But his ostentatious bravery that helped to blunt the German assault earned him a place in American legend.

3 June

He was a Marine who had survived a tour of duty in India. From 1747 to 1750 he had campaigned in the searing Indian heat, surviving enemy bullets as well as the disease, mud-choked trenches of a siege, heat stroke, and long sea voyages there and back. By the time he returned to Britain his legs were disfigured by the scars of battle. Like the men around him, he had survived the rigours of the campaign and battlefield wearing the redcoat of King George, but unlike them he had a shocking secret. Today in 1750 as he sat drinking in a London pub with his fellow Marines, he revealed that he, James Gray, was in fact a woman.

She later claimed that she announced to her speechless comrades, 'I am as much a woman as my mother ever was, and my real name is Hannah Snell.' Their response was refreshingly positive. They were supportive and encouraged her to fight for the pension due to her as a veteran even though she should never have been allowed to join up.

Hannah approached the favourite son of King George, the Duke of Cumberland, victor of Culloden, as he reviewed troops in St James's Park. He was enthralled with her story and made sure that she received a full lifetime pension. She supplemented that money by publishing a book, *The Female Soldier*, and appeared on the stage, telling the story of her life and demonstrating musket drills.

She lived another forty years and had at least two sons before, tragically, in her late sixties she had a mental breakdown and was admitted to Bethlem Hospital, 'Bedlam', in 1791. There she lived out her last six months. Among her fellow patients were fellow veterans for whom the trauma of battle had eventually proved too much, and who were suffering from 'shell shock', battle fatigue or post-traumatic stress disorder, long before any of these conditions were diagnosed.

4 June

Just after midnight a flare lit up the sky and an armoured vehicle entered the square. There were already reports of violence elsewhere in Beijing. Today in 1989, the Chinese government took back Tiananmen Square from the tens of thousands of protesters who had occupied it for weeks, crushing the peaceful revolution that looked as though it might sweep the Communist regime from power.

On the evening of 3 June large bodies of Chinese troops had approached the square. Barricades had been battered aside by armoured personnel carriers and crowds of civilians raked with machine-gun fire. In the early hours of 4 June, Chinese forces started entering the square. One of the first vehicles was set upon by the crowd. A hail of petrol bombs set it ablaze but the crew were rescued and shepherded to the student medical centre in the square. Over the next hour troops poured in from every angle. They sealed off the north and south and then fired on protesters trying to get into the square. More infantrymen surged out of the Great Hall of the People to the west, while on the eastern side soldiers emerged from the History Museum to complete the encirclement. The shouts of the crowd, the noise of helicopters, the protesters' loud-speaker system all mixed into a roar that witnesses say they will never forget.

Many protesters escaped, a hard core of several thousand gathered around the Monument to the People's Heroes in the centre of the square. At 2 a.m. machine guns were fired over their heads as the students begged the military to stop the use of force. By dawn, student leaders agreed to leave to avoid a massacre. Arms linked they marched away; diehard protesters were beaten or shot.

The following day the army reclaimed the streets and the world saw an unknown protester stand in front of a line of tanks; an image forever associated with the massive military response to peaceful democratic protests, an image still banned in China, like all mention of the Tiananmen Square protests.

5 June

It was a meeting of minds that helped to change the world. Today in 1833 Ada Lovelace met the 'father of computers' Charles Babbage for the first time. More even than Babbage himself, Lovelace appreciated what his Analytical Engine might achieve. The algorithm she published for the machine has led to her being called the world's first programmer.

Known as a child as Ada Byron, Lovelace was the only one of the philandering poet's *legitimate* children, even if she was not the 'glorious boy' for which he hoped. 'Is thy face like thy mother's my fair child!' he asked, and was never sure of the answer. Byron left England, and her, soon afterwards, dying when she was eight. In truth both parents neglected her and she was fortunate in having a doting maternal grandmother.

From her teenage years Ada was admired for her 'brilliant mind'. The focus on mathematics in her education owed much to her mother's determination to expunge what she regarded as Byron's insanity. But Ada's gifts were obvious and she thrived on it, so much so that her mother speculated that one day her daughter might become 'an original mathematical investigator, perhaps of first-rate eminence'.

She retained though a strong belief in the importance of poetical gifts in science – of intuition or imagination. It is something many great scientists would agree with. While Babbage's genius underpinned the design of his machine, it was she who saw its potential.

Ada died of cancer when she was only thirty-six and chose to be buried next to her great father at the Church of St Mary Magdalene in Hucknall, Nottinghamshire, having made a confession to her husband – of which the detail is unknown to this day – that caused him to abandon her bedside.

6 June

It was the largest fleet ever gathered. Veterans say, with forgivable exaggeration, that they could have walked across the Solent to the Isle of Wight from deck to deck. There were 7,000 vessels from eight different navies that would carry soldiers to the coast of occupied Europe, where in the early hours of today in 1944 they would begin the job of driving Hitler's forces out of France. It is known simply as D-Day. (The 'D' is to emphasise that particular day, just as the army would always say an assault began at 'H-hour'.)

Nothing was left to chance. D-Day followed years of meticulous preparation. The right moon and tidal conditions were selected, the beaches were investigated by special forces who brought back soil samples. The Germans had been bombarded with false intelligence. Aerial photography had identified nearly every German position. Tanks had been designed that would float to the beaches and then deploy a terrifying array of specialist weaponry. Airborne troops were going to drop inland. The French Resistance was mobilised. British bombers dropped tin foil and dummy parachutists to confuse the Germans. The custodians of the Bayeux Tapestry, that priceless record of another cross-Channel invasion, had been tipped off and it was safely stored away from the fighting.

At dawn, American, British, Canadian and other troops stormed ashore. On some beaches, after a short sharp initial battle, the Allies quickly pushed inland. On one beach, code-named Omaha, American infantrymen found themselves pinned down without tanks. Wave after wave of men were disgorged from landing craft only to be annihilated by machine-gun fire. Thousands were killed or wounded as they waded ashore in deep, cold water.

By the end of the day the Allies had landed more than 150,000 men in France. A stunning achievement. The Germans rushed troops to the beachhead. What followed was a battle for Normandy that would rival the First World War battles in its intensity and cost. D-Day was just the beginning.

7 June

The constituency of Old Sarum in Wiltshire had sent two Members to Parliament since the late thirteenth century. Back then it had been a thriving religious community. By 1832 it had been abandoned. Nobody lived there, the landowner decided who the two MPs would be by assigning voting rights to a handful of his mates. It was a 'rotten borough', a symbol of how the British constitution had failed to adjust to changing times. Manchester, the new industrial metropolis in the north did not have any MPs.

But reform is always tricky and it was only the spectre of even more radical change or even revolution that persuaded King William IV to assent to the Great Reform Act today in 1832.

The House of Commons had tried to pass the bill the year before but it had been crushed in the aristocratic, Tory-dominated House of Lords. Riots tore through places like Birmingham, Nottingham and Bristol, cities where a new middle class felt they were denied a voice in the running of the country. The Whigs in the Commons tried again, and now terrified by the spectre of revolution, the House of Lords and the king caved in. A long list of rotten boroughs was abolished and their representation given to the new towns and cities. The property qualification for voting was set at £10, which added hundreds of thousands of new voters to the roll, although still only around 4 per cent of British people could vote.

It was not democracy, but it was the beginning of a gradual, uneven process that saw Britain change over the next century into a modern representative democracy. It was also a reflection of the pragmatism of the aristocracy and monarchy, who avoided the bloody fate of so many of their European cousins by accepting this change rather than stubbornly resisting it.

8 June

Crowds pushed against the white railings at Epsom on race day in 1913. A woman carrying two flags had squeezed to the front, as the thunder of hooves came closer. The first wave of horses charged past and as the next approached, she flung herself before Anmer, King George V's horse, as the king himself watched on in horror.

The jockey was flung from his seat, and the horse continued to run down the track. The limp body of the woman lay helpless as onlookers rushed to her aid. Her name was Emily Wilding Davison, and she became the emblem of female emancipation after her fatal accident, today in 1913: the first woman to die for women's right to vote, for the Suffragettes.

Emily Wilding Davison fractured her skull in her collision with the king's horse, and died in hospital four days later, aged forty. The Suffragette movement had gone to extreme lengths to secure women's rights and Davison was one of its leading figures. In 1909 she was sentenced for throwing stones at the carriage of Lloyd George, then Chancellor of the Exchequer, and was arrested a further nine times while campaigning. She was treated brutally in prison and was force-fed forty-nine times. It is believed that her death was not deliberate, and that she had in fact been attempting to tie one of her flags to the bridle of Anmer as he hurtled past.

Her funeral was a huge event. People lined the streets as her coffin, mounted on a black carriage pulled by a black horse, processed through the streets of London, with 5,000 Suffragettes in white leading the procession. On her coffin were the words 'Fight on. God will give the victory.'

9 June

At 3.13 p.m. today in 1865, the Folkstone to London train was crossing a viaduct over the River Beult near Staplehurst, when it derailed, killing ten passengers and injuring forty. On board was the famous novelist Charles Dickens, who was travelling with his mistress Ellen Ternan and her mother in the first-class carriage.

The track over the viaduct was being repaired and the workmen had removed two of the tracks, not expecting the train to arrive for another two hours. The train was derailed and seven carriages ended up in the muddy riverbed below. The car that held Dickens and his companions hung perilously from the track at an angle. Dickens escaped with Ellen and her mother, Frances, but returned to snatch his flask of brandy and top hat before rushing down the bank to the wreck below.

Dickens filled his hat with water from the river and an eyewitness saw him, 'running about with it and doing his best to revive and comfort every poor creature he met who had sustained serious injury'. He pulled a young man from the wreckage, offered brandy to a dying man, and comforted a fatally injured woman as she passed away.

Before he left the wreckage, remarkably, Dickens returned again to his precariously suspended carriage. He had left his latest manuscript, *Our Mutual Friend*, in the pocket of his overcoat. On his return to London he was so traumatised by the experience, he lost his voice and experienced 'faint' and 'sick' sensations. His son believed he never recovered from the emotional impact of the crash, which left him 'greatly shaken' until his death on this day in 1870, exactly five years after the disaster at Staplehurst.

10 June

It was, according to a witness, 'as fine a day as our climate allows a June day to be'. In a world before electricity, television or modern transport, about twenty thousand people had turned out to watch the unusual event. Two crews of rowers, eight in each boat with a coxswain to steer, waited on the start line by Hambleden Lock on the River Thames. After one false start, they were ready to go at 7.55 p.m. The young men raced for pride and hard cash – the winning team would take home 500 guineas. Today in 1829, two teams, from two of the world's oldest universities, Oxford and Cambridge, were to compete in a race that had begun as a challenge between two friends who had studied together at Harrow.

The favourites, Cambridge, sat in a handsome pink boat, in matching white suits with pink waistbands. They had won the toss and chosen the Berkshire side of the river. Oxford in their green boat were dressed in dark blue. At the drop of a flag the crews heaved on their oars. The two crews seemed evenly matched; one journalist said that both 'put out the strength of their arms in excellent style'. Slowly Oxford pulled ahead and, despite a ferocious Cambridge counter-attack, maintained a lead through the rest of the race. When Oxford reached the bridge in Henley, after 2.25 miles, it was all over: they had won the inaugural Boat Race.

The race moved to London in 1839 and has been held annually since 1856 except during the two world wars, in which many of the race's alumni served, and several died. The peculiarly British institution is still shown on the BBC, making it one of the last high-profile amateur sporting events. Today the crews weigh on average over 25 kilograms more than their founding forebears, race almost twice the distance, in much faster, sleeker carbon fibre boats. Cambridge have ditched the pink, but Oxford still race in dark blue.

11 June

Eratosthenes of Cyrene was a genius. The chief librarian of one of the Hellenistic world's greatest treasures, the Library of Alexandria, he effectively invented geography. At the very end of the third century BC, he made the world's first, and stunningly accurate, calculation of the circumference of the earth, by comparing the altitudes of the sun at noon from two different places, Alexandria and Aswan, which were a known distance apart. He came up with a figure equivalent today to 24,900 miles (40,074 kilometres), which is only 41 miles (66 kilometres) out. Had Columbus used his figures rather than those of a fifteenth-century Italian astronomer, he would have known that the East Indies were a lot further away than he thought. Eratosthenes calculated the length of a year and the need for a leap day every four years; he was able to predict the occurrence of prime numbers and probably created the first map of the world, but one of his quirkier calculations saw him fix today as the date in 1183 BC for the legendary Fall of Troy.

The mythical, decade-long campaign by a coalition of Greek kings against the city of Troy in Asia Minor is told in the *Iliad*, one of the oldest works in Western literature. It was probably written down around five hundred years before Eratosthenes and may well have originated as an orally recited epic poem. It is attributed to Homer, about whom we know nothing for certain.

Given the lack of any evidence for the destruction of Troy as described by Homer at the end of the *Iliad*, it is hard to credit Eratosthenes with another success on this occasion. But his attempt to fix the events of that fateful night, when Odysseus smuggled a band of warriors inside Troy in a wooden horse, to then emerge and open the gates to the rest of the army, show just how foundational the *Iliad*, and its sequel, the *Odyssey*, had become. Their influence on the entire subsequent output of Western art and culture is impossible to underestimate.

12 June

It must have been an extraordinary sight. Today in 1817 along a rutted coach track between Mannheim and Schwetzingen an inventor called Karl Drais – Karl Friedrich Christian Ludwig Freiherr Drais von Sauerbronn to give him his full name – 'rode' an invention he described as a velocipede, a 'hobby' or 'dandy horse', or a '*Laufmaschine*' (a 'running machine').

It was so-called because the device was propelled by the rider, who ran along the ground then coasted between strides – at electrifying speeds of 6 or 7 miles per hour – not unlike a modern balance bike. To many people today what Drais had invented was the oldest ancestor of the bicycle.

Born in the German state of Baden, Drais was well connected (hence his lengthy name). His godfather was the grand duke. A serial inventor, he experimented with many familiar devices: a form of typewriter, a periscope and a system for recording piano music. But what obsessed him was travel without a horse.

Soon after the Napoleonic Wars he was ready to test his device, and then in Paris 'an immense concourse of spectators' watched the display that proved this machine 'went quicker than a man at full speed' while the 'conductors did not appear fatigued'. Not all were impressed. One sneered that Mr Drais 'deserves the gratitude of cobblers, for he has found an optimal way to wear out shoes'. But others hailed this 'simple idea, of impelling by the help of the feet a seat on wheels'. When it was later marketed it could incorporate, advertising stated, such accessories as a sail, an umbrella, or a lamp. Unfortunately rutted roads and hard wheels made using a 'draisienne' outdoors a tricky experience. Both London and New York banned them in 1819.

Drais himself meanwhile was unrecognised, impoverished and persecuted for his radicalism, after he renounced his aristocratic title and called himself 'Citizen Drais', in homage to the French Revolution. Only with the popularity of the modern bicycle has his invention received renewed acclaim.

13 June

It was a daring raid that rocked the English state. An embarrassing defeat was inflicted by the Dutch today in 1667 when they sailed up the River Medway and destroyed many of England's finest ships at their moorings.

King Charles II was dragging his feet over signing a peace treaty with the Dutch. The war was all but over, he had run out of money to pay for his fleet and most of his battleships were laid up in their base in Chatham. The Dutch planned a bold stroke to force him to make peace. Their fleet, under the brilliant Admiral Michiel de Ruyter, sailed into the Thames, risking disaster as the ships threaded their way through treacherous sandbanks and vicious tides. The target of the raid was the Royal Navy at Chatham. The Dutch smashed through a chain barrier across the River Medway and bombarded forts on the shore. They sacrificed old ships, loading them with flammable material, setting fire to them and sending the blazing ships upriver on the flood tide into the heart of the English fleet.

The Dutch managed to penetrate right up to Chatham dockyard. Three mighty English ships were burned to the waterline. Others were sunk to avoid capture. English crews abandoned their vessels, troops deserted and looted villages as they fled. News and rumour trickled back to London; the diarist Samuel Pepys wrote: 'I do fear so much that the whole kingdom is undone'. Fearing revolution, his family made a plan as to how they would survive the coming chaos.

King Charles's regime survived but he was utterly humiliated. He submitted to peace with the Dutch but immediately planned a resumption of hostilities. Particularly irksome was that his flagship, which bore his name, the *Royal Charles*, had been captured and was now a tourist attraction in Holland.

The lesson of the raid was clear. If Britain wanted to defend herself from invasion and dominate the world's oceans it required cold cash. King and Parliament would have to work together. Navies could not be run on the cheap.

14 June

It was an impregnable fortress, never taken by foreign prince or domestic foe. Yet today, in 1381, a rabble of rioters became the only people to ever storm the Tower of London. They dragged Simon Sudbury, the Archbishop of Canterbury, to Tower Green, where his head was hacked from his body. The Chancellor Robert Hales and other royal servants received the same treatment as the archbishop. Their heads were paraded through the streets and then fixed to London Bridge in the traditional treatment of traitors.

The summer of 1381 saw of a series of 'pitchfork' rebellions among the common people of England. The rebellion began in May, but came to a dramatic climax on 14 June when rebels poured into the City of London 'like the waves of the sea', and king and council fled to the Tower of London. In an attempt to placate the rebels, fourteen-year-old King Richard II left the Tower for Mile End, to negotiate with the mass of peasants, workmen and clergy. He left behind the desperately unpopular members of his court cowering in the chapel of the White Tower.

In the late morning a faction of the rebel force left Mile End and made for the Tower. It was undefended, the gates were open. Unopposed they swept in. To their delight, they discovered the king's mother, Lady Joan of Kent, hiding in the royal apartments; they apparently stole a kiss, before their bloody treatment of Sudbury and Hales.

It was the highpoint of the revolt. Its leader, Wat Tyler, was killed, royal revenge was swift and fierce. Sudbury's skull survives, in St Gregory's Church in Norwich, a grisly reminder of the momentary, but dramatic, shift in power between the working classes and the elite.

15 June

Foundation of constitutional government, or temporary tool of expediency? Historians have argued about Magna Carta, agreed to by King John today in 1215, for the last 800 years. Face to face with his rebel barons, the notoriously incompetent King John acquiesed to sixty-three clauses dealing with their grievances. He agreed to curtail his autocracy, and in doing so gave a glimpse of a new kind of royal power, one restrained by the law.

Murder, extortion, lechery, were just some of King John's crimes that had enraged his barons. Military failure combined with grasping financial demands turned King John's barons into rebels. After they seized London, John agreed to meet them at Runnymede between the king's Windsor stronghold and London. After five days of negotiating, John agreed, and a period of peace followed, lasting a whole nine weeks before the king repudiated this charter with its intolerable restrictions on his divinely appointed power. The barons realised that their only path to redress lay through the field of battle.

The following year King John died. 'Foul as it is, Hell itself is made fouler by the presence of John', wrote chronicler Matthew Paris. The rebel barons were happy to rally to his harmless nine-year-old son, Henry III, especially after the new king's advisers promised to reissue Magna Carta. Subsequent monarchs reaffirmed the status of the charter, helping to ensure that England developed a tradition that even royal power was restrained by the law, a cornerstone of modern constitutional government.

16 June

It was a magnificent spectacle. The entire valley near Guisnes, south of Calais, was swathed with gold fabric. Today in 1520 huge tents housed enormous feasts, there were jousts and musical soirées. This unprecedented display of wealth and majesty was all part of a diplomatic waltz between two young, glamorous kings to strengthen their alliance. For a fortnight Henry VIII of England and Francis I of France attempted to outshine each other in masculinity and kingship through sporting events, pageants and chivalry. The occasion became known as the Field of the Cloth of Gold.

Henry VIII had brought a party of almost 4,000. There were over 1,000 attendants for the queen, 200 halberd bearers and another 200 kitchen staff. In total, almost 3,000 tents needed to be constructed for the English alone, and a similar amount for the French court. Timber framework served as the structure for the mock palace and swathes of sumptuous, ornate material formed the walls and ceilings.

The events began on 4 June, when Cardinal Wolsey, the organiser of the meeting, preceded by a vast and elaborately dressed retinue, went to meet Francis. Three days later, both kings formally greeted each other and the celebrations began. Francis was charming to the queen, kissing her ladies, except those he considered to be 'too ugly'.

Both kings fell over each other in an effort to be courteous, and although it was agreed that they would not tilt against each other, Henry VIII could not resist the opportunity to compete with the French king. He challenged Francis to a wrestling match and was embarrassingly beaten. We are not certain how he took this humiliation, the rest of the event seems to have run smoothly. On 24 June the kings exchanged gifts and departed. Their diplomatic bond was as transitory as the golden field where it was forged; a year later they were at war.

17 June

The Junkers Ju 88 bombers set upon the British ships just before four o'clock in the afternoon today in 1940. The RMS *Lancastria*, a Cunard liner requisitioned by the military to help evacuate British nationals from France only a fortnight after soldiers had escaped from Dunkirk, was attacked just off the port of Saint-Nazaire, in the Loire estuary.

With no RAF fighters present and little anti-aircraft fire the pilots could take their time and the giant liner had no chance. Three bombs hit in quick succession, then one dropped down the smokestack and blew up in the engine room. After the bombs hit, the *Lancastria* quickly capsized while thousands of gallons of fuel poured out onto the surface of the sea where it was then ignited by further strafing from the aircraft.

The number of casualties is disputed. It seems certain that 4,000 people died but estimates have suggested twice that – at least as many as the *Titanic* and the *Lusitania* combined, though both disasters of course are much better known. The ship's normal quota was for approximately 2,500 passengers and crew, but the captain had been clearly instructed to ignore this: to 'load as many men as possible without regard to the limits set down under international law'.

This was Britain's worst-ever maritime disaster, and one of its least known. At the time the government imposed strict secrecy on the press and only in response to articles in the US media was it talked about at all, although the headline in the *Sunday Express* did mention the 'Last Moments of the Greatest Sea Tragedy of All Time'.

18 June

'Next to a battle lost the greatest misery is a battle gained', wrote the Duke of Wellington after the Battle of Waterloo, fought today in 1815. His army had held firm under the hammer blows of the French emperor, Napoleon Bonaparte, long enough for Wellington's Prussian ally to arrive on the battlefield in time to trap the French between them. It had been a long and terrible day. Across the battlefield 45,000 men lay dead and wounded. This evening in 1815 local people rifled through the piles of corpses, stripping their valuable clothes, stealing pocket watches and slitting the throats of the wounded. Wellington had lost members of staff and personal friends. He had always been where the fighting was fiercest, and ascribed his survival to divine protection. After sixteen hours in the saddle he slid off his horse and it kicked him.

The fighting had started at around midday. Thick mud had delayed Napoleon as he positioned his artillery. His plan had been to swat Wellington's army aside and occupy Brussels just a few miles to the north. Wellington described his own army as 'infamous'. It was, he warned, 'very weak and ill equipped'. Only around a third of the army were British, the rest were German, Dutch and Flemish. All day they withstood a battering from the emperor's guns and repeated infantry and cavalry assaults. Late in the day Napoleon threw his undefeated Imperial Guard at Wellington's men in a desperate attempt to defeat them before the Prussians arrived in overwhelming numbers. The Imperial Guard were repelled by ferocious musket volleys from Wellington's thin red line of defenders. As the Imperial Guard retreated, Napoleon's army collapsed. He had met his Waterloo.

It was 'the nearest run thing you ever saw in your life', admitted Wellington, then with a touch less modesty, 'By God! I don't think it would have done if I had not been there!'

19 June

The empire was at its greatest extent. The new emperor controlled millions of square miles and governed well over a hundred million subjects. His recent predecessors had ordered the construction of some of the world's finest buildings. The empire had weathered the climate crisis that had overwhelmed so many of its seventeenth-century competitors; it had, however, one terrible weakness: succession. Today in 1707, Bahadur Shah was crowned Mughal emperor in Delhi. There was no automatic assumption of primogeniture, so in order to obtain the throne Bahadur had killed his brothers and rebelled against his father. His father, Aurangzeb, though, could hardly object. When younger, he had also killed his brothers and rebelled against *his* father, Shah Jahan. Nor could Jahan object. He too had killed his brothers and rebelled against his father.

From the early sixteenth century, when Mughal armies (the name derives from the word Mongol) had swept through the Khyber Pass into modern India, they had dominated the region. They made a capital in Delhi and came to control what is now the northern half of India. Since in the Mongol world landed property (hard to divide) had been less important than animal herds (much easier), no system of primogeniture had ever evolved. But in the settled world that the Mughals inhabited, the lack of any system fostering orderly succession created turbulence. 'The sword,' wrote a British observer a hundred years later, 'was the grand arbiter of right and every son was prepared to try his fortune against his brothers.'

The additional fact that Muslim rulers had multiple legitimate wives only increased the likelihood of rival claimants. It is not surprising, therefore, that Bahadur Shah soon faced family plotting. His sons fought a bloody succession contest, only for the winner to be killed by a nephew. The empire would soon be undone by this lethal weakness.

20 June

In England we are wearily accustomed to the idea that football, while its origins might lie here, has for many years been played to a higher standard elsewhere. Well, it was today, on 20 June in 1867, that the first football match was played in South America, in modern Argentina (one such place) at the Buenos Aires Cricket Club.

A large resident British community had come to live in Buenos Aires during the nineteenth century, where they were often building railways – 'informal empire' as this has been called. Pastimes common in Britain travelled with them: cricket as well as football among them, one catching on in the region rather more than the other.

Two brothers, Thomas and James Hogg, organised this match, between one team wearing white caps and another wearing red (caps being then the common indicator of allegiance that shirts – in a world stripped of headgear – would later become). It was, said one report, a 'spirited contest', with the play of a Mr Barge in particular exciting 'great admiration' in a losing cause, even if the final 4–0 scoreline might suggest little uncertainty as to the result.

At that time the rules of football were still evolving, and the game was more an amalgam of rugby and football than either distinct sport as we know them now. There was no general agreement that the ball would be spherical as opposed to oval, there were not goals in the modern sense, and a general use of hands was permitted. Such fixity was for later. But the ball (if it was round) was rolling.

21 June

The *Empire Windrush* began life as a 500-foot-long German liner. Her passengers were indoctrinated with the joys of Nazism while cruising around the coast of Europe. Later she carried German troops to invade Norway and took Jews back across the North Sea to their deaths in the camps of the Third Reich. Captured by the British in 1945, she now carried British troops, largely along the great artery of empire from Southampton to the Far East via Suez.

In 1948 she stopped in Jamaica. A newspaper advert appeared encouraging Jamaicans to take up their right to live and work in the UK under the terms of the recent British Nationality Act, which allowed any UK or Commonwealth subject to settle in the mother country. Around five hundred Caribbean passengers, and a couple of stowaways, made the journey. Many had served in the RAF during the war and hoped to rejoin.

When they landed in Tilbury, just east of London, today in 1948 they were taken to an air-raid shelter in Clapham, and many sought work at the nearby labour exchange in Brixton. Their arrival was electrifying. There were howls of outrage, one politician claiming 'they won't last one winter in England'. The new arrivals experienced overt racism. Some were beaten up for dating white girls and landlords displayed signs saying 'No Blacks'. But many settled, stayed and thrived. Sam King became Mayor of Southwark.

Decades later, the 'Windrush generation' have become a symbol. No longer could nation states be presented as distinctive, ethnically homogeneous units. In the modern world, economies, politics, families and populations would be global. In 2018 the British Home Secretary was forced to resign over questioning the immigration status of some *Windrush* passengers. The British public were appalled; those young men and women had integrated themselves so completely into British life that their removal became unimaginable.

22 June

Two invasions of Russia, beginning today, 139 years apart, were hugely influential in shaping subsequent history. On 22 June 1941 German Führer Adolf Hitler launched the largest invasion force in the history of warfare against the Soviet Union. Three million men along a 2,000-mile front smashed through Soviet defences. On the same day in 1812 Napoleon Bonaparte, the French emperor, ruler of western and much of central Europe from Cadiz to Croatia and up to Kiel in the north, crossed the River Niemen into Russia. Typically, he wished to reconnoitre personally the best place for his vast army to cross. A hare spooked his horse and he was thrown from his saddle. His chief of staff thought this was a bad omen. He was right.

Both invasions were launched, after failure to defeat the British in the west, to secure dominance in central and eastern Europe, and negate Britain's control of the oceans by accessing India and Asia via the overland route. Both invasions were launched on the wildly optimistic premise that the Russian adversary would risk everything in a climactic decisive battle whereupon they would be defeated and collapse.

Napoleon and Hitler were both wrong. Russian armies did suffer appalling losses but roads turned to quagmires in autumn rains, hugely long supply chains struggled to supply the invading forces, and the Russian leadership stubbornly refused to collapse. Both Napoleon and Hitler won victories that would have annihilated any other opponent, but the Russians simply retreated and regrouped.

Napoleon captured Moscow, Hitler's men reached its outskirts. But winter was coming. Napoleon retreated, his army destroyed. By harnessing every technological advance of the intervening years, Hitler's armies managed to reinforce, resupply and survive not just one but three Russian winters, but the failure of the initial invasion to topple Stalin's regime was the decisive reverse of the Second World War.

If Napoleon had conquered Russia, and if Hitler had destroyed the USSR, the modern world would be a very different place.

23 June

The Scottish king knew that his army was watching as the English knight bore down on him. In an era of conspicuous battlefield leadership this single combat would either cement his reputation or break his cause. Today in 1314 Robert the Bruce faced down his enemy, and shattered Plantagenet dreams of a single British kingdom on the banks of Bannockburn.

Sir Henry de Bohun was hungry for renown. When he had spotted Robert the Bruce he lowered his lance and spurred his heavy warhorse into the charge. The Bruce calmly faced the onslaught, dodged the lance of de Bohun, and brought his battle-axe down onto his opponent's helmet, cleaving into his skull, killing him instantly. As so often on a medieval battlefield, the loss of a leader precipitated a rapid withdrawal; the English retreated. They would continue the battle the following day.

Robert the Bruce raised the spirits of his army with a speech, at which 'the hammered horns resounded, and the standards of war were spread out in the golden dawn'. Amid a hail of arrows, bloody hand-to-hand combat and cavalry charges, the English began to falter. The cry 'On them! On them! They fail!' rippled through Scottish ranks as the mighty English were driven back into the boggy ground around the burn. The slaughter was terrible. The war would go on, but England would never recover from this defeat, and Robert the Bruce's reputation as a warlord and saviour of Scotland was forged on the bloody field of Bannockburn.

24 June

The crowd was possessed. They danced, incoherent and frenzied, with no sense of control or rhythm. They lived only to twist, jump and spin. Today in 1374 crowds of people streamed into Aachen on the Rhine, where they danced before the altar of the Virgin.

This bizarre performance was the first recorded example of choreomania, a strange affliction that caused its victims to dance uncontrollably, often to the death. Monk and chronicler Petrus de Herenthal described both men and women to be 'so tormented by the Devil that in markets and churches as well as in their own homes, they danced and held each other's hands and leaped high into the air'. Modern scholars have failed to come up with a convincing explanation. Mushrooms, trauma, epilepsy, hedonism or a combination of all have been suggested.

It was contagious. By the Feast of the Apostles in July 1374, dancers had gathered in a forest in Trier, which began to resemble a small market town. There, they stripped half naked and set wreaths upon their heads, to dance and luxuriate in a bacchanalian orgy. This resulted in over one hundred conceptions. The 1374 epidemic reached its peak in Cologne with five hundred choreomaniacs taking part. After a few months, to the great relief of the Church authorities, it subsided.

The Church used exorcism aggressively to recover the souls of the dancers. Some were beyond salvation, those who perished from exhaustion and malnutrition were considered to be victims of the Devil. This particular epidemic became known as St John's Dance, for many of the affected called on John the Baptist, as well as the Virgin. There were minor outbreaks over the next two hundred years, another mass occurrence in the sixteenth century, and the Church has presumably finally admitted defeat with the unstoppable march of the modern electro dance scene.

25 June

The only survivor of the American force was a horse, called Comanche. Everyone else under the direct command of Lieutenant Colonel George Custer once the fighting started, was killed. Today in 1876, along the Little Bighorn River, took place the famous battle of the same name. There a leader known most commonly as Crazy Horse led a party of Lakota, Cheyenne and Arapaho Indians to a crushing victory over white settlers represented by the 7th Cavalry of the United States. It was their greatest victory. And it was their last.

The encroachment of white North Americans upon Native American lands has become one of the pre-eminent (and tragic) stories in the development of the United States. All too quickly the heart-warming stories of first thanksgivings turned to misgivings – on both sides. Initially forced to pick a favourite in the Anglo-French conflicts, Native American tribes almost invariably lost out, whoever they backed. And while Americans rebelled and then defeated the British, establishing their independence, this would only hasten the eclipse of the Native Americans.

During the nineteenth century the population of the United States soared, powered by the industrialising east, and a new state to the west could join the Union as soon as it could claim 60,000 inhabitants. Burgeoning communications – particularly railways – fostered westward expansion.

As the pressure of growing settlement told, tribes were pushed further west, across the Great Plains and then into reserves. Rare resistance – as at Little Bighorn – was dwarfed by the cases of deception and defeat. The last battle, at Wounded Knee in 1890, also called the Wounded Knee Massacre, saw hundreds of Native Americans slaughtered. One significant reason why Little Bighorn is so well known is that it was such a rare event.

26 June

King George IV was a man who devoted himself to socialising, womanising and collecting fine art. He embodied the gilded age of the pampered dandy. He became Prince Regent in 1811, taking over the king's duties during the reign of his father, George III, because of the king's debilitating mental illness. The Regency lent its name to an innovative period of change in architecture, fashion and art. George, the Regent, was known to be lazy, high-spending and dissolute by the entire country, but on his death today in 1830 it emerged that Britain's most public man had a very private secret.

Accounts of the 67-year-old's last days on earth are grim reading. He had been a handsome young man but wine and gluttony had caused him to balloon to well over twenty stone. His embarrassment about his weight and 55-inch waist turned him into a virtual recluse. He hid himself in Windsor Castle nursing a galaxy of ailments. The gout in his hand was so bad that he could not sign documents; he had arteriosclerosis and heart disease. He was almost entirely blind, and a huge tumour on his bladder was so painful that he became an opium addict to ease the pain. Death must have been a release.

When the time came to clear out the arch-follower of fashion's wardrobe, a surprising discovery was made. Among the rich frock-coats and silks were two nun's habits and a red petticoat. Perhaps we should not be surprised; *The Times* newspaper said he would always choose 'a girl and a bottle to politics and a sermon', and perhaps who can blame him.

27 June

It was the end of centuries of royal tradition. Today in 1743 a British king – George II – led an army in battle for the final time. It was at Dettingen, during what is known as the 'War of Austrian Succession', when British, Austrian and Hanoverian forces defeated the French. For over a thousand years, since their ancestor Cerdic, the first king of Wessex, fought an enemy king in single combat, English and British monarchs had seen themselves as lords of war. Many had fallen laughably short of an Alfred, Athelstan or Henry V, but George II was a good and experienced officer, praised by no less a judge than the Duke of Marlborough for having, during one major battle, 'distinguished himself extremely'.

And while it is true that George was German by birth and upbringing, he did impress many Britons with the loyalty he showed to his adopted country, as he does us by the devotion he showed to his wife at a time when royal marriages were much more likely to be ones of convenience. Whatever George's personal military distinction, though, there is little doubt – given the calibre of some of his descendants – that the end of any presumption of automatic royal leadership was a good thing.

George IV, for instance, had both a deep personal fascination with the military *and* the deluded sense of self-importance to think that he and Napoleon Bonaparte had been genuine rivals. He would, no doubt, have thrust himself eagerly forward. But he was never given the opportunity, the summit of his responsibility being the command of a 'pet' regiment in England, toy soldiers in human form – a limitation that was unquestionably good for the country at large.

28 June

People stood on furniture to peer into the packed Hall of Mirrors to catch a glimpse of the big moment. Today in 1919 the Treaty of Versailles was signed in the grandest room of King Louis XIV's palace – the treaty brought a formal end to the First World War. It was five years to the day since Archduke Franz Ferdinand, heir presumptive to the Austro-Hungarian throne, and his wife, Sophie, had been assassinated in Sarajevo by the Bosnian Serb Gavrilo Princip: the event that had triggered the devastating war.

The date, like the location, was carefully chosen. It took place in the Hall of Mirrors because it was here that the French had been obliged to recognise the birth of a united Germany in 1871: a good way of emphasising that the boot was now on the other foot. And on 28 June precisely, because this was the anniversary of the assassination of the Archduke and his wife.

Why it was that the murder of the Austrian heir in Sarajevo provoked a continent-wide war – lasting over four years and killing many millions – has been debated ever since. Some have emphasised long-term tensions between the 'great powers' in Europe, others short-term plans or misunderstandings. Some have squarely blamed the ambitions of Germany in particular. Today's treaty included the 'War Guilt' Clause 231, which stated that 'Germany accepts the responsibility of Germany and her allies for causing all the loss and damage to which the Allied and Associated Governments and their nationals have been subjected . . . as a consequence of the war imposed upon them by the aggression of Germany and her allies.' Others have either blamed someone else or denied any particular responsibility. Even now, over a century afterwards, there is no real consensus.

What does still seem ironic is that in the spring of 1914 few had suspected what lay just around the corner. One senior British diplomat had remarked then that since he had been at the Foreign Office he had never seen 'such calm waters'.

29 June

It was not one of Shakespeare's better plays. The playwright had less latitude when it came to recent history. The eponymous hero of *Henry VIII* lacked the depth and flaws of so many of Shakespeare's more celebrated characters, which is unsurprising given he was the late queen's father, and a great-great-uncle of the new king, James I. In fact, it would probably be almost entirely forgotten were it not for a spectacular performance of it, today in 1613. At a climactic moment in the play, a cannon was fired and sparks found their way into the thatched roof of the theatre where they caught on the dry rushes. The Globe theatre, which had hosted so many of the first performances of Shakespeare's plays, burned entirely to the ground. No one was hurt. One man's breeches caught fire but he was doused in beer by fellow theatregoers.

In a city of wood, catastrophic fire was not unusual, and besides, the theatre company, the Lord Chamberlain's Men, which Shakespeare co-owned, was no stranger to dramatic swings of fortune. They had built the Globe after falling out with a landlord in Shoreditch. During Christmas festivities in 1598 the actors had stolen it. They dismantled it beam by beam, and ferried it across the Thames and erected it in rural Southwark.

By the summer of 1599 it welcomed Londoners who made the journey across the river to the hedonistic south bank where a few coins could buy you drink, sex, cockfights, bear-baiting and plays. Dukes and paupers alike packed onto its wooden benches to watch the likes of *Julius Caesar*, *Hamlet*, *King Lear*, *Macbeth* and *Twelfth Night*.

Following the fire the Globe was rebuilt, but fires were easier to overcome than moral outrage. The Globe was finally closed in the 1640s by a regime which saw drama as sinful. This time it would take centuries before a band of players rebuilt it; far from sinful, Shakespeare was now regarded as an essential part of every citizen's cultural diet.

30 June

One eyewitness remembered that, as he sat at breakfast, 'the sky split in two and fire appeared high and wide over the forest'. A wave of intense heat ensued, while an enormous thump was followed by persistent noise 'as if rocks were falling or cannons were firing'. Lots of witnesses compared it to a sound like artillery. It was not a barrage of guns, it was worse; it was the largest impact event in recorded history – a meteor strike in Siberia, today in 1908 near the Tunguska river, from which it generally takes its name.

Though called an impact event, scientists think the meteor actually broke up several miles in the air, which would explain the lack of a crater. The immense good fortune that this took place over such an empty, uninhabited area meant that no human casualties were reported. Some 2,000 square miles of land were devastated and around 80 million trees destroyed.

One account spoke of trees crashing down, thunder, a wind so strong that it knocked people off their feet, and the earth shaking violently. From a clear sky, meanwhile, a 'strangely bright (impossible to look at) bluish-white heavenly body' descended before turning into a 'giant billow of black smoke'. Another witness wrote that 'All villagers were stricken with panic and took to the streets, women cried, thinking it was the end of the world.'

Not for many years did scientific analysis of the region reveal chemical signatures suggesting a vast extraterrestrial event, and levels of iridium, for instance, that are also seen on what is known as the 'Cretaceous-Paleogene boundary', where a mass extinction event is thought to have destroyed most of the world's species, including the dinosaurs.

JULY

1 July

Charlie May was terrified. A few days before the Big Push he had written to his wife, 'I do not want to die . . . the thought that I may never see you or our darling baby again turns my bowels to water.' By nightfall, today in 1916, Charlie May lay dead on the battlefield. Like the 20,000 other men killed on that one day, he would never see his loved ones again.

The first day of the Battle of the Somme was the bloodiest day in the history of the British Army. It was also an almost complete failure. The plans, timetables, training and vast assemblage of men and supplies had all failed to achieve any significant advance, let alone a breakthrough.

Around 1.7 million shells had been fired at German positions. The plan on 1 July was for the infantry to occupy a smashed moonscape. Instead the Germans survived the bombardment in deep shelters and slaughtered the British as they walked across no-man's-land. In one sector 780 Newfoundlanders attacked and within twenty minutes 80 per cent were killed or wounded. Only sixty-eight were fit for duty the following day. Further down the line a 'Pals Battalion' of men from the same neighbourhoods and workplaces, in Sheffield, was annihilated. 'Two years in the making, 10 minutes in the destroying, that was our history', said one survivor.

The battle ground on relentlessly, becoming the biggest-ever fought by the British Army. By its end in November over 400,000 British and Commonwealth troops had been killed or wounded, 200,000 Frenchmen and up to 500,000 Germans. The result of this industrialised slaughter was inconclusive. The British were able to learn valuable lessons that would help them eventually overcome the challenge of trench warfare – how to attack well-dug-in fixed positions – and defeat Germany, but at an awful cost.

2 July

Today most of us associate steam engines with railways. In fact, though, the first steam engine was patented earlier than is generally realised – in the seventeenth century, on this day in 1698. It was designed by a man called Thomas Savery not as a means of transport but as a way of pumping water out of a waterlogged mine: an issue that was becoming more urgent as mines went deeper. It was given the name 'the miner's friend'.

Thomas Savery was an engineer from Devon, fascinated by machines. The patent recognised today was for 'a new invention for raising of water and occasioning motion to all sorts of mill work by the impellent force of fire' – invaluable, the description promised, 'for draining mines, serving towns with water, and for the working of all sorts of mills where they have not the benefit of water nor constant winds'.

Savery's device had no piston – the moving part that again is particularly associated with early steam engines, invented only subsequently by a Frenchman called Denis Papin. Thomas Newcomen, also from the south-west – a man Savery had met – pioneered a later successful steam engine (which he then had to develop in cooperation with Savery and which utilised the latter's patent) which did make use of the piston and cylinder principle.

Savery's machine did have very serious drawbacks. It had an unfortunate tendency to explode, through its dependency on high-pressure steam causing soldered joints to rupture. And the engine had to be installed – and maintained – deep in a mine, close to the water that needed to be pumped out.

Still, it was a pioneering and important invention and illustrates the fact that steam power – which drove the Industrial Revolution – emerged from fertile competition rather than from the brainwave of a single genius.

3 July

War had changed. Generals had not. This became clear today in 1863 to anyone paying attention. The Industrial Revolution had transformed the battlefield. But sadly, few people paid attention.

General Robert E. Lee, leader of the Confederate forces, sensed victory. He was deep in enemy territory, only 85 miles from Washington, DC, capital of the United States. He had the Union Army almost surrounded. If he could destroy his foe, then President Lincoln would surely have to open peace negotiations with the Confederacy. He decided to unleash a massive frontal assault.

At 1 p.m. over 150 guns opened up in what would be the largest artillery bombardment of the American Civil War. One witness recalls how the guns 'vomited their iron hail', but the effect was limited. The fire was inaccurate and smoke obscured the Union lines.

Then, on the roasting July afternoon 12,500 Confederates stepped out into the open fields below their enemy positioned on the crest of a gentle ridge. Instantly cannonballs scythed through their ranks. As they got to within 400 metres, cannons switched to firing canister shot – a case of musket balls – turning them into giant shotguns. The Confederates were slaughtered, although some units got to grips with the enemy and there was hand-to-hand fighting. But they were too few in number. It was the high-water mark of the Confederacy.

The rebel troops broke and fled back to their start positions. They left half of their number behind them on the battlefield. Lee moved among survivors begging forgiveness. He saw one commander, General Pickett, and asked him to rally his division, to which Pickett replied, 'General, I have no division.'

'Pickett's Charge' was the decisive moment of the American Civil War; the Confederacy would never recover. Accurate, quick-firing rifles and explosive shells meant that the era of marching men towards the enemy in plain sight was over, but it would take decades for that lesson to be properly learned.

4 July

The fact that the organisers had even got representatives from thirteen of the British colonies in North America in the same room was itself cause for celebration. Then surely getting this Second Continental Congress to approve a resolution of independence from Great Britain on 2 July meant, as John Adams wrote, that the 2nd would 'be celebrated by succeeding generations as the great anniversary festival'.

Well, he was nearly right. Representatives now turned their attention to drawing up a formal Declaration of Independence, which provided their reasoning. It was approved today, on 4 July. And of course it is this anniversary, rather than that of the vote two days earlier, which has been the date celebrated by US citizens ever since as 'Independence Day'.

The text of the declaration was drawn up by a 'Committee of Five', of whom Thomas Jefferson acted as the principal author. Its words echo down the ages: 'We hold these truths to be self-evident, that all men are created equal, that they are endowed by their Creator with certain inalienable rights, that among these are Life, Liberty, and the Pursuit of Happiness . . .'

Colonists in North America, it asserted, were every bit the equal of men in Britain, not commodities to be taxed without their approval. The fact that the meaning of 'all men' would require long debate and often further brutal conflict – until it embraced both women and people of all races – does not diminish the power of the original sentiment.

By the time that independence was declared, the war in which the United States achieved its separation from Great Britain had begun. Already it looked – as it did duly prove – that the effort of imposing order upon unwilling colonists thousands of miles from home would prove too much.

5 July

It was the birth of an institution under whose auspices so many of us have, in turn, been born: the NHS.

Today in 1948 the charismatic health secretary Aneurin Bevan (a job previously considered rather lowly and not occupied by a cabinet minister) officially launched his grand, profoundly ambitious, and at the time highly contentious project: a National Health Service for the entire British population. It was to be funded by taxation and free at the point of delivery, under which all sorts of people – doctors, nurses, surgeons, dentists, opticians, to name a few – would be brought beneath one single organisation.

The launch began at Park Hospital in Manchester (known now as Trafford General). It was then that a thirteen-year-old girl named Sylvia Beckingham was admitted to the hospital for a liver condition, thereby becoming the first-ever patient to be admitted on the NHS.

Plenty decried the scheme. Some even deemed it the onset of 'National Socialism', so soon after the defeat of the Nazis in Germany. Nor were opponents simply Conservative Party MPs. Plenty in the Labour Party were hostile too, as well as many doctors, whose mouths, Bevan remarked, he had 'stuffed . . . with gold' in order to secure their cooperation.

Bevan made two major predictions, the first accurate and the second seriously inaccurate: he was confident that the initial rush upon NHS services would wane in the short-term; and he was sure that the high initial costs of the service would decline as the population became healthier.

As we all know now, of course, the spectacular success of the NHS contributed to increasing British life expectancy, while the cost of new medicines and treatments, as well as the number of NHS employees, sky-rocketed. Far from declining, the overall bill soared. So while affection for the institution has grown, funding it has become a headache.

6 July

The meeting attracted no publicity at the time, but in hindsight the introduction effected today in 1957 was one of the most important in popular culture.

It was then, at a village fete at a church hall – St Peter's Church in Woolton, an affluent suburb of Liverpool – that a sixteen-year-old John Lennon met a fifteen-year-old Paul McCartney. The day concluded with a 'Grand Dance' in the hall. John Lennon was performing with his group The Quarrymen (named after their school: Quarry Bank), having also played outdoors on the back of a flatbed truck. Paul came to watch, knowing one of Lennon's band.

Lennon, Paul remembers, looked and sounded the part – 'really looked suave', in his checked shirt and with slicked-back hair. And he has recalled too John's seemingly cool habit of inventing song lyrics. He thought it was done on purpose – old blues lyrics used in place of genuine ones – when often in fact he had simply failed to hear them properly in the first place.

Paul, meanwhile, impressed Lennon too with his knowledge of music and his way with a guitar. He demonstrated a Little Richard track, playing it left-handed on a right-handed guitar. They shared an obsession with the new wave of American music, from Elvis to Gene Vincent, and, of course, Buddy Holly.

While some have remembered that Paul then instantly joined the group, others recall a rather longer process, involving him coming to watch a rehearsal. Gradually, the other members left and a year later a lad called George joined. And what was now a threesome became a foursome when, shortly afterwards, they picked up a drummer, and after experimenting with names such as 'Johnny and the Moondogs', 'The Silver Beetles' and 'The Beatals', rechristened themselves 'The Beatles'. The rest, as they say, is history.

7 July

In the darkness of early morning, a Japanese soldier, Private Kikujiro, sneaked off to the loo today in 1937 at the Lugou Bridge at the edge of the Chinese capital of Beijing.

Unsure what had become of Kikujiro, his superior thought that he had been kidnapped by the Chinese – and in the fraught, knife-edge state of relations between the two countries, he ordered an attack on them. The incident marked the beginning of the Sino-Japanese War – and effectively marked the very first shots of the Second World War.

Since 1931 in particular – when the Japanese invaded and set up a puppet state called Manchukuo in Manchuria, Japan had exploited civil war in China to expand its grip on the country's north-eastern provinces. Japanese forces had moved ever further, greatly exceeding the limits put upon foreign military personnel under the Boxer Protocol agreed some decades earlier. Japan's soldiers effectively surrounded both the Chinese capital of Beijing and the important port of Tianjin.

Having refused a peremptory demand from the Japanese to search for the missing Private Kikujiro in the nearby walled town of Wanping, both the Chinese and the Japanese began to mobilise their forces, while the Japanese deployed reinforcements and surrounded the town. By the time Kikujiro had completed his task and returned to his regiment, both sides were mobilising and events were – in a desperately tense atmosphere – taking their course.

Chinese and Japanese forces fought over the nearby Lugou stone bridge with eleven arches, called the Marco Polo Bridge in the West, which the Chinese held only with great losses. Subsequent attempts to achieve a truce were stillborn, or short-lived, and when a Japanese naval officer was shot in Shanghai early in August what had been skirmishes became a full-blown war.

8 July

Like a phoenix, it came out of the flames. Today in 1579, in the Russian town of Kazan, survivors of a fire found a symbol of faith; they called it a miracle.

Our Lady of Kazan, a painting of the Virgin and Child, was discovered in the ashes of a fire. According to legend, a fire destroyed the house of a merchant and afterwards the merchant's young daughter began to dream of an icon of the Virgin Mary, hidden among the ruins. Her dream recurred and eventually she was compelled to search the rubble of her father's house. Amazingly, she discovered the painting, wrapped in an old cloth, in immaculate condition hidden deep beneath the ashes, apparently untouched by the inferno.

The painting quickly became famous and associated with further miracles after two blind men were said to have had their sight restored after standing in front of it. It quickly became the most important piece of religious art in Russia, even inspiring the construction of churches in its honour. *Our Lady of Kazan* was considered so potent that it went on tour during times of threat to the country, such as during the Napoleonic Wars, when it was paraded in full view to restore hope as Napoleon Bonaparte's army neared the Russian capital.

In 1904 the painting was stolen by thieves, and in the eyes of believers its disappearance has led to a series of disasters in the country, such as the Revolution of 1905. Rumours abound; it might have been burned, or buried. Although many copies have been made, claiming to be the original, the real *Lady of Kazan* is still missing to this day, having disappeared without a trace.

9 July

It was the world's first official lawn tennis tournament. Today in 1877 it began at Wimbledon, at the suggestion of the secretary of the All England Club. Only one event was put on: a Gentlemen's Singles. The hope was that the tournament would raise enough money to repair the broken roller, pulled by a pony, which was needed to maintain the lawns.

Other venues around London were inspected, but none was deemed more suitable than Wimbledon, whose croquet lawns were all converted into tennis courts for the purpose. On 9 June the tournament was announced in the *Field* magazine: 'The All England Croquet and Lawn Tennis Club, Wimbledon, propose to hold a lawn tennis meeting, open to all amateurs, on Monday, July 9th and following days'. 'The value of the prizes,' the notice declared, 'will depend on the number of entries.' The silver Field Cup was donated by the magazine for the winner.

The club had been founded purely for the sport of croquet, but interest in this demure pastime was waning along with membership. Nevertheless, with a croquet tournament held at the club the week before the tennis, croquet players had first choice of courts. Tennis players were advised that practice balls could be obtained from the club gardener for a shilling a ball.

Unified rules drawn up by the MCC – the Marylebone Cricket Club: also the governing body for rackets and real tennis – were altered for the tournament. The court was to be rectangular, not hour-glass shaped. The net height was lowered. A real tennis scoring sequence was adopted – 15, 30, 40 – with six games in a set, a match being the best of five sets. Servers would have two chances to deliver a correct service, keeping one foot behind the baseline. Little, of course, has changed since, apart from the number of competitions and the prize money.

10 July

It is a long, narrow valley enclosed by steep mountain ranges. The floor of the valley is nearly a hundred metres below sea level. As a result the heat is trapped and less than 1 centimetre of rain falls per year.

The Timbisha people called it *tumpisa* meaning 'rock paint', thanks to the red paint that can be made from the soft clay of the valley. For centuries they learned how to survive in one of the earth's most hostile environments. White settlers arrived in great numbers en route to the California Gold Rush in 1849 and called it simply Death Valley. This is understandable, as one early attempt to cross this low-lying desert by wagon train heading from Nevada to central California saw a dozen 'stampeders' (named after their habit of dashing wildly towards new gold strikes) die in soaring temperatures.

Its reputation as the world's hottest place was sealed today in 1913 when the US Weather Bureau recorded a temperature of 134 °F or 56.7 °C. This reading, made in what is now called Furnace Creek, still stands as the highest air temperature ever recorded on the surface of the earth. In 1972 the temperature of the ground itself reached an astonishing 201 °F or 93.9 °C.

Furnace Creek was the centre of the local mining operation, the valuable mineral borax was found there and despite the appalling working conditions it was mined until the early twentieth century. Profit trumped everything, and continues to do so as Furnace Creek now boasts a golf course. The green fairways are a testament to human ingenuity, but also our profligacy with natural resources. The impact we are having on our environment seems certain to mean that the world's hottest record is one that is soon to be broken.

11 July

London burned uncontrollably; houses, shops and churches were reduced to twisted and blackened stumps of wood. The fire destroyed 'the great part of the city'. Yet this was not the famous Great Fire of 1666, but a less-famous blaze in 1212, which incinerated a large part of medieval London.

It started in Southwark, gathering speed and force reached London Bridge, and remarkably travelled over the bridge across the Thames and engulfed the city. The main loss of life, and destruction, occurred on London Bridge. The prevailing south-westerly wind fed the fire with oxygen and blew the sparks from one timber-framed, straw-roofed building to the next. People fleeing the fire from Southwark swarmed onto the bridge but became trapped as the fire spread along the buildings that lined the bridge. Citizens threw themselves into the river to escape the flames. Many drowned and rescue boats were submerged by people desperately trying to climb on board them.

The earliest recorded fire in London was AD 60 when ancient Londinium was sacked by Boudicca. The inferno she ignited was so severe that a thick layer of buried ash is still used by archaeologists to date remains. Another blaze destroyed St Paul's Cathedral in 1087 and in 1135 the original wooden London Bridge was destroyed by fire.

In an environment where buildings were constructed largely of wood, in close proximity to one another, and where domestic life surrounded a hearth, it is not surprising that fires were a common occurrence in medieval London. The Great Fire in 1666 is the most famous but there were only six verified casualties. With up to 3,000 deaths in 1212, the lesser-known Fire of London was, in fact, far more destructive than its more recent equivalent.

12 July

The most powerful man in the world was humiliated today in 1807. Not by an enemy army, not by Machiavellian intrigue, not by an eloquent opponent, but by rabbits.

Napoleon Bonaparte, His Imperial and Royal Majesty, By the Grace of God and the Constitutions of the Republic, Emperor of the French, King of Italy, Mediator of the Swiss Confederation, Protector of the Confederation of the Rhine, dominated Europe from the border with Russia to the Atlantic coast. A few days before he had signed a treaty with the Russian tsar on a fine raft anchored in the middle of the Nieman river, carving up the continent and sealing a peace deal between the two great powers.

Bestriding the continent like no one before him since the Romans, it was clearly time for a party. His chief of staff organised a shoot. Grand picnics were laid on, beaters, loaders and other staff scurried around the sportsmen. The quarry today was rabbits. Thousands of them had been rounded up and they would be released and driven towards the waiting guns.

In the event, they did not need any encouragement. No one knows why but when the cages were opened hundreds of rabbits made a dash for Napoleon. With a tactical flair missing from his opponents on the battlefield they brought overwhelming numbers to bear in unison. Napoleon fled. Chased by rabbits he leapt into his coach and was driven away.

It turned out the rabbits were not wild, they had been brought from farms. They must have seen Napoleon as the source of food. Like Cnut and the tides, this bizarre tale is a reminder that imperial power is a human construct, to our animal cousins we are just another ape.

13 July

It could have been good luck or sound judgement. This morning in 1174 a detachment of English knights, feeling their way through a thick Northumbrian fog, found themselves at the encampment of the Scottish King William I who was besieging Alnwick Castle. William had been over-confident and had divided up his army to blockade the magnificent fortress from all directions. That tactic left him thinly spread, and when the English relief force, which had ridden overnight from Newcastle, came up from the south, they found the Scottish king and his bodyguard deeply vulnerable.

Charismatic battlefield leadership was the one trait that no medieval king could do without, and William knew what was expected of him, however desperate the situation. He leapt on his steed and roared 'Now we shall see which of us are good knights!' before launching himself in a reckless and badly coordinated attack on the English. He was absolutely right. Both sides did then see who was any good, and it was not William. Man and horse went crashing to the ground as he closed with his foe. The horse was killed and the king was captured.

While his leaderless army headed home, William was taken to Newcastle, and then eventually to Falaise in Normandy. King Henry II occupied Scotland. William was allowed to return but only after signing the humiliating Treaty of Falaise in which he pledged allegiance to Henry as his feudal lord, agreed to pay for the costs of the occupation and submitted the Scottish Church to English rule.

William is remembered as 'the Lion'. A generous epithet, one derived not from his prowess on the battlefield, but from his banner which featured a red lion rampant on a yellow background, still the Royal Banner of Scotland, and still worn by its rugby and football players to this day.

14 July

The ancient castle was no match for a furious mob of Parisians. Today in 1789 the fortress in Paris known as the Bastille was stormed and sacked. Combining roles as military stronghold, armoury and political prison, it seemed the ultimate representation of the old – the *ancien* – regime, in which a monarchy seen as decrepit and bankrupt ruled the state.

Most people know of the incident, and if they know the date it is largely because to this day, in France – still, of course, a republic – the '*quatorze juillet*', 'Bastille Day', is still honoured and celebrated. Not only does it mark the beginning of a seismic revolution (both famous and infamous at the same time), it also represents one of those rare moments in history that are truly epochal – like the outset of the First World War, or the attacks of September 11 – when nothing afterwards is ever quite the same again.

Beforehand, mounting tension was exacerbated by a worsening financial crisis that affected the French royal government. Decisions were then made that failed (understandably perhaps, given the unprecedented nature of events) to recognise a mood of general intransigence. As economic deprivation combined with social unrest to fan the flames, houses rumoured to harbour food or weaponry were plundered.

Unrest and social chaos worsened, the authorities panicked, reluctant to take measures which might have restored order. And the Bastille – a medieval fortress already marked for demolition and replacement by an open space – was attacked. Uncertain of their ability to hold out, the fortress's occupants soon surrendered: the commander and his officers were murdered.

When the king was apprised of events early the following day he is supposed to have enquired if it was a revolt, and was given the famous reply: 'No, sire, it's not a revolt; it's a revolution.'

15 July

After seven weeks of a gruelling siege, when the knights broke into the city they were in no mood for mercy. Today in 1099 a Christian army took Jerusalem and massacred Muslim and Jewish men, women and children. Described as 'the navel of the world' by a contemporary, Jerusalem was prized as holy by all three monotheistic religions and was festooned with sites sacred to one or all of them. The ferocity of the slaughter reflected the zealotry of the perpetrators.

The Crusader army assaulted the walls with two enormous siege engines, equipped with catapults, bridges and a battering ram. The defenders responded with Greek fire, a combustible compound. Lassos were used to pull the siege engines to the ground, and bales of burning hay were hurled at the Crusaders. They managed to set one engine on fire, but Flemish knights on the second managed to get into the city. Resistance collapsed and by midday the Crusaders were pouring into the city's streets.

The slaughter began. Massacres were not uncommon. Muslim forces had carried out many before, but the Crusaders appear to have inflicted another level of barbarism, perhaps in an attempt to cleanse the city of paganism and establish Jerusalem as a city solely for those of the true faith. Fugitives on Temple Mount were slaughtered; the blood ran above the ankles of their murderers. Many Muslims had their stomachs cut open, for it was rumoured that they would ingest their gold for safekeeping.

Jerusalem's travails were far from over, but it is notable that a century later when the Muslims recaptured it, there was no slaughter. While thousands were marched into slavery, those who could pay were able to ransom themselves and were escorted back to Crusader-held territory. But faith and affiliation were deeply complex. They were denied entry to Christian-controlled Tyre, and robbed and terrorised by their fellow Crusaders outside Tripoli. The Crusades were not a clear-cut clash of two, homogeneous antagonists neatly defined by religion, but a complicated, ever-shifting conflict in which personality, ambition, localism and cash were as important as faith.

16 July

The seventeenth century was when the Atlantic slave trade really took off. Over 1 million Africans were captured, transported and put to work in the Americas in appalling conditions. But slave raids were not confined to the west coast of Africa. North African states preyed on the Mediterranean and Atlantic coasts of Europe, carrying off slaves to serve in Africa. Perhaps as many as 1 million Europeans were abducted and served as slaves in the Barbary States of North Africa over a couple of centuries.

Today in 1627 the most spectacular raid of this period came to a climax as slave traders stormed ashore and rounded up hundreds of people, not where we might expect in Italy, Spain or even the south coast of England, but in Iceland. The commander of the slave ships was Murat Reis the Younger, who operated out of a port on the Atlantic coast of Morocco. To complicate matters he seems to have been Dutch originally, but converted to Islam after being enslaved himself, thus winning his freedom. With a crew of Arabs, Berbers and other converted Europeans, he headed north.

His ships sailed along Iceland's south coast, raiding until on 16 July they reached Vestmannaeyjar, a group of islands on which they landed. At first the locals tried to fight, but anyone resisting was slaughtered. With dozens of corpses littering the villages, the rest of the population, hundreds of men, women and children were rounded up and led aboard the ships. Between 400 and 800 Icelanders were captured. Among them was Guðríður Símonardóttir, a young mother and wife of a fisherman. She was sold in Algeria into sexual slavery, before being ransomed and returning home.

Perhaps the numbers of captives do not seem that high, but the population of Iceland was only 60,000 at the time, so something like 1 per cent of the population were taken in one raid. That is the same percentage loss that the UK suffered during the Second World War.

17 July

They had ruled Russia for three centuries. They had survived invasion, assassinations, riot, scandal and defeat. But today in 1918, finally, the Russian Romanov dynasty was utterly extinguished, in a gruesome mass murder.

In 1914, Tsar Nicholas II led Russia into the First World War. It was a disaster, the human losses and the strains it placed on Russian society bred discontent and eventually revolution. In 1917, Nicholas was forced to abdicate. Later that year radical Bolsheviks, led by Vladimir Lenin, seized power and held the imperial family captive.

It triggered a terrible civil war. By the summer of 1918 anti-Bolshevik forces were advancing on Yekaterinburg, where the Romanovs were being held and their gaolers were ordered to kill them to prevent their rescue. The family were woken late at night and told to dress. They were ushered down to the cellar of the house and lined up in two rows, supposedly for a photograph. As they awaited the camera flash, a group of armed men burst into the cellar and fired wildly into the terrified family. Drunkenness or incompetence meant that some of the victims had to be repeatedly stabbed to finish the job.

In 1991, in a forest nearby to Yekaterinburg, the remains of Tsar Nicholas, his wife and three of his children were exhumed, and two years later their identity was proven by DNA. The Soviet authorities were coy about their fates, fuelling a raft of conspiracy theories; one persistent myth is that Anastasia escaped and survived. Several women came forward claiming to be the lost princess, but none were proven to be anything other than impostors.

The deaths of the Russian royal family were just a handful of the tens of millions who were starved, murdered and brutalised in the catastrophe that followed the Russian Revolution.

18 July

The Hundred Years' War did not last a hundred years nor was it one continuous war. Fighting between England and France rumbled on and off for 116 years and there were significant lulls in the violence. One of them began today in 1389 when, after a month of negotiation, the three-year Truce of Leulinghem was agreed to just outside Calais.

England had a young king, Richard II, and he was short of money. The wars of his grandfather, Edward III, had strained England's ability to pay. Richard's revenue-raising techniques were proving ever more unpopular. France was struggling too. King Charles VI's mental collapse was dragging French internal politics into a state of chaos. The two countries needed a break. This truce marked Richard's assertion of his own royal power, a symbol of him ridding himself of those who had run the country during his childhood, like his influential uncle, John of Gaunt.

Freed from the grinding war in France, Richard sought to strengthen his position in England. His political enemies were either exiled, stripped of land and title, or executed, and his kingship became increasingly unpopular. In 1399, after the death of his wealthy uncle John of Gaunt, Richard seized his lands, which by right belonged to Gaunt's son, Henry of Bolingbroke, who had been conveniently exiled. In 1400, Bolingbroke invaded, supported by an army of Richard's enemies, deposed Richard, and installed himself as the first Lancastrian king. Richard was imprisoned, and probably murdered at Pontefract Castle.

Richard had hoped that peace with France would allow him to bolster his own position in England. He had miscalculated. His fractious nobles, lacking a foe to fight across the Channel, turned on their own king. There was peace in the fields of France but bloodshed within the English royal family.

19 July

It was a piece of basalt, unearthed during building work on an ancient fort at the mouth of the Nile. The French officer was a scholar as well as an engineer. Today in 1799 he stared at the intricate inscriptions on its surface and knew instantly that it was an important archaeological discovery. He deciphered three inscriptions, of similar lengths, but in different scripts. Lieutenant Pierre-François Bouchard lugged the four-foot-long stone back to his camp near the city of Rosetta. Henceforth the stone would bear the name of the place where it was discovered, becoming the Rosetta Stone.

The previous year Napoleon had invaded Egypt and instructed scholars to seize and examine all the cultural artefacts they encountered. Bouchard knew Napoleon was in Egypt for more than territorial aggrandisement. This was an expedition of scientists and Egyptologists as much as an invasion. The experts were electrified by the stone. It was the modern world's first example of an ancient Egyptian bilingual text. It offered the prospect of being a means to be able to finally translate the hieroglyphics of the Pharaohs.

When the British defeated Napoleon in Egypt in 1801, they promptly seized all the artefacts he had gathered, including the Rosetta Stone. It was taken to London where it has sat ever since in the British Museum as scholars in Britain and France competed to decipher the inscription. The squabbling over who cracked it first is epic. Suffice to say, it took a good twenty years, but the Rosetta Stone was indeed the key that unlocked the lost language of Pharonic Egypt . . .

20 July

Today in 1969 the first manned lunar module touched down in the Sea of Tranquillity on the surface of the Moon. Images broadcast, almost live, were watched by hundreds of millions all over a world temporarily united in this extraordinary human achievement. 'The Eagle,' the leading astronaut Neil Armstrong reported, 'has landed.' The *Eagle* – the national bird of the United States – was the name given to the lunar module, part of which was able subsequently to blast off from the Moon's surface to rejoin the expedition's command craft.

It was late in the day (UTC time) when the landing occurred, and given that it was some six hours before Armstrong emerged to climb down the nine-rung ladder and take his famous first steps on the Moon – when Buzz Aldrin then joined him – by general reckoning this happened on 21 July. Armstrong found the Moon's low gravity, one sixth of the Earth's, straightforward enough to walk in. He planted the American flag, which had a wire support to compensate for its lack of fluttering.

Thirty times Apollo (now without the rocket that had brought it here) had orbited the Moon before *Eagle* separated and began its descent. Not surprisingly, after the module had landed, Armstrong and Aldrin declared themselves far too alert to take advantage of the five-hour sleep period now planned and got directly to work planning the moonwalk.

Armstrong had opted to bring with him a piece of wood from the Wright brothers' 1903 aeroplane's left propeller (and a piece of fabric from its wing) – to commemorate another occasion in the same century when humankind had made a seismic technological leap. But unlike the flag, the Air and Space Museum wanted these artefacts brought back to Earth.

21 July

In the only surviving portrait of the warrior king Henry V he is depicted unconventionally, from his left side. This may be due to his sensitivity about a scar on his right cheek, a souvenir from the battlefield of Shrewsbury, where today in 1403 he was shot in the face by an arrow at the tender age of just sixteen.

Prince Henry had marched to Shrewsbury where he joined his father, King Henry IV, to crush Harry 'Hotspur' Percy, an aristocratic rebel. Percy had been a key ally of the House of Lancaster but he became disenchanted at the king's 'tyrannical government' and raised the standard of revolt.

It was the first time two armies wielding the lethal longbow would ever meet on the battlefield. The result was a hail of iron-tipped arrows that took a terrible toll on both sides. Prince Henry was hit, and it is likely that Harry Percy was killed by an arrow in the face.

Henry was more fortunate. The royal physician John Bradmore attended to the prince over several days. He later wrote a medical tract in which he claimed that the arrow had punched into the bone at 'the depth of six inches'. He managed to remove the arrow, using screws and tongs, and 'by moving it to and fro, little by little (with the help of God) I extracted the arrowhead'. He used honey as an antiseptic and washed the wound thoroughly with alcohol.

The doctor probably saved Henry's life. The prince never forgot the awesome power of the longbow. When he invaded France in 1415, he took a sizeable body of bowmen with him, and it was to them that he largely owed his greatest victory, on the field of Agincourt.

22 July

They may have been the largest wooden ships ever built. Beneath acres of sail, flying on nine masts, the mighty 'treasure ships' crept up the waterway to Nanjing. Today in 1433, after a sea voyage of two years and over ten thousand miles, the Xiafan Guanjun, Foreign Expeditionary Armada, arrived home.

The commander, Zheng Ho, brought his fleet safely to the walled city. They passed beneath the nine-storey octagonal pagoda, the Great Baoen Temple, where Buddhist monks gave thanks for another voyage completed. Zheng Ho had overseen its construction. His remarkable organisational skills were as sought after on land as on sea. He had been dispatched to 'go and instruct' the 'foreign countries, distantly located beyond the sea' who 'did not know' about the power of China, 'into deference and submission'. He had set off with what was probably the most powerful naval force to that date, over a hundred large ships, numerous smaller ones, and over 25,000 men on board. The biggest vessels were perhaps twice as long and three times as wide as HMS *Victory* and something like eight times heavier.

The fleet had travelled as far west as Hormuz in the Persian Gulf, stopping in places like Java, Sri Lanka and India. Its sheer might overawed everyone who saw it. Foreign rulers paid tribute, and the returning fleet was carrying giraffes, elephants and rich trade goods.

China was the world's great maritime power. But the glorious return of the Armada to Nanjing was the end of not just the seventh expedition into the Indian Ocean but of the entire era of transoceanic expeditions. China turned away from the sea. In 1436 the building of seagoing ships was banned. So when the Europeans, arrived in the East a couple of generations later, Chinese naval domination was a distant memory.

Europeans would conquer much of Asia, by controlling the ocean. Their ships would eventually push deep into China itself, during the *bǎinián guóchǐ*, the 'Century of Humiliation'. China paid a heavy price for ignoring the sea.

23 July

The usual date for the start of the Civil War is 22 August 1642, when the royal standard was raised at Nottingham Castle – it then blew over in a storm. This, though, is an Anglocentric view.

Some time before this, conflicts took place involving King Charles I's northern realm of Scotland: his Stuart dynasty's homeland (even if Charles himself spent little time there). Today, on Sunday 23 July 1637, for instance, the Civil War – or Civil Wars – could be said to have begun in Edinburgh, as female maidservants in St Giles's Cathedral rioted rather than submit to prayers from King Charles's new prayer book.

It was the year that William Laud, the Archbishop of Canterbury, oversaw the publication of a new Book of Common Prayer intended for introduction into the Church in Scotland. It was 'episcopalian' – assumed the authority of bishops – rather than 'presbyterian', to accord with majority Scottish practice. Anticipating its unpopularity, Laud attempted simply to impose (rather than to negotiate) uniformity of worship.

When the book was first read publicly, tumult ensued. There were general 'cursings and outcrys' while one market-woman famously hurled her stool at the minister's head, demanding whether he dared to 'say Mass in my [ear]'. For such presumption the Devil, she implored, should give him colic. Stones, sticks and Bibles were thrown. Service books were ripped. A full riot ensued as those thrown out hammered at the church's doors.

Rebellion in Scotland led to what was called a National Covenant being signed north of the border and ultimately, in 1639, to outright war. To confront it Charles needed money. And to get this he had no choice but to summon Parliament in London. It was his tactless handling of this that radicalised the king's political opponents in England and which led to the outbreak of war there too.

24 July

The first Olympic marathon was won – initially – in London by a diminutive Italian called Dorando Pietri today in 1908. It ended with a lap of the Olympic track in White City.

Pietri entered the stadium utterly exhausted, and first went the wrong way – until umpires put him right – and was then helped up several times when he collapsed. The final assisted 350 metres took him ten minutes. One American spectator effused afterwards that what he had witnessed was surely 'the greatest race of the century'.

When the second-place runner (American, Johnny Hayes) protested, Pietri was duly disqualified. But his achievement was revered all the same and drew plaudits from around the world. In spite of his removal from the official results, Queen Alexandra awarded him a special gilt cup.

Watching was the correspondent for the *Daily Mail* – and author of the Sherlock Holmes stories – Sir Arthur Conan Doyle. 'The Italian's great performance,' he wrote, 'can never be effaced from our record of sport, be the decision of the judges what it may.' At Conan Doyle's behest the *Mail* began a subscription with which to help Pietri open a bakery in his home town. Subsequent races were organised between Pietri and Hayes, as well as others, on an American tour.

This first Olympic marathon course ran from Windsor Castle to the White City stadium, through Eton, Slough and other places in west London: Harrow, Wembley, Willesden. The precise distance had not yet become established. Organisers had simply requested a race of about twenty-five miles.

The impossibility of entering the track by the royal entrance, and the need to preserve a good view of the finish, meant the final lap was run clockwise rather than the more usual anti-clockwise. For purely practical reasons, as a result, the final distance was '26 miles plus 385 yards on the track', though subsequently – so renowned had the race become – its arbitrary length became the standard.

25 July

No king in Europe's history better illustrates the terrible division unleashed by the Protestant Reformation than Henri IV, King of France and Navarre. Born a Catholic, raised a Protestant, he narrowly avoided assassination countless times, fought for his faith, made one of the great compromises by renouncing it, only to eventually be murdered by a fanatic. He is famous for his quip 'Paris is worth a Mass', an adage repeated ever since by politicians who have sacrificed their own beliefs on the altar of their ambition.

By 1593 France had been mired in three decades of chaos and civil war. Millions had died as an unstable succession coincided with bitter religious disputes caused by the adoption of Protestantism by factions within the French elite. In 1572 thousands of Protestants were slaughtered in Paris at the Saint Bartholomew's Day Massacre. Henri was lucky to escape with his life. In 1587 the Catholic League forced the weak French king to disinherit Henri who at that stage was the heir presumptive. This ignited another vicious bout of conflict, known as the War of the Three Henries, as three parties all led by an Henri fought for control of France.

Henri won significant victories on the battlefield, leaving him in pole position to succeed when the king died in 1589. His Protestantism left him illegitimate in the eyes of a swathe of his subjects and today in 1593, at the urging of his lover, Gabrielle d'Estrées, he renounced his Protestantism. Paris, and the throne of France, was indeed worth a Mass.

His rather mercenary conversion enraged Queen Elizabeth, his Protestant neighbour and donor who hoped that a Protestant France would leave England less isolated, but it seems to have convinced a majority of his subjects and his reign was regarded as a success, earning him the epithet 'Good King Henri'. A majority, but not all. In May 1610 a Catholic fanatic stabbed him to death when his carriage was stuck in traffic in Paris. In an age that demanded unambiguous religious purity, Henri's pragmatism provoked the enmity of both sides.

26 July

It was 'the greatest cricket match that was played in this part of England', one newspaper correspondent enthused. Today in 1745 on a common near Guildford in Surrey, two teams clashed in what was the first recorded women's cricket match in history.

The origins of the game of cricket are obscure, but most think it evolved in clearings in this part of England – initially as a game for children rather than adults. The oldest definite reference – to games of 'creckett' – is found in a court case very late in the sixteenth century, discussing events half a century earlier, and dealing with a land dispute in Guildford.

A little later the sport was certainly popular among women in the south-east: particularly in Surrey, Sussex and Hampshire. At this time (until the overarm action was pioneered late in the eighteenth century) the ball was bowled underarm. There is a story – sadly discredited – that the radical move was made by a woman keen not to snag her arm in a cumbersome skirt. It should be true.

The match in 1745 was played between 'eleven maids of Bramley and eleven maids of Hambledon, all dressed in white'. They were distinguished only by the colour of the ribbons in their hair: the Bramley 'maids' wearing blue while the Hambledon 'maids' wore red.

The team from Hambledon scored 127 'notches' or runs while their opponents could muster only 119. (In early matches, with no scorer, runs were often recorded with simple notches carved onto a stick.) They bowled, batted, and caught, the observer admitted – somewhat grudgingly – 'as well as most men could do'. Huge numbers watched – 'of both sexes the greatest number that ever was seen on such an occasion'. In fact, so good was it considered as a spectator sport that a return match was played later in the year – in Hambledon, on Tuesday 6 August.

27 July

In 1690 England was a basket case. Continentals joked that it was the Land of Revolutions. In the previous seventy-five years there had been several civil wars and insurgencies, one king had been executed, another fought off an invasion by his nephew before being chased into French exile by his son-in-law. London had been all but destroyed by fire, so had the Royal Navy. In 1690 a French fleet had defeated the navy again off Beachy Head and England was defenceless.

National fortunes were at their lowest ebb, yet, bizarrely, a mere thirty years later England would emerge, having forged a union with Scotland, as a dominant European power and on the way to global hegemony.

Desperation fosters innovation. England needed a fleet to secure its shores and protect its trade. Navies cost money and no one wanted to lend money to the government. So, today in 1694, a new institution was created, one that would transform government finances and be copied the world over: the Bank of England.

People would now lend money not directly to the crown but to the independent bank. They could be confident that it would be returned with interest because Parliament ring-fenced money from customs receipts to pay it back. It was a staggering success. In just twelve days £1.2 million was raised, and the list of subscribers is still on display in the bank, a group headed by the king and queen who put in £10,000 but also including working people, like 'skinner' Richard Atkinson who invested as little as £25.

Half of the money raised was spent on the navy. In the long term a stronger fleet protected Britain's merchant marine and revenue from taxes on trade went up. The birth of sophisticated government lending with rigorous oversight by Parliament was a financial revolution. More important than divine favour, ingenious tactics or heroism was money; the giant wars to come were won by the governments that could borrow vast sums at a reasonable rate of interest.

28 July

The emperor was an old man. In his mid-seventies, he had ruled over a divided, fractious empire for longer than nearly every sovereign in history. He had lost his son to suicide, his wife to an assassin's blade and now his nephew and heir to a terrorist sponsored by a neighbouring rogue state. Franz Joseph of Austria–Hungary had spent his life fighting an exhausting and ultimately futile battle to keep his empire intact. To the emperor and his advisers the involvement of Serbia in the assassination of his heir, Franz Ferdinand, and Sophie his wife, in Sarajevo in June 1914, was an act of war. Serbia was actively encouraging the Slavs of the empire to rebel. It would have to be crushed.

Some of the old emperor's advisers had their own particular reasons. Military supremo Franz Conrad von Hötzendorf was desperate to marry his mistress and thought glory on the battlefield would sweep aside any social obstacles. But all felt that the empire's integrity was threatened unless Serbia was dealt with.

So, today in 1914, Franz Joseph signed a declaration of war. It triggered one of history's most destructive conflicts, the First World War, because Serbia was not alone. It had a powerful backer in Russia; Austria on the other hand sought German support. A web of alliances threatened to draw in states all over Europe and beyond. On the same day Winston Churchill wrote to his wife saying, 'Everything tends towards catastrophe and collapse, I am interested, geared up and happy.' In Berlin Kaiser Wilhelm also felt the same inexorable slide into war, writing 'the ball is rolling and can no longer be stopped'. The handful of men who could have stopped it believed they should not or could not. The price of that failure was the destruction of their societies and their entire way of life.

29 July

Sailors feared nothing more than fire. Wooden ships were packed with flammable material, barrels of gunpowder, canvas sails, miles of ropes braided from plant fibre. Crews feared fire more than enemy cannonballs or autumn gales. So when lookouts spotted eight tongues of flame to the west in the early moments of today in 1588, all hell broke loose.

The Spanish fleet, or Armada, had anchored off Calais the day before. They had sailed from Spain to pick up a powerful army in the Low Countries, carry it across the Channel, invade England and depose the heretic Elizabeth I. The English fleet had harassed the Armada but could not derail its progress up the Channel towards its waiting army.

The English had to act. Eight old ships were packed with pitch, gunpowder and tar, their helms lashed, sails set and pointed at the Armada. Spanish ships scattered in a chaos of awkward manoeuvring in the dark. As the sun rose on 29 July the hulks of the fireships lay smoking on the beach; they had failed to ignite a single Spanish ship but turned the well-ordered Armada into a straggling shambles.

Like packs of wolves the smaller English ships overwhelmed the larger but isolated Spanish galleons. One Spanish flagship ran aground and English sailors swarmed aboard, two other galleons were battered into helplessness and were wrecked the following day. Many others were badly damaged. Desperate to escape they ran before the wind along the coast, pushed further and further from their army.

By 4 p.m. the English were running out of ammunition and broke off the battle. The defeated Spanish had to head into the North Sea and set a course for home around the north of the British Isles. Their battered ships would prove vulnerable to the gales on their return voyage. England was saved from invasion. The world's most powerful empire had been humiliated and the navy's victory became the founding myth for England's rise to global mastery.

30 July

Almost no one in England is unsure about the year that the country won the World Cup for the one and only time. The year 1966 is one of the most famous dates in English history. Non-English observers might even say that the English were unhealthily obsessed about it.

Even so, few could tell you the full date on which it happened. Well, it was on this day when the teams ran out onto the pitch at Wembley Stadium. The queen was there to present the trophy. In a mixed summer, the sun shone from a blue sky. And the match was watched by an all-time record TV audience of over 32 million: much more than half the country. Football really did come home. No wonder, perhaps, that the English bang on about it.

With both teams having looked strong during the previous matches, it was West Germany who scored first, in the 12th minute. For seven long minutes it was the Germans who were winning. Then it was tied at one apiece, until in the 77th minute the 'wingless wonders' of England – so-called because they used what then was an unconventional 4–4–2 formation – took the lead.

For twelve glorious minutes it remained 2–1. The World Cup looked set to be won on home turf, though West Germany pushed all the time for an equaliser. Then, agonisingly, in the final minute of ordinary time, they scored one, in a messy, chaotic scramble that legendary English goalkeeper Gordon Banks protested had involved a handball, though replays disproved this. Extra time loomed.

The events of that additional half an hour are well known: a third English goal shown subsequently not to have fully crossed the line, the fourth goal and the famous commentary it evoked: 'They think it's all over . . . it is now.' England had won the World Cup, the team members became legends, and despite the brief flare of hope in the summer of 2018 it has never happened again. Until it does so, the English will continue to obsess about that day in 1966.

31 July

The forgotten Treaty of Breda was signed today in 1667 between England and the Dutch Republic, and it does not deserve its obscurity. For it was by this agreement that the Dutch gained the small island of Run – one of the Banda Islands in Indonesia – in return for an island on the east coast of North America called Manhattan. It doesn't, with hindsight, seem a good swap.

To be fair, it was not as mad as it sounds. The treaty came at the end of the Second Anglo-Dutch War and it was the Dutch who had emerged on top, who called the shots. What the treaty did was largely recognise an existing situation.

In fact the English did offer to return New York in exchange for sugar factories in South America seized by the Dutch. But the offer was declined. Manhattan was a fairly unproductive colonial outpost requiring expenditure to protect it from surrounding English settlements. It had also been occupied by the English who seized it three years earlier. It was hard to see it remaining separate, so predominantly English were the surrounding population.

In the valuable, spice-growing islands of South East Asia, by contrast, a region in which they had struggled to compete, Run had been the only English settlement. It was sought after now by the Dutch because the Banda Islands in general (there were ten of them) were the home of all the world's nutmeg trees, and this was a spice immensely sought after. Nutmeg had been prized by Europeans, not only for its flavour but for its preservative and medicinal powers (it was thought to keep plague, that terror of the medieval world, at bay). Given that its previous passage to Europe involved levies being paid to Muslim traders, it seemed well worth the effort to obtain it directly.

From the nineteenth century nutmeg was also cultivated successfully in Malaysia and India, breaking the Bandas' lucrative monopoly. But by then, of course, England did not own Manhattan anyway.

AUGUST

1 August

The preacher saved souls on Sundays but spent Mondays engrossed in his other passion, science. Today in 1774, while conducting experiments in his laboratory in Wiltshire, the Reverend Dr Joseph Priestley made one of history's most important discoveries.

It was a sunny day. We know this because Priestley used a magnifying glass – a 'burning lens' – to focus the sun's rays onto a sample of mercuric or mercury (II) oxide. He collected the gas given off and found that a flame burned intensely within it, while a mouse could live four times longer than normal.

For some twenty-three centuries humans had accepted the ancient belief that 'air' was one of the four elements of creation – that it was, as Priestley called it, 'a simple elementary substance, indestructible and unalterable'. Increasingly, though, it was recognised that it was not: that in fact it was a 'composition' of gases, among which was this colourless, reactive one that he called 'dephlogisticated air' – 'pure air' – and to which, shortly afterwards, was given the more lasting label of 'oxygen'. Added to gases already discovered – hydrogen, nitrogen, carbon dioxide – it helped to build a picture of multiple separate 'elements', each with differing properties, which comprised the chemical world.

As a dissenter, Priestley was denied entry to Church of England universities like Oxford and Cambridge, and even subjected to violence in England. He was also a supporter of the American and the French Revolutions, and in 1794 he followed his sons by emigrating to Pennsylvania – welcoming the prospect of America achieving 'equal eminence' with its mother country. When he died a decade later, Thomas Jefferson hailed 'one of the few lives precious to mankind'.

2 August

Olivier de Clisson was not just killed, his body was also treated with contempt. Today in 1343 he was taken from his cell in Paris to Les Halles, the central marketplace, and beheaded for treason in front of a huge crowd. His corpse was then strung up on a gibbet while his head was despatched to his native Brittany where it was impaled on a spear and put on display over one of the principal gates of the city of Nantes.

His crime was supposedly betraying a town to the English with whom the French crown was locked in a struggle for supremacy. It was very unusual to execute a nobleman publicly without producing clear evidence of his crimes, and it was even more unusual to display his corpse like a common criminal. Many contemporaries were appalled, but his wife, Jeanne de Clisson, took her disapproval to another level.

When she saw her husband's impaled head, she swore revenge. And she meant it. She went to war against the King of France. She sold her estates, purchased three warships, painted their hulls black and their sails red. Then from the deck of her flagship, *My Revenge*, she scoured the Channel, hunting French ships. For thirteen years she captured ships, murdering everyone aboard, apart from one person she left as a witness so that the French king knew it was her. Friend and foe alike spoke in awe of the 'Lioness of Brittany'.

She survived battle, shipwreck and days adrift on a raft, but was never captured. She eventually married an English military commander and retired to a castle on the Breton coast. Her campaign of vengeance in a world dominated by men makes her truly extraordinary.

3 August

Giant swastika banners were bathed in afternoon sun. The venue, the pageantry, the military lustre all spoke of a resurgent Germany. The Berlin Olympics of 1936 was a propaganda opportunity for the Third Reich, a paean to the supremacy of Teutonic civilisation and manhood. The climax was the final of the 100-metre dash, and at 5.45 p.m. on 3 August that contest was won not by a blond-haired paragon of Hitler's mythical Aryan race, but by a 22-year-old African American. Jessie Owens crossed the line in a world-record-equalling 10.3 seconds. It was an inconvenient puncturing of the Nazi worldview in the very heart of the Nazi project.

What happened next has become as mythologised as the victory itself. Hitler was said to have deliberately snubbed the black athlete. It is certainly true that Hitler, in the words of his henchman Albert Speer, was privately 'highly annoyed by the series of triumphs by the marvellous coloured American runner, Jesse Owens'. Shrugging, he said that, 'People whose antecedents came from the jungle were primitive . . . their physiques were stronger than those of civilised whites and hence should be excluded from future games'. However, Jessie Owens insisted that on that day in the stadium their paths had crossed and Hitler 'waved at me and I waved back'. Owens was quick to call out Americans who sought to demonise Hitler to mask their own racism. 'Hitler didn't snub me – it was our president who snubbed me. The president didn't even send me a telegram,' he later said.

In Germany Owens had been allowed to stay in the same hotel as his white teammates, he had become the first African American athlete to receive sponsorship – a pair of Adidas shoes was pressed upon him by the company's founder. Back in America the fact that he was black meant that he could not enter the Waldorf Astoria hotel through the front door, and had to travel to his own victory party in the freight elevator.

History can be inconvenient, and not just for the Führer.

4 August

Simon de Montfort was trapped and outnumbered. The royal army of young Prince Edward had outmanoeuvred him. Nevertheless, today in 1265, de Montfort would fight. He had no choice. 'May the Lord have mercy on our souls,' he said, 'as our bodies are theirs.' The battle that followed, beside the town of Evesham, was the climax of one of medieval England's many civil wars as, once again, the Plantagenet family had to enforce their right to rule on the field of battle.

The Second Barons' War began in 1264 after Henry III's barons grew sick of his rule, as their forebears had of the rule of his father, John. Personal and political were entwined as Simon de Montfort, Earl of Leicester, married the king's sister Eleanor without royal consent and then lobbied hard for a greater baronial role in government, through regular meetings of so-called *parlements* ('an occasion for speaking'). Armed conflict followed at the Battle of Lewes, where King Henry and Prince Edward were captured. De Montfort was king in all but name. But Edward escaped, rallied support and moved like lightning; now he had the rebels at his mercy.

De Montfort's army made a bold cavalry attack, forcing back some of the royal forces. Edward counter-attacked and encircled de Montfort's army. It turned into a massacre. Rebel barons were slaughtered and de Montfort unhorsed and hacked to death. His corpse was beheaded, his testicles sliced off and hung either side of his nose. The barbaric trophy was then sent to his wife at Wigmore Castle.

Prince Edward had restored royal authority but the wrangle over exactly where power and authority lay within the English government would continue to shape his reign and that of his successors. De Montfort certainly lost the battle, but his championing of *parlements* means that he is now seen as a founding father of parliamentary democracy.

5 August

Harry Houdini was the most famous magician in the world. He had made an elephant disappear, escaped from a box with the lid nailed shut, eaten needles and blades and wriggled free from a straitjacket while suspended upside down. There seemed to be no end to the trickster's baffling abilities.

Today in 1926, Houdini performed what was arguably his greatest trick, just months before his death aged fifty-two. He emerged, alive, after ninety minutes locked in an underwater coffin. Prior to the performance of the stunt, which would be his greatest challenge, Houdini practised regulating his breath, taking short and shallow breaths in order to conserve the limited oxygen available to him. In rehearsals he managed up to seventy minutes, before signalling to his team that he felt he was about to suffocate.

The trick was performed in front of an excited audience of journalists at the Shelton Hotel in New York. Houdini was submerged in the swimming pool, inside a metal casket fitted with a safety buzzer. At ninety-one minutes Houdini buzzed his assistant to remove him from the coffin. He later explained that he 'commenced to see yellow lights' and had to stop himself going to sleep. To combat claustrophobia he moved his body as much as possible, awkwardly shifting around the minute space, to take the weight off his lungs.

Harry Houdini died a few months later, his death caused by a ruptured appendix. He had boasted that he could endure any man's punch to the gut with no injury. It turned out, in the end, that he couldn't.

6 August

It was only one aircraft. The citizens of Hiroshima had been dreading a vast armada of bombers like those that had destroyed the other Japanese cities. Today in 1945 they looked up and were relieved. Then came the blinding flash of heat and light. It only took one aircraft and one bomb to obliterate the entire city of Hiroshima. A new era – the *nuclear* era – had begun. The confused and often badly wounded survivors had little idea what had had happened. Only a few days afterwards, on 9 August, a second atomic bomb was dropped on the city of Nagasaki.

After the the surrender of the German forces the Allies had called for a similar, unconditional Japanese surrender. The alternative, they promised, would be 'prompt and utter destruction'. That call ignored, city after city suffered a conventional firebombing campaign. Invasion of the Japanese mainland was planned and rehearsed. Probable fierce Japanese resistance promised a drawn-out, bloody affair.

By August two types of atomic bomb were ready. Targets chosen were expected to be of sentimental as well as military significance, to be mostly intact, and large enough to display the bomb's power. Tokyo was 'all bombed and burned out'. Initially Kyoto had been top of the list, until the objection of the American war secretary, Henry Stimson, who had visited the ancient capital with its shrines and temples. Other possible targets were Kokura and Niigata, both ahead of Nagasaki (chosen for its great shipyards).

As it was, Hiroshima was selected as the first, 'largest untouched target'. The idea of a demonstration in an unpopulated area was quickly dismissed. This certainly was, as Stimson remarked, not simply a new weapon but 'a revolutionary change in the relations of man to the universe'.

7 August

The bullet sped out of the muzzle of the Lee–Enfield rifle, spinning on its axis towards the enemy at 744 metres per second. It was 7 August 1914, and the first British shot of the First World War had been fired. Appropriately for a war that would be a global conflict, this first shot was not fired on the Western Front, nor was it fired by a Briton. The man who pulled the trigger was Alhaji Grunshi, a soldier in the Gold Coast Regiment in West Africa, and he did so while invading German-held Togoland.

Togoland was an isolated German colony, surrounded by ocean to the south and by British and French-ruled territories to the north, west and east. It was wholly defenceless apart from its German-instructed police force. Nevertheless, it was strategically important because of the radio transmitters it possessed that allowed it to communicate both with other German colonies in south-west and eastern Africa and with German shipping in the South Atlantic.

When war was declared the British Empire sent the Gold Coast Regiment into Togoland. On 7 August the soldiers were met by a large group of the Togoland police force, which opened fire. Grunshi shot back, thereby firing the first British shots of the war.

On the following day resistance in Togoland began to collapse. Not long afterwards the radio transmitters were destroyed to ensure that they did not fall into British hands. The colony's formal surrender to the British and the French took place on 26 August, four days after the first British shot is thought to have been fired on the Western Front by Edward Thomas.

The first Commonwealth casualty of the war was Grunshi's comrade Private Bai, killed shortly after Grunshi's own claim to fame, though his name does not appear on the memorial to the fallen of the Gold Coast Regiment – because no African names did.

8 August

The president had long maintained that he knew nothing of any cover-ups. He had won the election fair and square, not by breaking the law. Yet today in 1974, the 37th President of the United States of America, Richard Milhous Nixon, announced his resignation.

Our perception of Nixon is so dominated by his ignominious end that few now recall the strength of his position. Only two years previously, in November 1972, he had been re-elected in one of the biggest landslides in US history. By then, though, the seeds of his downfall had been sown. In mid-June that year five men were caught breaking into the headquarters of the Democratic Party, at the Watergate complex in Washington, DC. Journalists using an informant linked the burglars to the Nixon administration, and it gradually became clear that the White House had been directly involved in an attempt to sabotage the Democratic campaign.

As details of the cover-up emerged, there was little doubt that Nixon had been complicit. 'People have got to know whether or not their President is a crook,' he said defiantly. A growing number thought that they did.

On 5 August 1974 a tape that became known as the 'Smoking Gun' was released, forcing Nixon to admit misleading the country about what he knew regarding White House involvement in the break-in. He now faced certain impeachment in the Senate, well shy of the votes needed to survive. His political base having collapsed, on 8 August Nixon made a radio broadcast from the Oval Office declaring his plan to resign and hand the presidency to his deputy, Gerald Ford – something he did formally the following day.

Subsequently he clung to the hope that history would forgive him and focus upon his achievements. 'You'll be here in the year 2000,' he told students, 'and we'll see how I'm regarded then.' But little had changed, and it still hasn't. He remains the only US president to be effectively forced out of office. For now . . .

9 August

No empire is eternal. Not even Rome. A battle fought today in AD 378 hastened the city's fall and the collapse of a swathe of its empire. An over-confident emperor took on the Goths at Adrianople and the result was utter defeat. The victorious Goths were free to roam around and settle within the bounds of the empire. Before long they would capture the city of Rome itself.

Adrianople (Hadrianopolis) is known today as Edirne and lies in European Turkey, near the Greek and Bulgarian borders. A large force of Goths had moved there hoping for land to settle. The Emperor of the Eastern Roman Empire, Valens, was jealous of the success of other Roman generals and wanted his own victory. He ignored advice to await support. He moved west, and paused in his capital, Constantinople, before moving on to Adrianople. The fact that it was a sweltering hot day meant that his men and horses went into battle exhausted and dehydrated.

There are conflicting accounts of Valens's demise. Some say he was burned to death. Elsewhere we read that he was struck by an arrow. Either way, the day ended badly for him. What is generally agreed is that Valens's career was distinguished only by having led to the demise of Roman territorial integrity – a fact that was recognised even at the time. It was his defeat and death in that battle that eased the path of 'barbarian' peoples like the Goths into the heart of the empire. This heralded the collapse of the Western Roman Empire: a major turning point in European history.

Ammianus Marcellinus, a soldier and historian who wrote the one of the very last major surviving histories of ancient Rome, commented that it was this defeat that marked 'the beginning of evils for the Roman empire then and thereafter'. Few since have disagreed.

10 August

One of England's greatest explorers was Italian. It's an awkward fact, which the English avoid by calling him John Cabot, rather than his actual name, Giovanni Caboto. Today in 1497 the Genoese-born seafarer returned to the court of King Henry VII, telling his royal employer that he had discovered new land to the west of Ireland: 'new found land'.

His little ship *Matthew* had arrived back in Bristol and he immediately continued east to the capital, taking a map and a globe that he had made to illustrate his journey. Using these he was highly convincing. 'He tells all this in such a way,' reported one ambassador, 'and makes everything so plain, that I . . . feel compelled to believe him.'

The king showered Cabot with rewards and the expectation of more. He was given £10. A pension was granted, it was said, until 'more will be known of this business'. In the streets outside he was treated like a major celebrity. The common people called him 'the Admiral' and chased him 'like madmen'. To his friends Cabot promised bishoprics, or islands, in the new world. He thought – he died thinking, just as Christopher Columbus did – that what he had found was the east of Asia.

For England, the discovery of America changed everything, but it did take a long time. After Henry VII had died, his son, Henry VIII, was not that interested, preferring to throw his weight around on the European stage. Other regions of Europe with an Atlantic coast – France, Brittany, the Basque country, Portugal – despatched more ships there more quickly.

Gradually, though, and particularly during the seventeenth century, the English went in great numbers – to live, not just to visit – and in the process they made this new continent a largely English place.

11 August

It is hard to achieve notoriety in the long, corrupt, debauched history of the medieval papacy, but that's exactly what Alexander VI, who became Pope today in 1492, managed to do. Rodrigo Borgia – an Italianised spelling of his Spanish name of Borja – was elected by a body of cardinals notoriously partial in their allegiance. His papacy was one of the most infamous in Rome's history, and his name has become synonymous with dissolution and lack of principle.

Borgia's papacy began as it went on. When Rodrigo became Pope he did so after bribing one cardinal, considered particularly influential, with four mule-loads of silver – and a mule can carry rather a lot of silver, if not perhaps as much as the value of benefices he was also granted.

Already his maternal uncle, whose name Rodrigo took, had brought the Borgia name to the papacy. It is he, though, who has become legendary for wantonness and rapacity, admitting fathering multiple children by various mistresses, at a time when the discoveries of Christopher Columbus had brought the Christian religion to an area of the world that had not encountered it before.

One of Borgia's cardinals, Cardinal Giovanni de' Medici (later to become Pope himself), is alleged to have declared shortly after Borgia's election: 'Now we are in the power of the wolf. The most rapacious perhaps this world has ever seen; and if we do not escape, he will inevitably devour us.'

One son Borgia made a duke. The other became a cardinal – not a bad promotion for a teenager. He had an array of mistresses. He did though enjoy and appreciate art and was in a position to extend it his patronage. Artists of the renown of Raphael and Michelangelo worked for him, and a new architectural era began in Rome.

12 August

The boy was playing on a street in Glasgow when he was run down by a horse and cart, today in 1865. He was badly injured, his lower left leg was fractured. At the accident ward at the Glasgow Royal Infirmary he was treated by a surgeon named Joseph Lister. On that day, for the first time ever, Lister performed surgery using a cleansing spirit, otherwise known as an antiseptic.

The boy was prescribed chloroform while the wound was treated with carbolic acid, and his leg was bandaged and braced with a splint. He recovered well over the course of a few weeks and his wound healed. He was discharged from care after six weeks.

Joseph Lister was the house surgeon at the Glasgow Infirmary and was experimenting with ways to treat the devastating mortality rate among post-operative patients, who died from a condition known as 'ward fever'. He was heavily influenced by the French scientist Louis Pasteur, who pioneered experiments with bacteria, and argued that infection was often the cause of death after surgery.

Lister made a detailed report of the boy's treatment in a medical journal but it was greeted with widespread derision. His ideas were criticised and he was openly mocked at one medical conference. But as his method produced better outcomes, it was impossible to doubt his techniques. His surgeons had to wash their hands, their instruments and the operating surface in a carbolic acid solution. His post-operative death rate dropped to just 15 per cent.

By the early twentieth century he had gone from being a laughing stock to becoming the father of modern surgery. In 1902 he agreed to come out of retirement for one last operation. King Edward VII had fallen gravely ill with appendicitis and surgeons refused to operate without Lister's advice. The 75-year-old outlined a strategy, which they followed to the letter. The king survived and thanked Lister personally, assuring him: 'I know that if it had not been for you and your work, I wouldn't be sitting here today.'

13 August

Most of the foreign diplomats fled the city when they heard the news. Today in 1920, the Soviet Red Army captured a key town on the outskirts of Warsaw and it was clear that this was the start of an all-out assault. The Battle of Warsaw that followed was one of the most important battles of the twentieth century.

Having gained the upper hand in the Russian Civil War, Vladimir Lenin had looked outwards, seeing Poland as a corridor through which communism – Bolshevism as the new phenomenon was often known – could be brought into first central then western Europe. The shortest route to Berlin and then to Paris, Russian Bolsheviks declared, lay through Warsaw.

Almost all observers feared they were right; capture of the Polish capital seeming a prelude to Soviet support for revolution in defeated, chaotic Germany. When, earlier that summer, the Soviet army invaded Poland, Polish forces had fallen back in disarray. As Polish supply lines shortened, though, the Russian ones grew longer. Desperation bred fierce resistance: for the country of Poland, this was a bid to ensure its survival soon after its rebirth, in the wake of the First World War – after more than a century of partition by foreign empires.

Plans were made to attack the Red Army from the south and from the north, encircling it, then coming at it from the rear as it assaulted the Polish capital. But generals and political leaders realised it was a huge gamble; that if Warsaw fell all would be lost. Many doubted Polish forces could regroup after their chaotic retreat – but saw little alternative.

As it happened, Polish plans worked better than could have been hoped, as the Soviets – struggling with communication, while their codes had been broken – suffered a complete collapse. Defeated again as they fell back, a negotiated peace was agreed, and the very real spectre of a communist takeover of Europe receded.

14 August

Duncan and Macbeth were made famous by William Shakespeare, but unlike some of his more fantastic creations, they actually existed, and today in 1040 they met in a pitched battle at Pitgaveny near Elgin, where Duncan was defeated and Macbeth won the Scottish crown.

Duncan was a weak and incompetent king. Macbeth was a powerful lord from the north of Scotland and had, importantly, an equal claim to the throne, through his mother. After forming an alliance with his cousin the Earl of Orkney, Macbeth led his army against Duncan and successfully usurped the throne.

Unlike the Macbeth portrayed in Shakespeare's tragedy, his seventeen-year kingship was relatively peaceful and he was considered to be a wise, pious and strong leader. Macbeth was so secure on the throne of Scotland, he even left it, in order to go on a pilgrimage to Rome in 1050.

Eventually, perhaps inevitably, he was challenged by Duncan's son, Malcolm, who had been biding his time in Northumbria. Eager for revenge, Malcolm gained the support of the Northumbrian earl, Siward, and in 1054 their united armies marched north to Scotland and faced Macbeth, at the Battle of Dunsinane. They were victorious, but Macbeth remained king. Instead of relinquishing his crown, he restored Malcolm's lands. The compromise could not last. Malcolm, hungry for his father's crown, fought Macbeth at Lumphanan, Aberdeenshire, on 15 August 1057. Almost exactly seventeen years after Duncan's defeat, Macbeth was finally killed in battle, and Malcolm seized the throne where his father had lost it, on the battlefield.

15 August

He was the grandson of the first Great Khan, heir to his vast empire, which stretched from the coast of south-east China, through Central Asia to the Black Sea. In practice his cousins ruled the western portions of that empire with almost complete autonomy but nominally Kublai Khan was the Khagan of the Mongol Empire, and his rule over most of east Asia made him the most powerful man in the world.

Believing he could cross the sea as easily as his horsemen had crossed the endless, rolling expanse of the Central Asian plains, he had set his eye on Japan. It was today in 1281 that hubris overtook the forces of Kublai Khan at the very easternmost point of the Mongol expansion. On 15 August his fleet was annihilated, not by the massed ranks of samurai gathered on the shores, but by a typhoon that wrecked his ships. The Japanese ascribed their salvation to the gods, calling the storm *kamikaze*, or 'divine wind'.

Kublai Khan's fleet had arrived off Japan in June but time and again he had been denied a foothold on land by stubborn resistance from the army of samurai. By early August the fleet of thousands of ships, carrying well over 100,000 men, was anchored in the Tsushima Straits ready to force its way ashore. It may well have been the largest invasion fleet in history until D-Day in 1944. Then on the 15th a storm tore through the straits and smashed the wooden ships to flotsam. Eighty per cent were sunk, their crews drowned or slaughtered in the shallows by samurai as they crawled ashore.

This miraculous storm proved a lasting deterrent to the Mongols, who never attempted another invasion. As the Japanese government faced certain defeat in the Second World War it harnessed the myth of a 'divine wind' to turn young aviators into *kamikaze* pilots who, they were promised, would sweep another invader from the oceans. This time though, the intervening centuries had produced warships that could withstand what the gods, elements or Japanese aviators could throw at them.

16 August

The cavalry charged, the ground shook at the pounding of hooves. The hussars and troopers hacked down on the helpless, terrified crowd. One of the units had fought its way through the Napoleonic Wars but today in 1819 on St Peter's Field in Manchester, their enemy was a crowd of their fellow countrymen and women. It has become known as the Peterloo Massacre: a landmark event in the centuries-long struggle for political liberty.

The cavalry charge at the large but peaceful outdoor political meeting caused the deaths of fifteen people, one a two-year-old boy, and the wounding of hundreds more. The name Peterloo was an ironic reference to the decisive recent battle of Waterloo. And indeed, in its long-term impact, it was comparable.

The huge cost and economic dislocation of the Napoleonic Wars had gripped a country which was in any case experiencing rapid change. The monied classes feared social upheaval. Individual protests were assumed to represent wider unrest: a part of what the leading magistrate at St Peter's Field called 'a great scheme'. Manchester – and the north in general – was a place whose expanding population had seen little rise in political representation. On this day, around sixty thousand people (women and children too) came to listen to radical speakers – like Henry Hunt – who demanded major electoral reform.

Alarmed by the size of the crowd, magistrates ordered that the speakers be arrested. In response the cavalry, untrained in dealing with such civil protest, charged, brandishing their sabres. The area was cleared of all but the bodies of the dead and badly wounded. In the short term it was a tactical victory. The meeting was broken up. In the longer term it fuelled outrage and made significant reform almost impossible to resist.

17 August

Even in August life in the Yukon is hard. The days are short-ening fast, the temperature at night plunges, the river water is icy cold. It took a certain type of person, tough, self-sufficient, crazy perhaps, to spend their lives in the Canadian north-west prospecting for gold and other minerals. George Carmack was one such person. Descended from European settlers, he preferred the company of the indigenous peoples. He was known as 'Squaw man' after marrying his Tagish wife, Shaaw Tláa, who accompanied him on this expedition together with her brother, Skookum Jim.

The day before, one of them, probably Skookum Jim, had found a nugget of gold in a creek bed. He was a legend even before his find, described as 'powerfully built with strong sloping shoulders, tapering . . . downwards to the waist, like a keystone'. He was regarded as 'the best hunter and trapper on the river, in fact he was a super-specimen'.

Today in 1896 they worked feverishly to stake out their claims. A hint of gold would bring an army of desperate men and they needed to show that this stretch of land was already claimed, and off-limits to others. They felled trees around a block of land along the creek, 500 feet by 2,000 feet. Next they staked out three more claims, the legal limit.

Then they made the 50-mile (80-kilometre) journey to the mouth of Forty Mile River and submitted their claims at the police post. Within hours the electrifying news was spreading. Their discovery launched history's last great goldrush. Within weeks a wave of prospectors arrived in what was rapidly renamed Bonanza Creek. Within months, 100,000 people would come, a giant invasion of one of the world's last great wildernesses. Most would never find a nugget of gold.

Carmack and Skookum Jim did find enough gold on their claims to become very wealthy, but both realised that the hunt was better than the finding, and both continued searching for the mother lode until the ravages of the prospecting life finally overcame them.

18 August

It was an auspicious moment, a morale-lifting success for a band of settlers embarked on an uncertain and laborious mission to build a new life in a hostile and unfamiliar land. Today in 1587 a child was born in Roanoke, Virginia. She was the first English child to be born on the western side of the Atlantic Ocean, in America. They called her Virginia, Virginia Dare. The settlers hoped that she was a symbol. A sign of a fertile new community that would multiply, expand, settle. But she wasn't.

It was the second attempt to plant a colony. The first had been evacuated. Fifteen had stayed behind, but a few years later the only sign of them was a skeleton. The second attempt appeared to be going better. Virginia's grandfather was the colony's governor. Just after her birth he decided to sail back to England to fetch reinforcements and supplies.

He left with the promise to return as fast as possible. But the weather, politics, technology and geography of the Atlantic world made promises hard to keep. England went to war with Spain. The supplies of shipping, food, recruits and raw materials all became badly disrupted.

He was forced to wait three years before returning. When he did in August 1590 he found the buildings collapsed and no sign of his daughter, granddaughter or any of the other 108 men, women and children he had left behind. There was no trace of a struggle. The colony had disappeared, and they have been known ever since as 'The Lost Colony'. Settlers would populate a New England, but not yet.

19 August

You can only keep technological advances secret for so long. Today in 1839, in Paris, the French government bowed to the inevitable and unveiled Louis Daguerre's invention to the world, along with full instructions. Prior to this, details of the invention had been carefully withheld. Daguerre was an accomplished artist and theatrical designer as well as an inventor. When he released the first of the images that became known as 'daguerreotypes', they were hailed as near miraculous.

Daguerre's images were not the very first 'photographs'; earlier techniques involved impractical exposure times of hours if not days – making the capture of people difficult if not impossible. While Daguerre's process also involved long exposure, his fundamental discovery was that an invisible 'latent' image – made much more quickly – could be 'developed' chemically into one that was visible.

Silver salts, it was known, were sensitive to light. What Daguerre found was that he could use salt solution to 'fix' an image left latent by light exposure upon a copper plate that was thinly coated with silver iodide, then made visible by fumes of mercury vapour. 'Fixing' essentially meant washing away the 'undeveloped', light-sensitive silver iodide. Once fixed, the highly delicate image was then protected by being covered by a plate of glass. For two decades this technology was commonly used, until it was superseded by less complicated, less cumbersome (and less poisonous) techniques.

After testing his technique, Daguerre is said to have exclaimed in rapture: 'I have seized the light – I have arrested its flight!' His name is one of (all male) French mathematicians, scientists and engineers inscribed – as an 'invocation of science' – upon the Eiffel Tower.

It is almost impossible, now, to conceive of a world in which there was no photography. But of course, this – for most of human history – was how it was.

20 August

Today in 1858, our understanding of the world and our place within it altered fundamentally and for ever. For it was then that Charles Darwin first published an outline of the theory of evolution. It was a terrible anticlimax. The scientific community largely ignored it and Darwin was utterly distracted by the death of his baby son weeks earlier from scarlet fever.

For more than twenty years he had worked on his theory: the possibility that species might change, or 'evolve', having occurred to him first during his five-year voyage on the ship *Beagle* (which returned in 1836). He was conscious, though, that he should answer every possible objection *prior* to the publication of a theory certain to be controversial. Darwin was distracted by publishing what were often geological findings from the *Beagle* expedition, then for almost a decade by conducting detailed research into the classification of barnacle species (which illustrated his general ideas).

In the end Darwin was prompted to hasten publication, having received word that another scientist – Alfred Russel Wallace – was on the verge of making a similar argument. He agreed to a joint paper, the one published today, in the journal of the Linnean Society. It was largely unnoticed. The society's president was unenthusiastic, remarking a few months later that the previous year had seen no revolutionary discoveries. Wallace's and Darwin's ideas did get at least one reviewer's attention, in a negative sense. Professor Haughton wrote that 'all that was new in them was false'.

Despite the unimpressive reception, Darwin, recuperating from his family's tragedy on the Isle of Wight, decided to embark on a short abstract of his big thesis. 'I rather hate,' he wrote, 'the idea of writing for priority, yet I certainly should be vexed if any one were to publish my doctrines before me.'

Thirteen months later it was ready for publication. He called it *On the Origin of Species*. In it he provided a unified concept of evolutionary adaptation through natural selection that is the basis for all scientific investigation into life on this planet.

21 August

He was on a roll. Today in 1897, only eleven days after he had first synthesised 'aspirin', the German research chemist Felix Hoffmann also synthesised 'heroin': two utterly familiar substances, one of the most beneficial to humankind, followed by one of the most potentially harmful.

In the latter nineteenth century the new state of Germany was the centre of a burgeoning chemical industry, one focus of which was the synthesis of dyes. Born in 1868, just before the country's unification, Hoffmann worked in pharmacies and studied chemistry in Munich, prior to starting work for the recently founded Bayer company. A vast number of chemicals were engineered first as by-products of the dye industry, then tested – by chemists using little that was more scientific than a hunch – to discover their properties.

While it had been known since ancient times that willow bark could help to relieve fever and pain, its active ingredient tended to irritate patients' stomachs. This problem, however, was found to be much improved by Hoffman's 'acetylating' it – adding the acetyl chemical group – which made it both more potent *and* easier to 'stomach'.

When Bayer's American factories were sold off in 1919, as part of Germany's reparations for the war, 'aspirin' (as this product was called) ceased to be trademarked and became freely and widely available – as it is still.

Soon afterwards Hoffman was instructed to 'acetylate' morphine, the aim being to produce the weaker substance known as 'codeine'. Instead what was produced was something subsequently labelled 'heroin'. It turned out to be a more powerful painkiller than morphine. Until it was discovered to be an extremely addictive drug, it was widely sold, for instance, for pain relief and in a cough syrup for children.

Felix Hoffman helped to create a world in which the use and misuse of drugs is now central to our existence as individuals and as societies.

22 August

The Old Etonian was perhaps a little over-confident at the wheel of his brand-new red Fiat. John Scott-Ellis cruised through the streets of Munich, today in 1931, without incident until he turned right and hit a pedestrian with a memorable crunch. The man brushed himself off, accepted Scott-Ellis's profuse apologies and walked off unhurt. Only later did the Englishman learn that the man he had hit was none other than Adolf Hitler.

It is a little-known event, and by bizarre coincidence in December of the same year another forgotten collision took place, this time in New York, the victim: one Winston Churchill. Bearing in mind the pre-eminent roles both men played in subsequent events, it is easy to imagine how different history might have been.

Although Hitler had not yet come to power, by this time the advance of the National Socialists, or Nazi Party, was well underway, and he was a famous figure. It is said that his German companion asked Scott-Ellis whether he knew who that man was with the small, square moustache that he had just knocked down. He had not the least idea.

Naturally enough the driver later thought about the incident: 'For a few seconds, perhaps, I held the history of Europe in my rather clumsy hands . . . [Hitler] was only shaken up, but had I killed him, it would have changed the history of the world.'

After Churchill was hit by a car he asked a friend who was a physics professor to calculate the impact and was informed that it was probably equivalent to a shotgun fired twice at close range. A good thing, he was teasingly told, that his weight had cushioned the blow.

23 August

It was to be a traitor's death. The sentenced man was taken straight from his trial in the Hall in the Palace of Westminster, stripped and dragged through the streets of London. His name was William Wallace; he had humiliated the English crown, and today in 1305 this 'robber, public traitor, outlaw, enemy and rebel against the king', in the words of one government record, would pay a terrible price.

Wallace was a knight, a member of the lesser nobility, who had risen to command the Scottish army, annihilating the English at the Battle of Stirling Bridge in 1297 and even raided deep into northern England. King Edward I marched north the following year to press his claim to the throne, and this time defeated Wallace at Falkirk, forcing him into exile and the Scottish lords to submit. Wallace returned a few years later, was betrayed and taken to London for trial.

His galaxy of crimes, according to Edward's government, included calling 'himself king of Scotland', he also 'slew the king's officials in Scotland, and also as an enemy led an army against the king'. Wallace replied simply that, 'I could not be a traitor to Edward, for I was never his subject.'

The punishment reserved for traitors was truly awful. In front of a crowd in Smithfield Market, Wallace was strangled, but released just before passing out. Then while he clung to consciousness, his genitals were cut off, he was eviscerated and his bowels were burned in front of his eyes. Finally he was beheaded. His head went on a spike above London Bridge, his body was quartered and sent to Newcastle, Stirling, Perth and Berwick.

The medieval world was built on a carefully maintained hierarchy of obedience to the king, and through him, God. Wallace had upended that arrangement and his very public, excruciating, torture, death and humiliation was a signal not to mess with the Plantagenets, as they attempted to bring all of Britain and Ireland under their rule.

24 August

The British were back. The American republic was only a few decades old when today in 1814 its former colonial masters, stormed its capital and burned its public buildings, including the official home of the American president, now known as the White House.

An ill-prepared militia had attempted to stop the British redcoats on the outskirts of town. It was all over in minutes. In 'the greatest disgrace ever dealt to American arms' the British army of about 4,500 men defeated the larger American force. The victors occupied the capital as the president, James Madison, and his entire government fled. They took refuge in a small town in Maryland called Brookeville, known subsequently as the 'United States Capital for a Day'.

The British torched all the public buildings, the Congress, executive offices and the Executive Mansion itself. Before they burned the White House, British officers sat down to eat Madison's dinner and helped themselves to his wine cellar. The damage was limited by the onset of a major storm which extinguished fires and forced the British back to their ships, an event regarded, and remembered, with religious veneration as the 'storm that saved Washington'. Damage done to the White House – which could have been far more significant – was repaired, allowing the president to move back in by the autumn of 1817.

'May none but honest and wise men ever rule under this roof', John Adams, the first president to live in the White House, had written. No comment.

25 August

'Great Astronomical Discoveries' roared the front page of the *New York Sun* today in 1835. The astronomer Sir John Herschel had discovered life on the surface of the moon. Not simple life either. Extraordinary, unbelievable animals were held to have been seen – goats, unicorns, humans with wings like bats, bison – through 'an immense telescope of an entirely new principle'. The piece did not elaborate on precisely what this 'entirely new principle' was. It was an article – or rather, series of articles – which now would be held to fall into the category of 'fake news'. What was the outcome? Circulation up. The paper's revenue up. And the public misinformed.

The articles were written, it seems, on the initiative of journalist Richard A. Locke, satirising the tendency to claim that extraordinary civilisations existed elsewhere in the universe. In one such essay the author had announced in all seriousness that he had seen one of the 'colossal buildings' erected by a civilisation upon the lunar surface. The tone of Locke's articles was similarly serious – avoiding the transparent comedy which marked some other spoof pieces, and which marred their plausibility.

The end to Herschel's remarkable observation, it was said, had been the destruction of this powerful new telescope by the strength of the sun's rays. Initially Sir John Herschel himself – the son of William Herschel, and a genuine astronomer – was amused by the hoax, but his amusement turned to annoyance when he was repeatedly asked about it by readers who had believed the story. He found it hard to credit (as we have been obliged to do) just how much people would be prepared to believe things they read in a newspaper.

26 August

The legionaries were reluctant until one standard bearer leapt into the sea and waded ashore with his eagle aloft. Today in 55 BC, the Romans arrived in Britain. They were led by Julius Caesar, one of history's greatest warrior statesmen.

Britain was an unknown. Three hundred years before, the island had been discovered by the Greek seafarer Pytheas of Massalia. His account, tragically, does not survive but it is quoted by later classical writers. Pytheas reported that Britain was cold, the inhabitants were 'of simple manners' and were perfectly happy eating plain food. Caesar needed more usable intelligence. He sent a ship to reconnoitre landing zones.

When Caesar's fleet arrived at Dubris (Dover), the British were massed along the cliffs forcing him to move north-east along the coast. The Britons followed him and opposed his landing, with legionaries having to disembark into deep water. After fierce fighting, the Romans were able to beat the Britons off and to establish a camp. Oddly this first recorded invasion is British history's only example of a contested invasion, where there was fighting on the beaches.

Caesar wrote a vivid description of Britons. They 'dye themselves with woad', he reported, 'which occasions a bluish colour, and thereby have a more terrible appearance in fight'. 'They wear their hair long,' he continued, 'and have every part of their body shaved except their head and upper lip.'

He did not linger. Winter drew near. Tides were higher than Mediterranean seafarers were comfortable with and a severe storm damaged his fleet. He was anxious to return to the continent. The expedition had not been a great success, but it was spun as one. Little, previously, had been known about these mysterious islands to the north from which resources like tin derived. Precious intelligence had been gathered, and alliances were made that were a genuine help during Caesar's second incursion. The actual Roman conquest had to wait for nearly a century. Ultimately Caesar, as the historian Tacitus remarked, 'revealed, rather than bequeathed' Britain.

27 August

On this day – and on *only* this day – took place what is believed to have been the shortest war in history, on 27 August in 1896. It took place between Great Britain and the tiny East African island state of Zanzibar. It lasted about forty minutes. This is not, like the First World War, a conflict over which the causes have been much debated. On the contrary, they are rather clear. It began when one (pro-British) sultan died and the succession did not go as was hoped in London.

At that time Zanzibar was next to a region where Germany and Britain were rivals – on the adjacent mainland German East Africa and British East Africa lay side by side. When a new sultan seized power who was unfriendly to Britain, the latter attempted initially to use diplomatic pressure. Ultimatums were despatched, demanding that the new sultan stand down. He, though, remained firmly ensconced within the palace, reinforcing the building with troops and artillery. It was time for some more diplomacy, this time with gunboats.

So small was the island that the palace was well within range of ships moored off the coast. Britain sent a small fleet of warships and landed Royal Marines to join Zanzibari troops loyal to Britain. During the night of 26/27 August, one consul wrote, 'the silence which hung over Zanzibar was appalling'.

In the morning the British flagship signalled that action would shortly commence. When the sultan maintained his defiance, five minutes later, at 9.02 a.m., a bombardment of the largely wooden palace began. By 9.40 the royal palace had been set on fire, its flag shot down and its occupants surrendered. While the sultan's forces suffered about 500 casualties, the British suffered only one. The sultan fled to German East Africa while the British established a rival, puppet government.

28 August

British ships had carried hundreds of thousands of enslaved Africans across the Atlantic for years until the practice was outlawed by Parliament in 1807. In the British colonies of the Caribbean, however, slavery continued. It was not until today in 1833 that William IV gave his royal assent to the Slavery Abolition Act, a law that prohibited slavery, and which went into effect the following year.

As with most laws, it was the product of passion and pragmatism. Anti-slavery campaigners had maintained the pressure on the British government after their success in ending the slave trade. The problem was that while slave traders had been powerful, they were small in number, but the slave-owning lobby was vast. Hundreds of influential British families were involved in the production of sugar, tobacco and other crops, which depended on slave labour. The slaves were their property. For owners abolition was arbitrary confiscation by the government; rebellions had flared up over less.

Lofty idealism may have eventually persuaded MPs, but on this occasion it was given a significant boost by a widespread slave revolt that broke out in Jamaica in 1831. The human and economic cost meant that Parliament could not ignore it, or the inhumane conditions that caused it. Slavery would have to go; to get the act passed, lawmakers came up with a giant compensation package. The largest bailout in British history, £20 million (an estimated £17 billion today) was paid to slaveholders. It was 40 per cent of the Treasury's annual income. The British government had to turn to the Rothschilds to raise such a huge amount.

Not a penny of that went to the former slaves, most of whom were quickly re-employed under not dissimilar conditions. It would prove a lot easier to amend the legal status of the slaves than rebalance the entire planter economies of the Caribbean.

29 August

The people of Oroville, California, did not like the look of the dark-skinned, wild-looking man who had suddenly appeared today in 1911 seemingly intent on finding food. They called the local sheriff and the officer took the man into custody 'for his own protection' before people took the law into their own hands.

The fifty-year-old man in question was Ishi, the last surviving member of the Yahi people. They had lived as hunter-gatherers in small, autonomous bands with no central authority in the mountainous Sierra Nevada until they were wiped out at the end of the nineteenth century by white settlers who brought firearms and disease as they searched for gold.

Ishi had lived for many years alone, until, close to starvation, he wandered into a settlement, becoming, in the parlance of the time, 'the last wild Indian in America' to come into contact with white Americans.

Ishi became an object of fascination, both to thousands of curious tourists but also to the academic establishment. Anthropologists from the University of California in Berkeley housed him on the campus, where he helped them with their research and taught them about Yahi traditions. He was often ill, ravaged by diseases against which he had no immunity, until he died of tuberculosis in 1916.

As the last Native American to live in the United States with no contact with white people, Ishi is a symbol of the catastrophe that engulfed the aboriginal population of the continent as they were overwhelmed by a set of challenges that pushed them to the brink of extinction.

30 August

The chairman of the Council of People's Commissars of the Russian Soviet Federative Socialist Republic had already survived one assassination attempt that year. In January 1918 Vladimir Ilyich Ulyanov, or Lenin, as he preferred to be known, was saved from a hail of bullets by a colleague who forced his head down in their car. Only just in time, the bullets grazed the tops of his saviour's hands. Today in 1918, an assassin came even closer to ending the life of one of the twentieth century's most transformative figures.

The leader of the young, fragile Bolshevik state had just delivered a rousing speech to the workers at the Hammer and Sickle factory in Moscow. As he left, Fanya Kaplan, a long-time revolutionary activist, called out his name and fired three shots with a Browning pistol. One tore through his coat, another sliced through his neck and became embedded in his collarbone and the third hit his left shoulder.

Lenin was rushed to the Kremlin, which he refused to leave, even to seek medical help. Doctors attended but were unable to remove the bullets without a full operating theatre. Kaplan confessed to shooting Lenin, who, she said, had betrayed the Revolution by banning opposition parties and dissolving the Constituent Assembly, after the Bolsheviks had failed to win a majority. Three days later she was executed.

The assassination attempt spurred the Bolsheviks to unleash a campaign of mass repression known as the Red Terror. Thousands of political opponents were murdered over the coming months as Russia slipped into an ever-deepening civil war. Millions more would be killed, starved and imprisoned in the years that followed as Lenin's criminal, paranoid regime clung to power. We will never know to what extent the assassin's bullets accelerated Lenin's journey from radical activist to blood-slaked dictator, but comrades noted that his physical and mental health would never fully recover from Kaplan's attack.

31 August

It was a death and an accession that changed the fate of England and France. Today in 1422, a nine-month-old baby became 'King of England, Heir and Regent of France and Lord of Ireland'. His father, Henry V, died a terrible death from dysentery. The personification of the chivalric ideal of warrior kingship was no match for a gruesome bacterial infection that he had contracted in May. After three months of vomiting, wasting away and blood-filled diarrhoea his fragile corpse was taken back to London and buried in Westminster Abbey. England had lost its formidable king. The only certainty was now conflict, with enemies abroad, and between the king's relatives at home. People feared the worst. And they were right.

Henry VI was raised by a council of nobles and his young mother Catherine of Valois. It soon became clear that the lottery of primogeniture had failed as spectacularly with the son as it had triumphed with his father. Henry VI showed little interest in the crown or war. A pious, studious and gentle recluse, Henry VI is now chiefly remembered for his tragic mental collapse.

In 1453, Henry VI was struck down with a 'malady' that caused him to fall into a state of inertia; he even remained comatose at the news of the birth of his son. Royal doctors tried shaving his head, purges and administering an enema. He lapsed in and out of this state for the rest of his life, allowing powerful opponents like his cousin Richard Duke of York to assume many of the powers of the crown. The vacuum at the heart of government led to civil war. The Wars of the Roses pitted royal cousins against each other yet again.

SEPTEMBER

1 September

Mr C. F. Herbert was a gold miner in Australia. He would never forget the night of 1 September 1859. The sky was on fire. Auroras filled the heavens with dancing sheets of colour. Talking years later in 1909 he said, 'The rationalist and pantheist saw nature in her most exquisite robes, recognising the divine immanence, immutable law, cause and effect. The superstitious and the fanatical had dire forebodings and thought it a foreshadowing of Armageddon and final dissolution.'

He was witnessing the biggest geomagnetic storm in recorded history. He was not alone. The astronomer Richard Carrington had spent that morning looking up at the sun through clear skies just outside London. Through his brass telescope he saw 'two patches of intensely bright and white light' break from the sun's surface. He had just become the first human to see a solar storm, a giant flare, with the energy of 10 billion atomic bombs, which would soon make itself felt on earth.

That evening the Northern Lights were seen as far south as the Caribbean, while in New England in the United States people were able to read by the power of their light. To their amazement telegraph operators found they could continue to operate their machines even after disconnecting them from their power supplies.

The 'Carrington Event' struck the earth at a time before transistors and computers; it has been estimated that the cost of an equivalent event today would be profound social disruption and over $1 trillion dollars. Modern human civilisation is fragile, built in the blink of an eye, exploiting climatic and solar conditions that are disturbingly changeable.

2 September

It is the ultimate example of the chasm that separated the modern industrial world of the late nineteenth century from the societies that had been left behind. Today in 1898 British imperial forces, armed with modern weapons, carried by steamer and railway, sustained with tinned food and networked by telegram cables, utterly destroyed a large Sudanese army at Omdurman just outside Khartoum in Sudan.

Sudan had been controlled by the forces of the *Mahdi*, Muhammad Ahmad, the messianic, self-appointed saviour of Islam, since he had driven out Egyptian occupiers and their British allies in the 1880s. He had died, leaving his successor to deal with the British and Egyptians. They were determined to reconquer Sudan – a volatile Islamic regime could not be allowed to threaten the Suez Canal and Britain's link with India.

The invasion, when it came in 1896, was a stunning demonstration of modern military might. Herbert Kitchener, the British commander, personally wielded a pick as his army built a railway through the hostile Western Desert. Steam-powered gunboats shadowed the army along the Nile.

When the Sudanese forces hurled themselves at British lines at dawn on 2 September 1898 they were decimated by artillery firing exploding shells, machine guns and rapid infantry volleys of new hollow bullets that expanded on impact to inflict appalling wounds. Armed with antique muskets, spears and swords, the Sudanese were slaughtered. By the end of the day over 10,000 had been killed with a similar number wounded. In return the British force sustained less than 50 dead with a few hundred wounded.

By 1900, Europe, or Europe's former colonies in the Americas, had conquered nearly every other society on earth. The Battle of Omdurman illustrates how this unprecedented global domination was achieved. Never before or since would the technological, and therefore military, balance be so spectacularly skewed in their favour.

3 September

At 11.15 a.m. on 3 September 1939, the prime minister, Neville Chamberlain, came on the radio. For people in Britain at the time, there was only one station. An announcement was expected. Austria, had been invaded, as had Czechoslovakia and now Poland. People knew that war was probably coming.

Across the country they tuned in, and listened, with heavy hearts, but also with a largely unquestioning conviction that war was right: that there was no alternative. Chamberlain spoke: 'This morning the British Ambassador in Berlin Nevile Henderson handed the German government a final note stating that unless we heard from them by eleven o'clock, that they were prepared at once to withdraw their troops from Poland, that a state of war would exist between us. I have to tell you now that no such undertaking has been received, and that consequently this country is at war with Germany.'

These days this broadcast seems to mark the beginning of a great struggle for global freedom, with the forces of darkness that Adolf Hitler, and Nazi Germany, represented. For most listeners at the time, though, it was the affirmation, simply, of British determination to maintain her independence and global position.

Many of us have forgotten that days later the USSR also invaded Poland in accordance with the Nazi–Soviet Pact. Why didn't Great Britain also declare war on the USSR? In truth this was a conflict driven by national interest and real politik more than morality. A 'secret protocol' in the Anglo-Polish treaty meant Britain was only obliged to protect Poland from *German* aggression – so it was only from *German* aggression that it did so.

The First World War is remembered as futile, yet Britain achieved her stated war aim, to protect the sovereignty of Belgium. The Second World War is hailed as a victory, but Poland, the land for which Britain went to war, finished the war in 1945 occupied, swathes of territory annexed and its people oppressed by a regime scarcely less evil than the Nazis.

4 September

It underpins modern work, recreation, dating, shopping, argument, travel and the writing of history books. Its name is one of the most widely used words in the English language; it is one of the world's most valuable companies. Yet, only a few decades ago, it did not exist. It was only born today, in 1998. Google has become so fundamental to our lives that we regularly ask each other what we did before it existed.

In the late twentieth century it became clear that the Internet was going to contain the sum total of all knowledge ever accumulated by the whole of the human race. Two students realised that this colossal assemblage was next to worthless without a gatekeeper, a way of searching it. In 1995 Larry Page attended an open day at Stanford where he was shown around by a computer science student who had moved to America as a child from the Soviet Union, called Sergey Brin.

They became close friends, cramming their rooms with inexpensive (often disassembled) computers, and creating a search engine far superior to others that used links within web pages as a means of establishing the importance of other pages on the World Wide Web: their celebrated 'PageRank Algorithm'. Their initial name for the engine was 'Backrub'. They suspended their studies in order to found it as a venture.

By the late summer of 1998 they were noticed by Silicon Valley, and received their first significant investment – a cheque for $100,000 – which allowed them to move into their first office: a garage in California. The company was given a new name: Google, after Googol, the name for the vast number written as a 1 followed by one hundred zeros. The search page was kept distinctively plain and simple, in part because they could not afford a software designer, and in part to accelerate the engine's speed.

The impact made upon culture, and upon the population's access to information (and misinformation), has been as profound as Gutenberg's invention of the printing press, and the technology is still in its infancy . . .

5 September

The condemned man was brought out at dawn, just after 5 a.m. An unwilling firing squad of eleven soldiers who had served alongside him had been assembled. Today in 1917, they were going to shoot one of their mates for the crime of desertion.

Private Jimmy Smith was a decorated veteran, having fought with distinction. He had survived a bloody beach assault on Gallipoli, and he had fought at the Somme. There, in October 1916, he had been buried alive by a blast and terribly wounded. The mental damage was even greater; he was horribly traumatised. In England he discharged himself from hospital and tried to hide in his mum's terraced house in Bolton, but was dragged out by military police. Back on the front line he refused to obey orders, and in July 1917 he walked out of the trenches.

He was given a sham trial. He did not speak. He was not represented. No consideration was given to the mental trauma that army doctors had acknowledged. He received the death penalty. General Douglas Haig confirmed it, and on the morning of 5 September he was tied to a chair, a blindfold was placed over his eyes and a white piece of paper pinned as a target over his heart.

His comrades fired. No one wanted to hit him and instead of being killed outright he was wounded and lay writhing on the floor. The young officer in charge was supposed to finish him with a revolver but baulked and ordered Private Richard Blundell, a particular friend of Jimmy's, to take the revolver. At 5.51 a.m., as the sun rose above the battlefield, Blundell shot his mate in the temple. Blundell carried the trauma to his grave. On his deathbed, age ninety-six, his daughter reports that just before the end he shouted, 'Jimmy Smith'.

The British Army condemned 3,000 people to death in the First World War, but carried out just over 300 executions. Many of these men are now believed to have been carrying mental wounds sustained in the appalling conditions of the industrial battlefield. In 2006 all of them received a government pardon.

6 September

It was the last journey of a national treasure. Like Samson shorn of his locks, the ship had lost its cannon, its masts, rigging, chain plates, anchor cable and much of its ballast. Now a squat, ungainly hulk, it beetled up the Thames today in 1838, a sadly reduced relic of the mighty ship it had once been.

During the Napoleonic Wars, three decades earlier, the battleship had surged across oceans, her bows throwing white spray high in the air as she was driven along by acres of canvas hanging from three towering masts. Built from 5,000 oak trees, carrying 98 guns, *Temeraire* had followed close behind HMS *Victory* at Trafalgar. She had rescued her flagship as it was surrounded by enemy ships, firing a massive double-shotted broadside into the French *Redoutable* which left it a floating wreck.

Now tugboats hauled it up the oily Thames towards Rotherhithe. It has always been more convenient to toast war heroes than to care for them. By 1838 she was falling apart, and was sold to the breaker John Beatson for £5,530. Today she was being dragged to his yard for breaking up and recycling. Watching, apparently, was an artist. He was so taken by the symbolism of the journey that he painted it. His name was J. M. W. Turner.

Turner always called his painting *The Fighting Temeraire Tugged to Her Last Berth to be Broken Up, 1838* 'my darling'. It is an allegory; the setting sun, the ancient sailing ship dragged to its fate by steam-powered tugs; nostalgia in an era of rapid technological change. The inevitability of decay. Every one, and everything, even the once state-of-the-art victor of Trafalgar, eventually gets a tow to the breaker's yard.

7 September

Today in 1978 Georgi Ivanov Markov felt a sharp sting, like an insect bite, as he crossed Waterloo Bridge on his way to his job at the BBC. He looked around and saw a man fumbling with an umbrella. There was no sign of rain. He continued on his way to work at the World Service where he was employed to broadcast radio programmes aimed at his native Bulgaria. He had been a writer and playwright but had defected to the West in 1971. His withering criticism of the Bulgarian regime and its cult of personality around the Communist Party leader, Todor Zhivkov, marked him out as an enemy and a target for assassination.

By the time he arrived at the office, he had a welt on the back of his right thigh. He mentioned the incident, and the umbrella, to colleagues as the pain grew worse through the day. By that evening he had a fever and went to a hospital in Balham. He never left. Four days later he died.

A post-mortem revealed a metal pellet the size of a pinhead embedded in the dead man's leg. Tiny cavities in it had been filled with ricin, a potent toxin, for which at the time there was no known antidote. The tiny projectile was fired by a mechanism inside the umbrella. KGB defectors later confirmed that they helped to arrange the assassination.

No one has ever been charged in connection with the murder. The ingenious delivery system and unstoppable toxin combined to make this the most infamous of Cold War assassinations, one that has helped to give the conflict its enduring reputation as a game played by gadget-wielding spies and hitmen.

8 September

Statues are always political. Today in 1504 the people of
Florence crowded to see Michelangelo's latest masterpiece
positioned at the entrance of the town hall, the seat of civic
government, in the heart of the republic, the Palazzo Vecchio.
David, hero of the chosen people, the Israelites, loomed over
the palazzo, his eyes flashing defiantly in the direction of Rome.
The biblical hero who had humbled the mighty Goliath was
now the symbol of Florence's determination to preserve its
liberty from its enemies, be they the Medici, so recently
expelled from Florence, or the Borgias whose ambitions to
enlarge the Papal States around Rome seemed limitless.

The statue had been commissioned forty years before
Michelangelo completed it, and was initially awarded to
another sculptor, and then another. Both sculptors rejected the
commission due to 'taroli' or imperfections in the marble.
Aged only twenty-six, Michelangelo took on the task of
sculpting the huge block of marble and two years later
produced the massive figure, seventeen feet high, weighing
over five tons, which at the time was considered to be a revolutionary portrayal.

Unusually Michelangelo chose to portray him as a man,
rather than a boy, and before he faces Goliath, rather than
after with the giant's severed head as a trophy. His sling rests
over his shoulder, his hand grips the rock. The curls, muscles
and veins on this astonishing masterpiece are so lifelike that
people joked that Michelangelo had been asked to sculpt David,
not bring him back to life.

9 September

It was thought to be impossible. Maybe that's why he tried it. Today in 1913, the Russian pilot Pyotr Nesterov became the first person ever to fly an aerial 'loop the loop'. Although the achievement made him famous, Nesterov's superiors were far from impressed: he was punished 'for risking government property' and given ten days of close arrest – unlike a French pilot who did it afterwards, and was given a medal.

From his days training in the artillery Nesterov had become fascinated by the science of aviation, pioneered by the Wright brothers among others shortly after the turn of the twentieth century. He was sent to serve in a balloon regiment as an observer. He built a glider and learned how to fly it. And he took flight training at the St Petersburg aviation school before qualifying as a military pilot.

During the summer of 1913, a year before the outbreak of the First World War, Nesterov became the leader of an aviation detachment based in Kiev. Convinced that an aircraft would be able to fly a loop – a feat never previously accomplished – Nesterov felt sufficiently confident to put his life on the line by piloting the plane that did it himself. Many watched as he did so, at Syretzk aerodrome near Kiev.

Not content with one unprecedented achievement, shortly after war broke out Nesterov became the first pilot to destroy an enemy aircraft in flight. Since planes were not yet armed, he rammed the Austrian plane with his, fatally damaging both. Again he took a terrible risk, and this time it did not pay off. Nesterov died the next day from the injuries that he sustained at the age of twenty-seven. The fact that one Ukrainian town was renamed Nesterov in his honour seems scant recompense for his bravery.

10 September

He is simply *El Liberador*, the Liberator. Simón José Antonio de la Santísima Trinidad Bolívar Palacios Ponte y Blanco, generally known as Simón Bolívar, is one of the few men in history after whom a nation has been named. At the start of the nineteenth century Bolívar took the lead in severing the link between Spain and its possessions in South America, fighting a series of battles that ended Spanish dominance and led to the establishment of Venezuela, Bolivia, Columbia, Ecuador and Peru. Today in 1824 the revolutionary National Assembly in Quito gave Bolívar supreme authority to bring the war of independence to a decisive close. With his characteristic political deftness he accepted the appointment but rejected a salary of 50,000 pesos.

Spain's huge American empire rotted from the head. Since the start of the century Spain had lurched from crisis to crisis. Napoleon had invaded and installed his brother on the throne. The long, brutal Peninsular War followed, which pitted Spaniard against Spaniard as well as against the French invader. Liberation brought fresh instability. Liberals clashed with reactionaries as Spain sought renewal. Governments and constitutions came and went, lurching between political extremes. The effect of all this in Latin America was a confusing range of responses from ultra-loyalism to a desire for a complete severance, with everything in between. Loyalists switched to rebels and back again as governments in Madrid came and went.

By 1824 Bolívar had liberated huge areas of the continent. Following his appointment he led a campaign to deal with the last vestige of Spanish power. In just three months his forces provoked a major battle with the Spanish army in Ayacucho in Peru. The Spanish were utterly routed. The viceroy, José de la Serna, the Count of the Andes, was wounded and captured. It was the end of centuries of Spanish rule in South America. Bolívar was showered with titles and praise but became deeply disillusioned as the constituent parts of the liberated Americas bickered, split and eventually fought each other. His dream of a southern United States would never be realised.

11 September

This date, 11 September, will always be remembered for the terrorist attack in New York in 2001: one of those rare events which changed everything and, as a result of which, almost everyone then alive remembers what they were doing at the time.

Still, one should not forget other momentous things that have happened on the same date: such as the dreadful explosion at the Prince of Wales colliery at Abercarn, in south Wales, which caused the deaths of 268 miners – men and boys – over a century earlier, in 1879. Coal-mining in south Wales was fundamental to Britain's Industrial Revolution, in particular during the nineteenth and early twentieth centuries. If the revolution was powered by steam, the burning of high-quality coal – which burned at high heat, leaving a relatively small amount of residue – was critical.

Steam engines powered railway locomotives, ships and factory engines. They needed coal, and the seams in south Wales – accessed deep underground – were one of the UK's predominant sources. The extraction of coal, though, was a very risky business, renowned both for danger as well as the long-term health problems it produced in miners.

Just before noon on 11 September 1878 more than three hundred miners were working underground when a huge explosion tore through the mines at Abercarn, ignited, probably, when firedamp – naturally occurring flammable gas, particularly methane – came into contact with a 'safety' lamp (which reduced the dangers of using a naked flame but did not eliminate them). Fires were ignited underground and numerous miners were trapped and unable to escape – around ninety being rescued by brave attempts made in spite of the risk of further explosions.

12 September

General James Wolfe was facing disgrace and ridicule. His powerful army had been carried by the Royal Navy up the supposedly impassable St Lawrence River into the heart of France's huge North American empire. It was still early in the summer of 1759. The fall of Québec, its capital, should have been relatively straightforward. Instead the army had struggled. Wolfe found himself trapped in a war of ambush by Native Americans and Canadian (French colonial) militiamen, his battalions were eviscerated by disease and unable to land on the well-defended north bank of the river and storm into the city.

By the end of August, Wolfe himself was life-threateningly ill. He had fallen out with his fellow commanders. The young general, so full of promise, looked like he would join a long list of British officers who had been broken by the challenge of war in the North American wilderness. Then, on 12 September 1759, Wolfe launched an assault that would change the course of history and lead him to death and immortality.

Perhaps out of desperation as the prospect of winter neared, Wolfe ordered his infantry into small boats and at night they drifted down the current towards a little inlet near Québec. The oars and rowlocks were muffled with cloth. French speakers sat in the bows answering challenges from the bank. Perfectly judging the moon, weather and tide, the British keels crunched in the gravel at L'Anse au Foulon, and immediately scaled the riverbank; kilt-clad Scottish Highlanders at home on the steep, wooded slope. Just before dawn the British burst out onto the Plains of Abraham, scattering a small French force.

The British had got ashore. The French had no choice but to come out of Québec to drive them off. A battle followed in which Wolfe was killed at the moment of victory. Québec fell to the British, the vast expanse of New France soon followed. Wolfe's daring night attack had won a continent for Britain, and given the British their first great imperial martyr.

13 September

The four condemned women were forced to kneel. One account reports that the two weeping British prisoners held hands. Another states that the darker-skinned woman had been badly beaten, but despite this her last word was '*Liberté*'. Death was sudden. At dawn, today in 1944, each of them was shot by a member of the SS through the back of the neck. The corpses were searched for jewellery and the SS then burned the corpses of Yolande Beekman, Madeleine Damerment, Elaine Plewman and of Noor Inayat Khan, Britain's first female Muslim war hero.

Noor Inayat Khan had the blood of warrior princes in her veins. She was descended from Tipu Sultan, the Tiger of Mysore, one of British India's greatest opponents. Her Indian father had married an American and she enjoyed a privileged upbringing in London and Paris. Following the German Blitzkrieg in 1940 she had escaped to Britain where she volunteered for the armed forces. By 1943 she was a member of the Special Operations Executive, Churchill's pet organisation of spies and saboteurs designed to set occupied Europe ablaze.

Khan was trained for the extremely dangerous job of radio operator. She would liaise between local Resistance fighters and London. She received mixed reports but her instructor wrote that she 'was longing to do something more active in the prosecution of the war, something that would demand more sacrifice'. She got her wish.

She was inserted into France in June 1943, the first female wireless operator in occupied Europe. In October she was betrayed. The Gestapo imprisoned her and two attempted escapes earned her solitary confinement and constant shackles. She never told her gaolers anything but other inmates heard her weeping at night. In summer 1944 she was transferred to Dachau concentration camp.

For her bravery, in 1949, Noor Inayat Khan, an Indian, a British officer, and a Muslim, was awarded the George Cross for 'the most conspicuous courage' and the nation had a new kind of hero.

14 September

Today, in 1752, Britain and her empire awoke on 14 September, the previous day having been the 2nd. Some were unsettled. Others, like Benjamin Franklin, were sanguine, joking that it was pleasant for an old man 'to go to bed on September 2, and not have to get up until September 14'.

During the first half of the eighteenth century Britain, as other Protestant and Orthodox countries, continued to use the 'Julian' Calendar, named for Julius Caesar, as opposed to the newer 'Gregorian' one introduced by Pope Gregory XIII in 1582 and imposed by papal bull throughout Catholic Europe.

While the motivation had been religious – to align the date of Easter with that celebrated by the early Church – and was denounced by the Church of England as a popish monstrosity (previous attempts to introduce it in Protestant England having been defeated) – it was recognised by scientists as superior.

The old calendar *did* miscalculate the length of a year by eleven minutes, causing slippage over time. Parliament accepted their arguments, lamenting too the 'frequent mistakes' caused by the use of the Julian calendar while many neighbours used the Gregorian one.

The transition did involve practical issues. What if your birthday fell during those missing eleven days? Some actually moved their birthday. Contracts specifying payment dates, or delivery dates or even prison-release dates were all affected – though Parliament clarified that contractual payment dates should remain as under the Julian calendar.

Simultaneously New Year's Day was moved, from 25 March (Old Style) to 1 January (New Style), meaning that 1751 would be particularly short: 282 days, from 25 March to 31 December. The following year, 1752, was also short – 355 days – having lost the period between 2 and 14 September.

While it has been claimed that riots occurred – some demanding the return of their 'eleven days' – it is thought now that this is a myth.

15 September

It was the dawn of the era of mechanised transport so perhaps appropriately it did not go entirely to plan. Today in 1830, a railway running between Liverpool and Manchester formally opened: it was the first fully locomotive-pulled railway to connect two major cities.

It was a massive event. The prime minister, the Duke of Wellington, took his place on one of eight special trains to set out from Liverpool. Crowds lined the track and gathered in Manchester where the trains were expected to arrive.

Naturally there were delays. One of the trains derailed and the train behind collided with it, though no one was badly hurt. Much more seriously, around the mid-point of the journey – as the trains paused to take on water – many passengers got off. One of them was a former cabinet minister called William Huskisson, who went to pay his respects to the duke. Shaking the duke's hand, and talking with him, Huskisson failed to see a train approaching on the adjacent track. He was hit by it and suffered serious leg injuries from which later that night he died.

While Wellington felt remaining events should be cancelled, and a return made to Liverpool, by now the crowds in Manchester were becoming drunken and unruly, and he was persuaded to continue. By the time he arrived, any atmosphere of celebration had turned to hostility. Far from cheering and waving flags, the crowd threw vegetables at the duke. He refused to disembark, returning instead to the comfort of a stately home outside Liverpool where he arrived over six hours late. For him personally, it had been a horror show. He did not travel by train again for over a decade.

For all its tragedy, though, the sudden death of William Huskisson caused massive publicity. The line soon became very successful. The technology was transformative. 'The world,' the railway's secretary rightly declared, 'has received a new impulse.' This short stretch of track was the start of a global rail network that now stretches to over 620,000 miles (1 million kilometres).

16 September

To many, he is the last true prince. Today in 1400, Owain Glyndwr was declared Prince of Wales, the last time the title was adopted by someone who was actually a native of Wales. It was an act of rebellion against English rule and the start of a bitter conflict that raged for more than a decade.

Descended from the princes of Powys, Glyndwr was from a family of borderland gentry – Anglo-Welsh, and moving easily, as such, between the two societies. He studied for a time in London, serving in the army of the man who would become King Henry IV. He gained military and diplomatic experience at the side of some of the most accomplished generals and statesmen of the age. But when he returned to Wales he was appalled by the damage caused by English rule.

A bitter feud with a well-connected neighbour escalated quickly into a national struggle for freedom. Glyndwr defeated enemy forces on the battlefield, limiting the king's writ to a few scattered castles, while his charisma and vision for the future of Wales brought distinguished supporters flocking to his banner. Welsh students at Oxford University abandoned their studies to join the cause. He held court, established an independent Welsh parliament, tried to establish two Welsh universities, believed in a separate Welsh church and advocated a return to traditional Welsh law. He sought alliances with rebel Englishmen and even convinced the French king to send an expeditionary force to support his cause.

Gradually, though, the unrelenting enmity of King Henry IV's teenage son (who became the indomitable warrior king, Henry V) ground down the revolt. Glyndwr's strongholds fell. But his supporters never betrayed him. He went into hiding and was never found; his one final act of resistance against English rule. He did, though, have the last laugh. Not only is he personally revered, but Glyndwr's cousins bore the name 'ap Tudur'. In time his family would produce a dynasty which, if it did not restore Welsh independence, did see a Welshman rule, not just in Wales but in England too.

17 September

The space rocket was rolled out of a giant hangar at Palmdale, southern California, in front of a crowd of politicians, well-wishers and celebrities. On hand were a group of actors from the TV show *Star Trek*. Today in 1976 the NASA administrator Dr James Fletcher stood beside 'Bones', 'Sulu', 'Scotty' and 'Spock' as they watched the unveiling of the world's first reusable spacecraft. The actors were there because the president had changed the name of the prototype from *Constitution* to *Enterprise* after a vast write-in campaign from *Star Trek* fans.

It was the launch of the Space Shuttle, which would undergo more tests and improvements before blasting into space on operational missions six years later. The Shuttle team had worked for a decade in the build-up to today's unveiling. The costs of each of the Apollo Moon-landing missions had been vast; one way of reducing that was to employ a reusable vehicle. Journalists gathered at the event described it as a 'spaceplane' and they had a point. The spacecraft would be fired into space by rocket boosters which were jettisoned and recovered; and it had its own engines for adjusting its orbit and re-entering the Earth's atmosphere. On its final approach the Shuttle effectively glided towards the Earth.

Over the next thirty-five years five Shuttles were built which flew 135 missions. They launched satellites, conducted experiments, helped build the International Space Station and launched the Hubble Space Telescope and various interplanetary probes. Combined they have travelled around 500 million miles, and apart from *Challenger*, which broke up seconds into its tenth mission, they have all flown further than the distance between Earth and the Sun.

For three critical decades between the first generation of spacecraft and the modern proliferation of private companies operating an array of different vehicles, the Shuttle programme was the workhorse of manned space experimentation and exploration.

18 September

Until the late twentieth century referenda were considered distinctly un-British. The constitution has an unresolved question at its unwritten core: who or what exactly is in charge? The theoretical answer is Queen in Parliament, a compromise which melds three traditional sources of authority into one body: the people, whose will is expressed through their elected representatives in the House of Commons, the Lords, and the sovereign. Referenda blast this settlement apart. They are an unavoidable, decisive assertion of popular sovereignty. As such, they were avoided wherever possible by British governments. Only three national referenda have ever taken place so far; two of them were held to define the nature of Britain's relationship with Europe. There have been other referenda within specific parts of the country, and they have nearly all addressed a similar question: what level of autonomy or even outright independence do electors wish to have? The most dramatic of these plebiscites was held today in 2014 as the people of Scotland were asked if they wished to stay inside the United Kingdom.

They did. Just. An astonishing 85 per cent of eligible voters turned out, around 20 per cent higher than a run-of-the-mill general election. By 55 per cent to 45 per cent the electorate voted to remain. It was the first time in history that any of the citizens of England, Wales or Scotland had been asked to pass judgement on their membership of a country that has evolved in composition countless times over the centuries.

Campaigners for continued membership of the UK complained that it was impossible to counter the utopian rhetoric of the pro-Independence campaign, who promised a future made infinitely brighter by the return of sovereignty to the people of Scotland. They should not have been surprised. Subsuming oneself in a wider political union has always been a tough sell. A leading politician who witnessed the union of the two nations in 1707 wrote, 'Never did a treaty produce more ultimate advantage to a nation; never was any received with such a general and thorough hatred.'

19 September

He is the greatest general that no one has ever heard of, and one whose legacy endures. Today in AD 634, the city of Damascus – one of the oldest continually inhabited cities in the world, and bastion of the Roman Empire in the east – fell to a commander calling himself the 'Drawn Sword of Allah'. It was one of the first times that a major city had fallen to the Muslim forces outside their heartland in the Arabian Peninsula. It would not be the last.

Only two years previously, Muhammed – the prophet who had founded the Islamic religion – had died, and was succeeded by Abu Bakr, his companion, adviser, and father-in-law, though his entitlement to be 'caliph' has divided the Muslim world ever since. Abu it was who led the invasion of Syria, but the victory belonged to Khalid ibn al-Walid, the genius who fought over two hundred engagements and never lost a single one.

Inside information, it seems, permitted the Muslim forces to launch a surprise attack on a strong but lightly defended segment of the city walls. Ropes allowed around one hundred specially selected soldiers to climb up, to overwhelm the guards and to open the city's East Gate.

There was dispute, in the confusion, about whether the city had surrendered or been captured, but it was agreed that three days of peace should be guaranteed: 'They have this guarantee on behalf of Allah, the Messenger of Allah, the Caliph and the Muslims, from whom they shall receive nothing but good so long as they pay the Jizya [a tax levied by Muslims upon non-Muslim subjects].'

It was the start of a period of extraordinary expansion in which the Muslim armies conquered the Levant, Persia and Egypt. What Hugh Kennedy has written of the conquest of Egypt is true more broadly: 'seldom in history can so massive a political change have happened so swiftly and been so long lasting'.

20 September

No one gave them a chance against the legendary discipline of the Prussian infantry. But today in 1792, French revolutionary forces repelled a Prussian invasion at Valmy. It was certainly not a substantial battle. But it was one of history's most important: saving *la Révolution*, which in turn changed everything.

It was a result very few had expected. The Prussian army had marched into France with the support of all the great European powers when the French Revolution seemed to be sliding towards radicalism and republicanism. When the Prussian-led force pushed into France, the French army, stripped of many of its experienced aristocratic officers, seemed unable to stop the Prussians marching straight into Paris.

Around half the army was made up of enthusiastic volunteers but, critically, the artillery was full of veterans who knew their business. The French commander chose an imposing ridge, lined it with guns and hoped the Prussians would arrogantly march straight at them. His enemy obliged. As the morning mist cleared the French cannon blasted the Prussians as they laboured up the hill. They wavered, and the French general roared '*Vive la Nation!*' The cry was taken up by the entire line, the 'Marseillaise' was sung by tens of thousands of voices. The Prussians fled. It was a turning point in the history of warfare. An unenthused force of conscripts drawn from a polyglot collection of provinces, motivated only by a fear of the sergeant's musket butt, fighting for the hereditary rights of some distant prince or duke suddenly felt anachronistic. The watching German poet Goethe recognised how significant it was. 'From this day forth,' he wrote, 'begins a new era in the history of the world.'

Over the next two days, as the Prussians hastened for the Rhine, the French National Assembly, emboldened by the news of victory, abolished the French monarchy and proclaimed the French Republic. Valmy had saved the Revolution at its most vulnerable; within a few years there was nowhere in Europe that would not feel the effect of its searing radicalism.

21 September

Like so many others, Richard de Clare's family had found themselves on the wrong side of the civil war that had followed the death of Henry I. His father, the Earl of Pembroke, one of Norman England's most powerful magnates, had sided with King Stephen rather than Henry's daughter, Matilda. While Stephen sat on the throne the choice appeared a wise one. But when Matilda's son, Henry Plantagenet, invaded and forced Stephen to anoint him as his successor, it put the de Clare family in a difficult position. Richard was a young man when his father died and the new king, Henry II, refused to allow him to inherit the earldom.

In 1168 he met an exiled king who gave him the chance of redemption. The meeting would transform his fortunes, but also, more importantly, the entire course of Anglo-Irish history. Diarmait Mac Murchada had ruled the kingdom of Leinster before he intemperately stole the wife of another Irish king and was banished by the High King of Ireland, Ruaidrí Ua Conchobair. Like many an exiled lord before and since, he trod a weary path looking for sponsors, men and ships to put him back on the throne. After a fruitless search through royal and lordly courts across Britain and France he met de Clare in Wales. De Clare drove a hard bargain. He would become Mac Murchada's heir, and take his daughter's hand in marriage.

In 1169 the first troops crossed the Irish Sea, the following summer de Clare joined them. A lightning advance brought his army to the walls of Dublin, which he stormed today in 1170. Henry II was deeply unnerved by his vassal's success. He promised to restore him to favour if he surrendered key Irish strongholds to the English crown. De Clare agreed, the path to his father's earldom led through Ireland. As royal troops arrived to garrison Dublin, Waterford and other fortresses, it was the start of English rule in Ireland, which endures, in a much altered form, to this day.

22 September

The Portuguese had led the way. Ships loaded with spices from the East had earned their owners astronomical sums upon their return. English seafarers, emboldened by their victory over the Spanish Armada, dreamed of making similar voyages, and profits. It was too risky for any one individual, so today in 1599 a group of merchants met in London and outlined their plan 'to venture in the pretended voyage to the East Indies (which it may please the Lord to prosper)', and together agreed to invest the sum of £30,000. They followed up with an appeal to the queen for her patronage. Which, after a few attempts, she deigned to bestow.

The following year, Queen Elizabeth I granted a royal charter to the 'Governor and Company of Merchants of London trading with the East Indies'. The East India Company was born, by far the most famous of the so-called 'joint stock' companies. For fifteen years, the charter stated, the company would be granted a monopoly on all English trade with lands east of the southern tip of Africa and west of the southern tip of South America. So significant did the company become that for many years its fortunes were tied to those of the British Empire, which dominated so much of the world until its dissolution during the twentieth century.

In companies of the medieval world, merchants shared ship-space, defended themselves as a group against attack by pirates or hostile states, and shared privileges or permissions granted by foreign governments that were easier to negotiate as a body. But they traded essentially for themselves. Now an enduring, corporate fellowship was created. Investors could own a piece of the business, a 'share', and could profit while remaining aloof from day-to-day management. Money could be advanced without significant risk to their livelihood. Representatives would be hired to buy and sell purely for the company, *not* trading individually: representatives who were *employees*.

It was a simple but utterly revolutionary idea – a way to raise capital from a much wider pool and the ancestor of every modern company.

23 September

She was not an old ship but she had done too many years of service on the Spanish Main where warm water and humid air turned oak to sponge as ship worm munched its way through the planks of the hull. Today in 1641, *Merchant Royal* was finally nearing her native England but her crew were fighting a minute-by-minute, unceasing battle with the rising water in the bilge as seawater seeped in unstoppably. As they so often do, an Atlantic gale crashed into the continental shelf off Land's End, the sea piled up into steep mountains of waves and the south-westerly drove everything inexorably towards the jagged reefs of the Isles of Scilly and Cornwall.

The weakened ship fought the gale and lost. Her pumps failed and she sank on 23 September. Eighteen men died, while forty others made it into the boats and were rescued. More than human lives were lost. In fact an English government report stated that the loss was 'the greatest that was ever sustained in one ship'. When she sank the *Merchant Royal* had been weighed down with gold and silver. It is estimated that there were 100,000 pounds of gold aboard, valued at around £1 billion in today's money, 400 bars of silver, and perhaps half a million coins. The cash was the wages for the Spanish army fighting in Flanders, and threatened Spain's entire position in northern Europe.

It is one of the most valuable wrecks of all time. It has never been found.

24 September

Despite the rain, the floods, the appalling roads, the mud that sucked down the heavy cannon to their axles, the sickness that inevitably accompanied a marching army, the force that arrived outside the walls of Vienna today in 1529 still provoked a sense of awe. The splendidly mounted *sipahi* of Anatolia and the Balkans rode alongside the rough Arab skirmishers. North Africans rode camels, bands of Moldavians and Serbians marched beside the elite Janissaries, slave warriors who owed absolute loyalty to the Ottoman sultan.

Suleiman the Magnificent, ruler of an empire of tens of millions, stretching from Algeria to the Persian Gulf, had arrived in the heart of Europe. Vienna, the seat of the Habsburgs, lay before them. Never before had Ottoman forces penetrated so far into Europe. If Vienna fell, all Germany lay at Suleiman's feet.

Vienna's defences were not up to a modern siege. The 300-year-old walls were thin, built before cannon transformed warfare. All summer a seventy-year-old German mercenary had done what he could to prepare the city. Houses next to the walls were demolished, replaced by great supporting ramparts of earth. The gates were blocked up.

But Suleiman's force was not as potent as it looked. Torrential rain had forced him to abandon his heaviest guns on mud-choked roads. It did not abate. The autumn was brutal. Cold, wet weather forced him to make a quick decision. In mid-October he threw his men into an assault on the city but was beaten back. He had no choice but to retreat before winter set in.

The smaller, poorer, weaker Christian states had been saved from a superpower from the east by the rain. In the years that followed, however, those states underwent a transformation that meant they no longer needed the uncertain protection of the weather. Within a couple of centuries the balance of power was inverted and invading forces appeared beneath the walls not of Vienna, but of Constantinople.

25 September

It was a titanic clash for the crown of England between two great warriors, and two peoples who had been fighting over Britain for centuries. Today in 1066 at the Battle of Stamford Bridge, Harold of England routed a Viking army in a battle that effectively brought to a close the Scandinavian challenge to the English throne once and for all. It would be remembered as one of the most decisive battles in British history, were it not followed by an even greater battle just a few weeks later.

The giant king of Norway, Harald Hardrada, had already captured York. On hearing that there were Norse longboats in the Humber, the newly crowned Harold had made a lightning march north, where he caught Hardrada totally by surprise. The Vikings were without armour, split either side of the River Derwent. Scrambling to concentrate his forces, Hardrada ordered his detachment on the far side of the river to cross the Stamford Bridge, a narrow, wooden structure.

One enormous Viking axeman won eternal renown by single-handedly blocking the bridge to give his mates time to form their battle lines. His axe accounted for forty Englishmen as he held back Harold's army before a wily spearman floated himself under the bridge in a barrel and thrust his weapon into the unprotected groin of the Viking.

The English surged across. Hardrada was felled with an arrow to the throat. His army wiped out. A few solitary ships carried home the survivors of the last full-scale Viking invasion of England. King Harold had little time to celebrate. Only three days after this terrible battle in the north, William, Duke of Normandy landed in the south. To defend his crown, Harold would need to fight again.

26 September

It was the birth of modern physics. In 1905, four articles on space, time, energy and mass were published that transformed human understanding of the universe. It was hailed as an *annus mirabilis*, an 'extraordinary year'. What was truly extraordinary is that these articles came not from the world's most learned physicists at Cambridge, Berlin or Harvard, but from the pen of one man: a 26-year-old who had failed to find a teaching job and who had been passed over for promotion at his job in the patent office in Bern, Switzerland. His name was Albert Einstein.

Today in 1905 Einstein published the third of his four papers. It was titled, 'On the Electrodynamics of Moving Bodies' and in it he overturned Newton's ideas about the speed of light in a theory known to history as Einstein's special theory of relativity.

With his articles, Einstein soared to prominence. This provincial young man with no academic status was suddenly offered a succession of academic posts. Within a decade he was world famous. He would win the Nobel Prize for Physics in 1921 for one of the papers he wrote in 1905, but it was not for his theory of relativity or his deduction of the world's most famous equation, $E = mc^2$, but for explaining the photoelectric effect, the energy of light.

The fruit of that extraordinary year's work would allow scientists to predict how much energy will be released or consumed by nuclear reactions, convinced people about the reality of atoms, and transformed our understanding of space, energy, mass and time, which is pretty much everything.

27 September

Today in 1672, one of the most notorious business enterprises in English (or British) history was granted a new and broader charter from the king, Charles II, who personally invested along with his brother James. Thereafter it was known, as it is known still, as the 'Royal African Company'. Founded to trade along the African west coast, its initial focus was on the gold for which the region (the 'Gold Coast', as part of it became known) was renowned. It is for this reason that coins in England became known as 'guineas'. But it also quickly became absorbed in the growing trade in slaves.

The company's charter gave it the right to set up forts and 'factories', to exercise martial law and to maintain troops, granting it the 'whole, entire and only trade' in the region. By the 1680s the company is believed to have been transporting 5,000 slaves every year across the Atlantic, sponsoring hundreds of voyages. While the numbers grew larger – and most people tend to think of the Atlantic slave trade as an eighteenth- and early nineteenth-century phenomenon, concentrating particularly on the period of abolition – this was the critical period during which the trade became established.

Often captured slaves were branded on their chests, either with 'DY' for the 'Duke of York' – James, who would succeed Charles as king in 1685, and who was the company's governor – or with 'RAC', for 'Royal African Company'. Between 1672 and the end of the 1680s the company shipped around 100,000 slaves. Its profits boosted the growing financial power of the City of London, while major cities on England's west coast – Bristol, Liverpool – also flourished from slavery.

It lost its royal monopoly with the Glorious Revolution which swept James from the throne yet the company remained active in the slave trade until the 1730s, and its legacy endured far longer.

28 September

'When I woke up just after dawn on September 28, 1928,' wrote the Scottish physician Alexander Fleming, 'I certainly didn't plan to revolutionise all medicine by discovering the world's first antibiotic.' 'But I suppose,' he continued, 'that was exactly what I did.'

In truth it was not – nor would he have claimed – him alone. But it was Fleming who made the famous early discovery, returning from holiday (having failed, as often, to do his washing-up) to find on his laboratory bench a Petri dish of *Staphylococcus* bacteria wiped out by a mysterious fungus. 'That's funny', he is supposed to have said.

The mould, he discovered, was from the genus *Penicillium*, while the substance it released he labelled *penicillin*. He was not optimistic initially about its importance, finding it difficult to produce in quantity and fearing that it would not be effective in the human body.

Although he published his findings, there was not the fanfare we might now imagine. Throughout the 1930s he attempted to refine it into a form in which it could be mass-produced, but failed to do so and in 1940, after the outbreak of the Second World War – he had served in the Medical Corps throughout the first one – he abandoned it.

Fortunately, for Fleming and for humanity, the attempt was taken up by others who did succeed in manufacturing it in a purified form, in time to treat the wounded soldiers after D-Day. The problem the world faces now, of microbial resistance to antibiotics, is one that Fleming himself foresaw, cautioning against the use of too little antibiotic, for too little time. 'I hope,' he said, 'this evil can be averted.' Today, we are still hoping.

29 September

No one knew what it was, or how it spread. But they quickly learned what it did. Today in 1348 the Black Death came to London. One of the most devastating pandemics in human history, it seems to have arrived at the docks of Southampton that summer having spread across Eurasia. The narrow, filth-ridden streets, packed with people who had little knowledge of sanitation and none of how disease was transmitted, were the ideal conditions for the pestilence to spread. Once it hit London, its spread and severity were unprecedented.

Now known to be the bacterium *Yersinia pestis*, the Black Death or bubonic plague was carried by fleas that hitched a ride on the black rats that roamed the streets of medieval London. The plague had no sense of hierarchy: noblemen, clergy and royalty were among the victims. Two ex-chancellors and three archbishops of Canterbury all died of the disease, and the first wife of John of Gaunt, Blanche, Duchess of Lancaster succumbed at only twenty-three years old.

So many Londoners died that a vast plague pit was dug in Spitalfields. When that was filled a second was opened nearby. By the spring, the plague was claiming two hundred lives a day and mass graves were stacked five bodies deep. Around 50 per cent of Londoners, or 40,000 people, are thought to have died, a slightly higher proportion it is believed than for the rest of England.

The most appalling public health crisis in British history changed every aspect of life from wages to religion and architecture, but perhaps most importantly it demonstrated the resilience of fourteenth-century England. Even under unimaginable pressure the crown, church and society at large may have bent but they did not break.

30 September

Between 31 August and 9 November 1888 an infamous murderer walked the streets of Whitechapel in London, where it is believed that he took the lives of at least five victims. In the early hours of 30 September 1888 the mutilated bodies of Elizabeth Stride and Catherine Eddowes were discovered. Two more victims of a person known as 'Jack the Ripper'. The murders of Stride and Eddowes became known as the 'double event', a night where Jack the Ripper's murderous frenzy sparked panic in the world's biggest city.

At around 12.45 a.m., Israel Schwartz turned onto Berner Street where he witnessed a dispute. A man threw the woman onto the ground, where she screamed three times. Schwartz felt threatened and fled what he assumed was a case of domestic abuse. This was the last probable sighting of 44-year-old prostitute Elizabeth Stride before she was discovered with her throat slashed and her body heavily bruised.

An hour later the mutilated body of Catherine Eddowes, a 46-year-old casual labourer, who had been on her way to see her daughter in Bermondsey, was discovered by PC Edward Watkins in Mitre Square. Watkins had only walked through the square fifteen minutes earlier. The murderer had managed to slash Catherine's throat, remove the tip of her nose, part of her ear, and her womb and left kidney in that sliver of time. Earlier that night Eddowes had been arrested for being drunk, but after a few hours she had been released. She would have been safer in the cells than on the streets.

The identity of Jack the Ripper has never been conclusively determined. But his myth exploded into a cult obsession known as 'Ripperology'. Tourists, authors, researchers and eccentrics comb over the evidence again and again, trying to shed light on the crimes of history's most famous serial killer.

OCTOBER

1 October

Alexander saw the gap open in the Persian line. It was his chance. At the head of his elite Companion Cavalry he unleashed the greatest mounted offensive in history straight at his enemy, the 'Great King, King of the World', Darius of Persia.

Today in 331 BC, 25-year-old Alexander of Macedon, which had traditionally been a peripheral, weak state in northern Greece, annihilated the army of the world's most powerful empire and became Lord of Asia. On a battlefield near Gaugamela in modern Iraqi Kurdistan, Alexander's personal leadership was the key ingredient in a victory that made him master of much of the known world.

The Persian army was perhaps two or three times the size of the Macedonian-led force. There were war elephants, scythed chariots, swarms of fast, lightly armed infantry and the legendary Immortals or heavy infantry. In response, Alexander's plan was simple, he would decapitate the Persian army with an assault on Darius himself, but its execution would require exquisite timing, cohesion and leadership.

Alexander always placed himself in the thick of the action. It was said that his insatiable desire to outdo his almost superhuman father drove him to reckless acts of bravery. He had been astonishingly lucky to survive his first battle in Asia when, leading the attack on the enemy's centre, an axe blow split his helmet, his skull saved only by a matter of millimetres.

Today when he spotted the gap in the centre of the Persian line, Alexander swerved his superb horsemen through a sharp turn and aimed for it, right at the spot where Darius had stationed himself. The Persian ruler saw death in the frothing, screaming mass of men and horses, and according to a Greek source, as he 'had already long been in a state of fear . . . he was the first to turn and flee'.

His army disintegrated and he was later murdered. Alexander's victory won him an empire that was the largest to that point in human history. Even this was not enough, and he marched on.

2 October

After almost a decade of negotiations, the Infanta of Spain, Catherine of Aragon, landed in England at 3 p.m. today in 1501. Catherine had come to marry the Prince of Wales, heir to the English throne, a tall, handsome, intelligent young man who showed every sign of living up to his name and who would usher in new golden age, Prince Arthur Tudor.

A marriage alliance with the Spanish superpower was a great achievement for the Tudor family, who had grabbed the throne with the weakest of claims. Henry VII had worked hard to forge a deal that legitimised the Tudors as the equal of the greatest dynasties in Europe. To celebrate, he organised the most elaborate pageant ever seen in England.

Crossing the Bay of Biscay was uncomfortable and dangerous. Catherine was heartily glad to set foot ashore in Plymouth. From there she travelled to London, and was greeted with six separate spectacles as she made her way through the city; at Southwark she was met by an image of St Catherine. On Gracechurch Street there was a mock castle, housing Catherine depicted as Hesperia, a bright star, and her future husband, Arthur as Arcturus, the star that accompanied the birth of the prince.

Further pageants alluded to the fact both Catherine and Arthur were descended from the royal line of English kings through John of Gaunt and compared the Tudor court to the celestial court of heaven, with Henry VII presiding as God. As Catherine approached St Paul's Cathedral the ceremony ended with a woman portraying Honour addressing Catherine with the words: 'Noble princess, if this you'll purse, together with your excellent spouse, then, with us you'll reign in eternal prosperity.'

But things did not work out quite like that. Four months later Catherine and Arthur were afflicted by an unknown illness; Catherine recovered but Arthur did not. He was just fifteen years old. Henry VII forced Catherine to marry his second son, Henry. Even so, after bearing him a daughter rather than the desired son, Catherine was put aside by Henry VIII in history's most notorious divorce proceedings.

3 October

It was a strange place for a pacifist. Clambering over battlefield detritus, ducking down as machine-gun fire tore, crouching as shells crashed around him, 26-year-old Bill Coltman was not here to fight, but to rescue the wounded.

Today in 1918 the First World War was coming to an end, but it did not feel like it on the Western Front. The front-line soldiers knew little of the talk in distant palaces. The German army was retreating but was still a fearsome war machine. After one failed British assault the wounded lay screaming in no-man's-land. Coltman was a member of the Plymouth Brethren, a small evangelical sect for whom pacifism was a core belief. Nevertheless he had volunteered for active service as a stretcher bearer and had won an extraordinary number of gallantry awards for the many times he had dragged the wounded back to safety.

For forty-eight hours from the afternoon of 3 October Coltman performed his most courageous service yet. Time and again he crawled forward to treat the wounded, applying bandages and tourniquets, dispensing morphine, and hauling them back to the safety of British lines.

Shortly after, he learned that he was being awarded the Victoria Cross for his bravery. King George V pinned it to his chest at Buckingham Palace in 1919. It sat alongside the two Distinguished Conduct Medals and the two Military Medals, making Lance Corporal Bill Coltman the most highly decorated soldier in the British Empire. The bravest and most celebrated soldier in Britain's bloodiest war was one who never fired a shot or took a life.

Bill Coltman returned to civilian life as a gardener, and his modesty meant that he avoided the subject of his wartime service.

4 October

In February 1555, John Rogers was burned at the stake in Smithfield. His execution was ordered by the staunchly Catholic queen, Mary Tudor. Rogers received the death sentence for heresy and denial of the Church of Rome. The first Protestant martyr of her reign, he was sentenced largely for the part he played in the development of the Matthew Bible, which was printed today in 1537.

The Matthew Bible is one of the first nearly complete Bibles in English. It was translated by William Tyndale and Miles Coverdale under the pseudonym 'Thomas Matthew'. Before his capture and imprisonment, John Rogers had worked tirelessly with William Tyndale to translate the New Testament, and parts of the Old Testament, directly from the original Greek and Hebrew.

The Catholic Church conducted all services in Latin, and was wary of Bibles translated into vernacular languages. This made it easier to protect the Church's unity even if it meant that most parishioners could not understand church doctrine. Priests were therefore the mediators between the worshippers and God, a position of power that those such as William Tyndale disputed.

Vernacular Bibles were illegal in England, but copies were secretly owned; the word of God, coveted in private. The William Tyndale and John Rogers translations continue to shape the English we speak to this day, with expressions such as 'the salt of the earth' and 'eat, drink and be merry'.

William Tyndale was burned alive in Belgium in 1536. It was intended that he would be initially strangled so he would not suffer the agony of his execution, however the flames resuscitated him and he bore the excruciating pain silently. John Rogers was caught and suffered the same fate. It may have been some comfort to these men to learn that centuries later the Bible would be the most translated text in history, and is now available in over a thousand languages.

5 October

They called themselves Crusaders. The 200 men who left the Tyneside town of Jarrow today in 1936 bound for London were fighting for a higher cause, the survival of their community and way of life. Their journey south became the Jarrow March. Where once rebel armies had marched on London to install their candidate on the throne, now working men marched to make their voices heard and to force politicians to improve wages, working practices and conditions for Britain's industrial classes.

Jarrow's population had increased tenfold in just a few decades in the second half of the nineteenth century as shipbuilding became a boom industry on the banks of the Tyne. At the time the British built 80 per cent of the world's big ships, a figure that fell back to around half of the world's output in the 1930s as other nations developed the capacity. By 1934 the main shipyard in town was shut and the population were desperate. It was, said one campaigner, 'a workhouse without walls'.

A group of workers met Walter Runciman, president of the Board of Trade, and were told, with icy formality, that 'Jarrow must work out its own salvation.' The march was their attempt to do so. They walked to London, welcomed in some places like Nottingham as heroes, and given food and supplies, while in others, such as Market Harborough, treated with utter disregard.

They arrived in London through streets lined with supporters and handed a petition to MPs asking for help for Jarrow. Then they returned home by train. The government did nothing. One marcher called it a 'waste of time' but 'great fun'.

The marchers may have failed in their short-term objectives but the Jarrow March helped to shift attitudes in Britain and create the necessary preconditions for the transition to a welfare state. The post-war Labour government, drawing on totemic moments of struggle like the march, constructed a framework of social provision that institutionalised many of the marchers' demands and hoped to banish for ever the deprivation experienced by the unemployed of Jarrow.

6 October

The commanding officer of HMS *Endeavour* had come a long way. Born into rural poverty in North Yorkshire, with only a few years of education in the village school, he had risen to lead one of the most famous and important voyages of discovery in British history. Today in 1769, having travelled 15,000 miles, Lieutenant James Cook spotted a landmass he identified as New Zealand. Two days later he became the first European to land there, at Teoneroa near the north-east tip of North Island.

Aotearoa or 'Land of the Long White Cloud' had been sighted but not explored by a Dutch expedition led by Abel Tasman 127 years earlier. He had named it Nova Zeelandia after a Dutch province. Now Cook became not only the first explorer to go ashore but the first to circumnavigate it, and chart its coast. It was first spotted by keen young eyes belonging to the surgeon's boy, Nicholas Young, from the masthead. Having dropped anchor, Cook took two small boats ashore. They had an altercation with a hostile Maori force, which ended when one of Cook's men shot one of them. It was not a good start.

The following day Cook took gifts and attempted to communicate. Sadly this meeting also broke up violently. Next Cook tried bringing some Maoris aboard the ship, where they were treated respectfully and returned ashore in a more conciliatory mood. Even so, Cook was disappointed by the first encounters and frustrated in his search for fresh provisions, so he named it Poverty Bay and continued on his journey. He spent another six months surveying the coast, naming bays and prominent features.

The Maoris were right to be suspicious of the Europeans. Cook's expedition would bring traders, settlers, invasive species and modern technology that would radically transform every aspect of their life. Cook ensured that Aotearoa would become New Zealand, a colonial facsimile of the mother country, on the far side of the world.

7 October

The prisoners could sense the end approaching. After years of hopeless incarceration in the Auschwitz-Birkenau Complex, rumours of liberation gave the inmates a sliver of hope. The Soviet Red Army had thrust deep into Poland, there was news of an uprising by the people of Warsaw and American planes bombed nearby factories. This news kindled a spirit of resistance among the desperate prisoners and today in 1944 they rose up, determined to free themselves or die in the attempt.

In the Auschwitz Complex's munitions factory, young Jewish female prisoners worked to supply the German war machine. From mid-1944 women like Regina Safirsztain and Ala Gertner began smuggling out small quantities of gunpowder. These were then passed to the squads of prisoners forced to work in the camp's crematoria. Their intention was that, when they had a sufficient amount, the squad would blow up the instruments of genocide – the crematoria and gas chambers – and launch the revolt.

But they ran out of time. On 7 October the squad at Crematorium IV learnt that they were about to be murdered by the SS. They had no choice but to act. With unimaginable courage they attempted to blow up the crematorium, attacking the guards with anything that came to hand. Seeing the flames and confusion, the rest of the camp joined the uprising. Several SS guards were killed, the perimeter wire was breached and hundreds of inmates escaped while their comrades fought Hitler's heavily armed paramilitaries with rocks, clubs and fists.

The SS regained control and inflicted a characteristically savage retribution. Almost every escaped prisoner was rounded up and killed; hundreds of those who had stayed to fight were executed. Safirsztain, Gertner and the other women were arrested and tortured, but they all refused to name their co-conspirators and were hanged three months later. One of them, Róza Robota, managed to get a final message to the Polish resistance: '*Hazak v'ematz*'. Be strong and have courage.

8 October

His men called him 'Pappy' because he was an old-timer. Major Ralph Shelton was in his late thirties and a veteran of counter-insurgency. As a US Special Forces Green Beret he had fought Communist guerrillas in Laos, after being wounded during the Korean War. Today in 1967 he closed the net on one of the world's most wanted men, an Argentinian Marxist named Ernesto Guevara, a man whose charisma and ability made him the terror of the CIA and regimes across South America, a man better known by his nickname 'Che'.

Pappy had been in Bolivia training local soldiers as soon as word had reached Washington that Che had abandoned the revolutionary struggle in the Congo and returned to the continent of his birth. The veteran Marxist had fallen out with his Cuban comrades and now sought to spread revolution throughout South America. He raised a small force in the rural south-east of Bolivia. Tipped off by an informant, Pappy surrounded Che's ragtag army and unleashed a hail of fire. Che was wounded twice and as the Bolivians approached, shouted, 'Do not shoot! I am Che Guevara and I am worth more to you alive than dead!'

The Bolivian government certainly did not agree. Che was held in a local village for two days, before his captors were ordered to kill him and make it look like he had died in combat. Witnesses remember that during that brief imprisonment he conducted himself with great dignity despite his shredded clothes, matted hair and the trauma of his wounds. He refused to speak to any Bolivian officer, but talked of revolution to the enlisted men.

Che's legend spread after his death. His face still adorns posters and flags the world over, but Pappy never doubted his role, saying years later, 'That man is famous now, but he killed lots of innocent people and we were glad to help put him out of business.'

9 October

The great Crusader was leaving the Holy Land, his job incomplete, forced home by treachery. Today in 1192, Richard the Lionheart boarded a ship; his departure marked the end of the Third Crusade.

Earlier that year Richard had received word that there was a conspiracy in Europe, between his brother John and Philip Augustus, King of France. Richard was urged to return home to protect his dominions from a foreign enemy and a rapacious brother. Yet he had still not captured his ultimate prize, Jerusalem. He had however strengthened the Crusader state in the Holy Land. He had captured the strongholds of Acre and Jaffa. But just as he was preparing to leave, the latter had come under attack by Saladin's forces. In July, Saladin's troops forced their way into Jaffa, slaughtering Crusaders in the streets and besieging an obstinate group of defenders in the Citadel. Richard acted fast, returning to Jaffa only to find it apparently securely in the hands of the Muslims.

It seems that Richard accepted his stronghold had been lost, until a priest swam to his ship, having slipped out of the Citadel. He told the king that a band of defenders was holding out, and the battle was not over. Richard stormed ashore, wielding his trademark battle-axe; his men followed their charismatic commander. Saladin was forced to withdraw from Jaffa, leaving 700 men and 1,500 horses dead on the battlefield.

Richard and Saladin both needed a respite. They agreed a three-year truce and Richard embarked on his return journey. It would take a lot longer and prove a lot more expensive than he had reckoned on. He would have to overcome shipwreck and months of captivity before he reached England and home.

10 October

'You turn if you want to,' Margaret Thatcher famously told the Conservative Party Conference today in 1980, 'the lady is not for turning.'

The early period of Thatcher's premiership (she had become prime minister in May 1979) was one of economic disquiet and uncertainty. Not long after the infamous 'winter of discontent' of 1978/79, which saw widespread strikes and union unrest during a bitterly cold winter, she had embarked upon a liberalisation of the economy. At first, however, far from bringing an improvement, economic statistics got worse. Unemployment rose – from 1.5 million to 2 million that autumn, and continued to do so. Some commentators, and some prominent members within her own party, had urged her to back off, but while she did profess concern, she refused.

Thatcher's speechwriter for seven years had been the playwright Sir Ronald Millar. His intention, he admitted, was that the truly memorable line in the speech would be the pun 'You turn if you want to', coming soon after a reference to the media's obsession with the pusillanimous U-turn. He did not expect the subsequent phrase – 'the lady is not for turning', which made punning reference to an earlier play *The Lady's Not for Burning* (though most, including Thatcher herself, missed the reference) – would prove anything like so memorable.

The speech was immediately successful – the standing ovation that she received in the conference hall lasting for more than five minutes – and the 'lady is not for turning' phrase in particular has become emblazoned in political mythology, representative of a first female prime minister who was famously, some might say notoriously, strong-minded in the attitude that she took towards opposition.

Thatcher was also christened the 'Iron Lady' – this one coined by a Soviet analyst. A week later she acknowledged the term in a speech to Finchley Conservatives and compared it to the Duke of Wellington's nickname, the 'Iron Duke'.

11 October

In the long and brutal history of English atrocities in Ireland, none are remembered as keenly as one that occurred today in 1649 when Oliver Cromwell, Lord Protector of England, slaughtered thousands of soldiers and civilians in Wexford.

The port of Wexford in the south-east of Ireland sheltered a nest of privateers who preyed upon British ships as they entered the Irish Sea or sailed up the Welsh coast. The town was also held by rebel Catholic forces, who had expelled eighty Protestants, crowding them onto a ship which promptly sank after it left the harbour. Cromwell's victory in the English Civil War meant he could now turn the full attention of his battle-hardened New Model Army on Ireland where diehard Royalists had made common cause with Catholic rebels.

Cromwell's guns blasted holes in the town's defences and the defenders began to negotiate a surrender. During the talks, Cromwell's men suddenly stormed forward. Irish forces were unprepared and there was panic. The defenders fled, pursued by Cromwell's troops, who chased them into the River Slaney where hundreds drowned, including the town's governor and lead negotiator, David Sinnot. Priests were hunted down and butchered, and all control was lost in an anarchy of murder, looting and brutality. Nearly 5,000 Irish were killed, whereas there were 20 lost on the English side.

Cromwell denied giving the order to attack, but he made little effort to regain control of his men. Pro-Cromwell propagandists later claimed that it was righteous revenge for the town's history of raiding and for the deaths of the Protestant refugees. The horror of the slaughter at Wexford was seared into Irish consciousness. It is an enduring stain on Cromwell's reputation. Whether or not it was a deliberate decision, the massacre came to symbolise the murderous nature of British imperialism in Ireland.

12 October

Of all the seismic moments in the history of European exploration none is more important than what occurred today in
1492 when Christopher Columbus landed on San Salvador, in
the Bahamas, beginning the European discovery of America.

Late in the fifteenth century a sailor from northern Italy
had an idea that would transform the world. But of course
it wasn't deliberate. Columbus never imagined that he would
discover a new continent.

From his youth Columbus had worked as a sailor and
merchant, going as far south as the west coast of Africa and
north as far as Iceland. Though no scholar, he pored over
books of geography. He knew – most did – that the world was
round. Only fathers of the Church had believed it flat because
they could put Jerusalem, that Christian city, in the centre.

Columbus did think, though, that the earth was smaller than
it is, the equator shorter and the landmass of Eurasia longer.
He concluded that by heading west he should arrive fairly
quickly in Asia. European statesmen and their experts rejected
his ideas: the journey to Asia would be far too long. The
Portuguese said no. So too did the Venetians. And the English.
At first the Spanish did too. Columbus left their court dejected
and on the verge of giving up.

Only afterwards was he stopped by a rider and ordered back
to see King Ferdinand and Queen Isabella, who were convinced
that God was behind them. At last, after years of trying,
Columbus got the money he needed, and embarked on his
voyage. After five weeks, early in the morning, a lookout yelled
'land'. Cannon were fired to proclaim the discovery. The natives
proved friendly and, helpfully, had plenty of gold for jewellery
yet no iron for weapons. It was one of the most significant
moments in the history of humanity.

Columbus always thought it Asia, and called it the 'Indies.'
It was in fact an entirely new landmass, the Americas. The fact
that he was wrong scarcely makes it a less remarkable achievement.

13 October

'It's been a bit of a long shift,' joked Luis Urzúa. In fact it was a world record. Weeks before he and his team of thirty-three miners in the San José mine beneath Chile's Atacama Desert had been trapped by a rockfall, nearly 700 metres beneath the surface. The leadership shown by Urzúa, the shift supervisor, had held the group together and it was typical that today in 2010, after sixty-nine days underground, he insisted on waiting until all his men had been rescued before making his own bid for freedom.

On the afternoon of 5 August the group of miners had been trapped by a tunnel collapse in a mine that had recently failed various safety inspections. After searching for an escape route, Urzúa divided up the food and kept the men's spirits up. On 22 August a boring machine broke through to ascertain whether there were any survivors. They attached a note to the drill bit with insulation tape. *'Estamos bien en el refugio los 33'* ('We are well in the 33rd refuge').

This electrifying news initiated a vast rescue attempt involving national governments, mining conglomerates and NASA. On 5 September a borehole wide enough for a capsule that could carry a human was begun. Just before midnight on the 12th the first miner climbed into the 53-centimetre diameter pod and began the slow climb to the surface. Each had been prescribed a liquid diet rich in minerals, sugars and potassium. Each had taken an aspirin to avert blood clots. They wore a girdle to stabilise blood pressure, and sunglasses to protect them from the sudden sunlight. They reached the surface in nine to eighteen minutes. There they were greeted by TV crews transmitting to a global audience of 1 billion viewers and Chile's president, Sebastián Piñera.

At 9.56 p.m. on 13 October, 54-year-old Luis Urzúa was the last to reach the surface. Their record-breaking ordeal, and history's most complex underground rescue attempt, was over.

14 October

The analysts at the Defence Intelligence Agency were seeing a familiar pattern. A worrying one. By the autumn of 1962 the Communist regime in Cuba had been working closely with the USSR since the revolution three years before. The Soviet military had deployed advisers and equipment to the Caribbean island, only a hundred miles off the coast of Florida, but this looked altogether more threatening. Poring over aerial photographs they were struck by the layout of the surface-to-air missile sites that were being constructed. They were very similar to those used by Soviet forces to protect their ballistic missile bases. Did this mean that these sites were being prepared for the arrival of nuclear weapons?

Today in 1962, after days of poor weather in California had kept the planes grounded, Major Richard Heyser climbed into a 'Dragon Lady', an ultra-high-altitude U-2 reconnaissance aircraft. He took off just after midnight, watched the sun come up over the Gulf of Mexico, and approached Cuba from the south at his maximum altitude of over 70,000 feet. He turned on his camera as he tore across the island. In seven minutes it was all over, he was through Cuban airspace without a sign of an enemy fighter or a surface-to-air missile rearing up at him.

He landed in Florida at 9.20 a.m.; another plane whisked the roll of nearly a thousand photos straight to Washington, DC, where they were driven under armed guard to the National Photographic Intelligence Centre. By midday the worst suspicions had been confirmed. Heyer's photographs clearly showed transporters for the Soviet R-12 Dvina ballistic missile. If Cuba did not already have nuclear weapons on its soil, they were expected imminently.

President Kennedy was told thirty-six hours later. It was the start of the Cuban Missile Crisis, the nearest the human race has come to obliteration in recorded history. President Kennedy said later that the chance of all-out nuclear war had been 'between 1 in 2 and 1 in 3'.

15 October

His enemies called him 'the other king'. He had hauled himself up the precipitous social ladder of Tudor England from an artisan family to become Lord Chancellor, Archbishop, Primate of England and Cardinal. It was said that he dreamed of sitting on St Peter's throne in Rome itself. Ultimately however all power flowed from the actual king and when Thomas Wolsey fell from favour with his sovereign, Henry VIII, his fall was even steeper than his climb.

Henry VIII seized Cardinal Wolsey's grand home, York Place, and went on to transform the house, turning it into Whitehall Palace. Like any house renovation by a wealthy narcissist locked in a mid-life crisis, games and sports was at its heart. There was an indoor tennis court, a tiltyard, and a bowling alley, which was completed today in 1530.

The palace continued to be developed after Henry's death. The first Banqueting House was added by Elizabeth I, who endured a procession of disappointed suitors beneath paintings of fruit and vines, ironic celebrations of fertility. James I commissioned Inigo Jones to design the grand Banqueting House, which survives to this day.

Jones astonished the king with his perfectly proportioned honey-coloured facade, and grand interior. Thrilled, James I hosted the sick in his Banqueting House, performing the 'Royal healing ceremony', in which he touched those suffering from 'the King's evil', a skin disorder, probably scrofula. Charles II is said to have touched 7,000 desperate sufferers at Whitehall in the months following the Restoration.

In 1698, disaster struck and a fire consumed almost all of the palace. The diarist John Evelyn lamented, 'Whitehall burnt! Nothing but walls and ruins left.' The Banqueting House is the only major portion that survives. Henry VIII's tennis courts and sports complex remain beneath the present-day Cabinet Office, and perhaps his bowling alley too.

16 October

Parliament had centuries of useless wooden 'tally sticks' to get rid of. These notched and carved shards of wood were records of ancient financial transactions, records of long dead taxpayers. Today in 1843, the clerk of works at Westminster Palace decided to burn two cartloads in the basement of the House of Lords. By late afternoon visitors to the Lords commented that smoke was rising through the floorboards. These reports were ignored and the palace was closed as usual at 5 p.m. An hour later, the medieval royal palace was consumed by an inferno. Onlookers watched, dumbstruck, as one of Britain's most important buildings was devoured in an uncontrollable blaze.

MPs, Lords, and other volunteers manned water pumps and desperately tried to fight the flames. One artist opted to paint instead. J. M. W. Turner rushed to the banks of the River Thames and furiously sketched the blaze, even renting a boat in order to get closer to the heat of the fire, determined as ever to feel the power of the subject before transmitting that energy to the canvas.

At 1.30 a.m. the tide of the Thames was high enough to bring the floating fire engine close enough to make headway in the fight against the fire. Wet ash replaced roaring flames. The Houses of Commons and Lords had been completely destroyed, thankfully the magnificent Westminster Hall had survived. Treasures were lost, a thirteenth-century painted chamber where Parliament had opened for centuries, and where the death warrant for Charles I had been signed in 1649, had been obliterated.

The exhausted firefighters were rewarded for their courage with free beer. Westminster would be rebuilt, in conservative, Gothic style to reinforce the time-hallowed, medieval roots of the British constitution rather than a fresh neoclassical design, which would have had a definite whiff of modernity, and even republicanism.

17 October

The London Beer Flood, rather like the Boston Molasses Disaster, sounds like an opportunity to be flippant. In truth, though, neither event was any laughing matter. What began at the Meux and Company Brewery in Tottenham Court Road on 17 October 1814 left eight people between the ages of three and sixty dead.

First a huge vat containing 135,000 imperial gallons (610,000 litres) of beer ruptured. As beer gushed out, it tore through other vats. As a result more than 323,000 imperial gallons (1,470,000 litres) were released. The result was a tidal wave of beer – more than half the volume that would fit into an Olympic-sized swimming pool – which knocked down walls, cascaded into the street and destroyed everything in its wake.

As *The Times* reported, the destruction of brick walls caused roof timbers to tumble. Houses were flooded and even wholly destroyed. Eleanor Cooper, a barmaid at the nearby Tavistock Arms pub (you could hardly make it up), was killed after being buried under the resulting rubble.

In the neighbouring slum of St Giles, people lived squashed together in poor-quality houses that were demolished by the waves, and for all the wry talk – the reality, perhaps – of people lapping frantically at pools of beer, the destruction done was very severe indeed. In the aftermath people hushed their voices so that they could hear any noise made by trapped victims.

The smell of stale beer in the area lasted for months, as did the job of clearing up and treating those who were wounded, if not killed, by the flood. It was, *The Times* noted, a distressing task deserving 'warm approbation'.

18 October

It was one of history's greatest acts of vandalism. One that every Chinese pupil learns about in great detail. Today in 1860, during the Second Opium War, British and French troops burned and looted the Chinese Empire's beautiful 'Summer Palace'.

To this day art collections in Britain and France testify to the riches then robbed, and to the wanton destruction of so much else. While the damage was not wholly unprovoked, it is scarcely Britain's finest hour.

In a bid to 'open up' China to Western (particularly of course to British) trade a second 'Opium War', as it is known, was fought from 1856. The British refused to allow China to keep out shipments of Indian opium. France joined the British side while the Chinese regime, facing the massive Taiping Rebellion, was unable to mount significant resistance.

As Anglo-French forces approached Beijing, an advance delegation, sent to negotiate, was imprisoned, tortured and effectively murdered. In retaliation, the British high commissioner, Lord Elgin (son of the 7th Earl of 'Elgin Marble' notoriety), ordered the Summer Palace's destruction. Eight times larger than Vatican City, its grounds contained pavilions, palaces, temples, bridges and halls nestling amid gardens and lakes. For over a century and a half, work had continued constructing elaborate waterworks, buildings and lanscapes (with appealing names like the 'Courtyard of Universal Happiness').

That autumn the complex was empty, apart from eunuchs and other servants, the imperial entourage having retreated. Thousands of troops kindled fires that lasted for days and which killed servants hiding within the buildings. One Pekinese dog was seized and presented to Queen Victoria, which she named 'Looty'.

'You can scarcely imagine,' wrote one British participant, 'the beauty and magnificence of the places we burnt.' He called it 'wretchedly demoralising work', and in this history has tended to agree with him.

19 October

Rainwater sheeted down the castle walls and thunder cracked overhead as a king lay dying. It was a fitting context for the death of one of England's least impressive monarchs. By the time King John eventually died, today in 1216, his empire, which had once spread across the British Isles and parts of western France, consisted of the East Midlands. Prince Louis of France occupied much of his kingdom, welcomed by a nobility driven to rebellion by John's misgovernment.

Attempts to rehabilitate King John stumble on the unambiguous accounts left by contemporaries. 'He was a very bad man,' wrote one, 'he was greatly hated. Whenever he could he told lies rather than the truth . . . He hated and was jealous of all honourable men.' These characteristics had already alienated key allies and that was before his demands for ever-more taxation to fight disastrous wars to defend Normandy. Defeated, he invited further opposition by refusing to honour Magna Carta, precipitating rebellion and foreign invasion.

Just before his death he had travelled across the Wash to Lincolnshire where his baggage train was lost in the quicksands. Men, goods, holy relics and animals were washed away with the tide; even the crown jewels were apparently swallowed by the mud. Shorn of his kingdom and his treasure, the hopeless king had only his life left. Dysentery soon relieved him even of that.

Retiring for the last days of his life to Newark Castle, he died a gut-wrenching death. Given his unpopularity it was rumoured that he was poisoned (or according to other sources, had drunk bad ale or even a 'surfeit of peaches'). If it was dysentery, it saved his dynasty. With the hated John dead, his nine-year-old son suddenly looked a more attractive option than a French prince, and nobles rallied once again to the Plantagenet cause.

20 October

Maria Theresa's father had denied her an education. She was not allowed to ride a horse. She was not allowed to discuss affairs of state. She was encouraged to draw, paint, play musical instruments and dance. It was a very poor training for a woman who would become one of the most important rulers of Europe, today in 1740, when her father, the Holy Roman Emperor Charles VI, died and left her as his heir.

At the age of twenty-three Maria Theresa found herself, she later recalled, 'without money, without credit, without army, without experience and knowledge of my own and finally, also without any counsel'. She would need all of the above. Within weeks of her accession, several of Europe's strongest states refused to recognise her right to rule and her empire was plunged into war.

Enemy armies swarmed across some of her most precious territory. King Frederick of Prussia immediately invaded the province of Silesia, turning Prussia into a leading European power and himself into 'The Great'. Maria Theresa was determined to fight. She taught herself to ride to impress her Hungarian subjects and won their support in an emotional session of the Parliament in Budapest. She forced reluctant commanders to go on the offensive and against fierce odds maintained the Habsburg grip over most of its territory.

The War of Austrian Succession lasted eight years. In that time Maria Theresa had seven children. Few warlords in history have had to overcome challenges like those placed in her path, yet she preserved and reinvigorated her empire, giving it the strength to survive into the twentieth century when it had appeared to be on the verge of disintegration.

21 October

She became 'The Lady with the Lamp', a 'ministering angel' who 'glided' through hospital wards tending to wounded soldiers. She was one of the first celebrities created by Britain's mass media, the perfect vessel for a heady blend of beauty, patriotism, piety and devotion. Today in 1854 that journey began as Florence Nightingale left Britain with a team of volunteer nurses that she had trained herself. She was bound for Scutari (now absorbed by modern Istanbul) and the hospitals packed with the wounded and sick of the Crimean War.

Nightingale had inherited money and social conscience from her humanitarian parents. Travel stoked this instinct to use her wealth and position to help others. Surrounded by the majestic ruins of ancient Egypt she felt that she was being 'called to God'. She immediately enrolled for a spell of rudimentary medical training in Germany. Returning to England she worked as the superintendent at the Institute for the Care of Sick Gentlewomen before the outbreak of war gave her the opportunity to tend to those less fortunate than herself.

When she arrived in Scutari she found squalid wards packed with men. Hygiene and sanitation were ignored and preventable diseases tore through the weakened patients. She improved food and imposed basic hygiene practices like the washing of hands. She used *The Times* newspaper to address the British public and politicians alike. She shamed the authorities into sending out a team to fix the sanitation and was central to their decision to get Isambard Kingdom Brunel to construct a prefabricated hospital and ship it out.

After the war, her fame gave her the ability to fundraise and influence government policy. She effectively invented the modern nursing profession by founding the first proper training institute in London. She lobbied for better sanitary conditions in hospitals and slums alike. Her battle for clean, hygienic hospitals, homes and workplaces is thought to have boosted life expectancy in Britain as much as any single nineteenth-century medical breakthrough.

22 October

The passage had been brutal. Gales had battered the fleet ever since it had left the Mediterranean. Poor visibility and high seas meant that the commander, Admiral of the Fleet Sir Cloudesley Shovell, was uncertain about their precise position. Today in 1707 he hove to and had his ships check the seabed, its depth and composition. The leadsmen, standing on the side of the ship, legs wrapped around the shrouds for stability, dropped their lead plummets into the water and called out the depth at which they hit the bottom, then they hauled them in and examined the tallow on the lead which would bring up a specimen of the seabed, mud, sand, or clean, meaning it was rock. From these readings the navigators felt confident that they were in the Channel and could now run east towards Portsmouth with the gale at their backs.

At 8 p.m. sharp-sighted lookouts spotted waves breaking over submerged rocks and the glow of a lighthouse. With horror experienced hands realised that it must be the lighthouse on St Agnes, the southernmost of the larger islands in the Scilly archipelago. The Scillies are a graveyard of ships. Inaccurately placed on charts of the time, the jumble of reefs, rocks and islands lay in wait for battered ships and crews at the end of long voyages. They have destroyed thousands of vessels over millennia and were about to claim their most famous victims.

Warning shots were fired to alert the other ships but the lumbering square-riggers were impossible to manoeuvre as wind and current forced them towards the jagged lines of rocks. Shovell's flagship, HMS *Association*, went down with all hands, the *Eagle* hit 'Tearing Ledge' and sank with no survivors. As many as 2,000 men died, four powerful ships were lost; it was one of the worst maritime tragedies in British history.

Yet it led to a great advance in navigational technology. Such was the outcry that Parliament set up a prize for anyone who could accurately determine longitude at sea. As so often, tragedy spurred innovation.

23 October

In an age of omens, this was a bad one. Today in 1091, as the Conqueror's son sat on the English throne, a freak tornado struck his capital and destroyed the wooden London Bridge, along with numerous churches and hundreds of houses. It was a terrifying, bewildering event.

The course of the lower Thames is marshy and flat. The site of the first London bridge was the most downstream point where a permanent crossing was viable. London as a settlement depended upon its bridge and it was only when this was built by the Romans (guarded by a permanent garrison) that a trading community expanded into Britannia's capital.

There have been many London bridges since the Romans spanned the Thames. The first stone bridge was built by the penitent King Henry II, with a chapel to Thomas Becket, his murdered archbishop (and a popular Londoner), in the centre. It was known as the Chapel of St Thomas-on-the-Bridge.

Henry II's bridge was completed, after more than three decades, under King John, his successor but one. It was in part to recoup the costs that building upon it was encouraged and the medieval bridge is known for the more than one hundred shops that lined it (along with the toilets whose users perched above the river). It is known too for the impact its nineteen arches had upon the flow of water, meaning both that the river surface was more likely to freeze during cold winters and that a difference in water level on either side made 'shooting it' perilous. The bridge, it was said, was 'for wise men to pass over, and for fools to pass under'.

By early in the nineteenth century the need for a new bridge was clear, and one was built during the 1830s before Queen Elizabeth II opened the current one, sadly unencumbered with shops and chapels, in 1973.

24 October

It was the end of a war, and the beginning of a new world order. Today in 1648, the Treaty of Westphalia marked the end of one of the most devastating and prolonged conflicts in European history: the Thirty Years' War.

It had begun as a religious conflict within the Habsburg Empire. Protestant subjects of the Catholic emperor had famously thrown his representatives out of a window in Prague. He had responded with repression and Protestants around Europe rallied in support. It coincided with a period of global cooling that ruined harvests, created hardship and ensured there was an audience of desperate, hungry people willing to serve in armies or listen to preachers of violence.

The great powers of Europe, which rarely needed much provocation to try to seize territory and booty from their neighbours, threw themselves into the fighting and the resulting conflict cost the lives of hundreds of thousands, while millions more died from the famine and disease.

The peace process was glacial. There were 194 states represented by 179 plenipotentiaries. For the first six months there was an impasse over protocol, seating plans and orders of precedence. It took three weeks to organise today's signing ceremony alone. The terms of the treaty had ramifications for the future history of the continent arguably as significant as the war that produced it. Private freedom of conscience was guaranteed, the ability of states to set their religion free from interference by the emperor was strengthened, Habsburg power in Germany was curtailed, Spain's period of hegemony was brought to an end and France looked set to replace it. Above all, the treaty represented the birth of the idea of a community of sovereign states governed by a mutually agreed set of rules.

Away from the celebratory banquets, however, large areas of central Europe were blighted for generations. It was a Great War remembered for centuries, until it was eclipsed by first one, then a second, even greater war.

25 October

'It is magnificent,' quipped one veteran witness, 'but it is not war.' Today in 1854, British cavalrymen launched a suicidal and utterly pointless assault against Russian lines during the Crimean War, known as 'The Charge of the Light Brigade'.

During a battle outside the city of Balaklava in the Crimea, a farcical series of misunderstandings, miscommunications and inexperienced commanders hungry for honour sent 676 men and horses of the Light Brigade rampaging towards Russian artillery, which enjoyed a clear field of fire. The astonishingly brave cavalrymen, in neat lines, broke into a trot down a valley. Russian troops on the high ground on either side opened up a withering crossfire. A trooper in the 17th Lancers said later it was as if 'Hell had opened upon us from front and either flank'.

They forged on and broke into a full gallop as they neared the Russian guns at the end of the valley, which responded by blasting them with grapeshot – thousands of small projectiles that scythed down men and horses – at point-blank range. Remarkably they overran the guns, but lacking the ability to disable or drag them off, they had no choice but to run the gauntlet of the valley again, back to their start point. The Light Brigade suffered 40 per cent casualties and 475 horses were lost.

Blame for the misunderstanding leading to the slaughter has remained controversial as the original order was vague and the officer who delivered it died in the first minute of the assault. The event was subsequently immortalised by poet Alfred Lord Tennyson in 'The Charge of the Light Brigade'. The British, who love nothing better than spectacular, heroic, amateurish failure, instantly adopted it as one of their most beloved national poems.

26 October

There has been a Lionheart, a Bloody, a Conqueror and an Unready (or more accurately Poorly Advised). But there has only been one king in English history who is simply 'the Great'. Today in 899, Alfred the Great of Wessex, first King of the Anglo-Saxons, breathed his last in his most important city, Winchester.

Posterity has been particularly kind to Alfred; it was only in the sixteenth century that he was referred to as 'the Great' when his interest in seapower, promotion of English and defiance towards continental foes put him very much in vogue. But there is no question that he earned his epithet. Alfred saved Wessex, the last surviving Anglo-Saxon kingdom, from occupation by the Vikings.

In 878 a surprise assault sent Alfred fleeing into the marshes at Altheney in Somerset. Anglo-Saxon England was reduced to a few square miles of swamp, a refugee king and a handful of supporters. From this slenderest of foundations, Alfred rebuilt an army, forged weapons, boosted morale with guerrilla strikes against the Vikings and counter-attacked.

By May he had gathered an army together and struck boldly. He found a Viking force in Wiltshire and routed them at the decisive Battle of Ethandun. Generous in victory, he persuaded their leader, Guthrum, to be baptised, at which ceremony Alfred himself stood as Guthrum's godfather. He then agreed a peace treaty with the Vikings: they could keep East Anglia but must withdraw from Alfred's beloved Wessex.

The case for 'Great' is built on much more than this one brilliant campaign. Seeing the value of education to statesmen and soldiers, he founded a school. He built fortified towns, boosted tax revenue, launched a fleet of ships and professionalised his army. He was a devout Christian under whom the Church flourished, and a lover of books and law. Alfred provided his successors with a strong foundation to move north and east into Viking-held land. He, his son and grandsons not only survived the Viking onslaught but eventually brought the whole of England, for the first time, under one Anglo-Saxon king.

27 October

It is a legend. But in war and statecraft, legends matter. Today in 312 Constantine saw a cross of light in the sky, above the sun, with the words in Greek 'In this sign, conquer'. That night in a dream, Constantine was visited by Christ who told him to use the sign of the cross against his enemies. The next day Constantine ordered his men to carve a cross on their shields. He duly won an astounding victory at the Battle of Milvian Bridge, killing his enemy Maxentius.

Days later Constantine staged a carefully managed triumphal entry into Rome. Maxentius's body was decapitated, and his head was paraded through the streets. Constantine attributed his victory to God. His triumphal arch bore an inscription attributing his success to 'divine instigation'.

Although early accounts differ regarding the authenticity of Constantine's vision, the version that endured was the one he was careful to foster. He went on to practise Christianity and encourage it within the Roman Empire, while allowing all cults and religions to exist. Previous emperors had ruthlessly persecuted Christians, and Constantine himself had sampled other religions before settling on the Christian God. By the end of his reign Constantine considered himself to be the thirteenth Apostle of Christ. He saw to it that his new capital, Constantinople, was protected by Christian relics.

On his death Christianity became the official religion of the Roman Empire. What had been an obscure cult was now adopted by the dominant power in Europe, North Africa and the Near East. It was a decisive milestone in its journey to becoming the world's most adhered to religion, and Constantine the Great has understandably been revered, some would say worshipped, as a saint ever since.

28 October

'Universally read from the cabinet council to the nursery,' remarked Alexander Pope about the ageless satire *Gulliver's Travels*, which was first published on this day in 1726. It came simply as a travelogue penned by 'Lemuel Gulliver, First a Surgeon, and then a Captain of Several Ships'. Few, though, were taken in. The tales were too far-fetched for that, and it was instantly known by its abbreviated, familiar title.

From Ireland, Swift was familiar with the bemused and patronising tone English travellers adopted when faced with difference. At times he satirised both specific individuals and phenomena, like English imperialism in Ireland.

The book oscillates between low comedy and profound satire; his targets were instantly recognisable to his audience. Gulliver travels to different realms – among them Lilliput, Brobdingnag, Balnibarbi and the land of the Houyhnhnms – each with distinct peculiarities in terms of the inhabitants' physical size or appearance and their habits. All of which lampooned an aspect of contemporary life in the early eighteenth century.

In his first (and most famous) visit to Lilliput, for instance, Gulliver is surprised by islanders only six inches tall who are spiteful and worry over seemingly trivial questions, such as which end of an egg to break. In Brobdingnag it is he who is tiny, kept in a 'travelling box' and exhibited. In Balnibarbi 'scientists' attempt ludicrous endeavours, like the extraction of sunbeams from cucumbers, while elsewhere the Houyhnhnms are wise, talking horses who care for a race of savage, humanoid Yahoos.

The book put satire at the heart of British political and cultural life. Immediately after publication one widely read magazine started referring to parliamentary proceedings as 'Debates in the Senate of Lilliput'. It fostered a uniquely British, vicious tradition of satire that shocked visitors from more deferential cultures from nineteenth-century Russians to twentieth-century Americans who were appalled at the depiction of an ailing President Reagan on *Spitting Image*. Swift armed those denied a decision with derision.

29 October

It was the original black day. 'Black Tuesday', 29 October 1929: the day Wall Street crashed. A financial disaster so memorable it gave rise to a host of similar sombre-hued days. At the time, it followed 'Black Thursday' (24 October), then 'Black Monday' (28 October), though as it transpired it is Tuesday that seems the blackest. Before that there had been a long period of uncertainty, the hope being (as with previous events, like the 'Panic of 1907') that it would pass.

It didn't. Some 16 million shares were traded on the Tuesday, a volume not surpassed for almost four decades. Within a couple of days the market had lost more than $30 billion. After a brief rally, a long and steady slide resulted, until by the summer of 1932 prices stood at their lowest point in the twentieth century.

After the misery of the First World War, the 1920s are remembered as a time of expansion, optimism, excess and debt – as 'the Roaring Twenties'. Prices on the stock market had risen solidly for nine years, prompting one infamous assessment that they had reached 'a permanently high plateau'. Few chose to believe the gloomier (though wiser) prediction that a 'crash was coming'.

When it did, it marked the beginning, famously, of the 'Great Depression' – more than a decade of economic turmoil – which saw the rise of extremist governments followed by the descent into the Second World War. It was, it could be safely said, a bad day. With hindsight it all seems grimly inevitable, as of course, with hindsight, such crashes generally do.

'We are reaping,' declared one bank president, 'the natural fruit of the orgy of speculation in which millions of people have indulged.'

30 October

Today in 1961 the USSR tested on its northern, Arctic archipelago of Novaya Zemlya what in the West was nicknamed 'Tsar Bomba' (codenames also include Vanya or Big Ivan): the largest nuclear weapon ever detonated. The blast was more than 1,500 times the combined force of the bombs that destroyed both Hiroshima and Nagasaki. It also, astonishingly, contained more than ten times the energy of *all* the conventional explosives used in the Second World War.

All this, and it was significantly less powerful than it might have been. Measures were taken to reduce its power given that resulting 'fallout' would largely have come down upon Soviet, populated territory, and given the difficulty a pilot who dropped the bomb would face in escaping the resulting explosion. As it was, the chances of the 'release team' surviving were rated at only 50 per cent.

Both the plane itself, and an accompanying observer aircraft, were painted a reflective white in order to minimise heat damage. They were able to fly around 28 miles (45 kilometres) from where the vast bomb was dropped – but even so the plane dropped a kilometre in the air as a result of the shock wave.

The mushroom cloud that resulted from the blast, meanwhile, reached 64 kilometres into the air: more than seven times the altitude of Mount Everest. The intense heat would have caused third-degree burns a hundred kilometres from 'ground zero'. Sensors were still detecting the shock waves after the latter had travelled around the globe three times.

Nothing illustrates better the threat of nuclear Armageddon that faced the world during the latter half of the twentieth century. While the United States denied that it too had broken a voluntary suspension of nuclear tests, in fact it had conducted five tests that same month.

31 October

It was an eccentric way to start a revolution. Today in 1517, history's turbulent priest Martin Luther is said to have nailed his Ninety-five Theses to a church door in Wittenberg, a moment that lit the touchpaper for the Protestant Reformation. The celebrated incident may not even have occurred, but he was certainly a protester and his work sparked an upheaval in ideas.

The document contained a list of ninety-five points that he wanted to raise with the Church about its practices, corruption, ritual, and particularly about the granting of indulgences, which allowed people to avoid purgatory in the next life for a donation in this one. His theses instantly went viral, with the newly invented printing presses replicating and disseminating the news on a vast scale. Previous protesters the Church could refute, silence or ignore, but Luther's brilliance allied to new technology meant that this time they had a problem.

The story goes that Luther was inspired to publish his criticisms while on the toilet; severe constipation had put him in a bad mood with, well, everything probably, but certainly the Church as it was then constituted. Luther admitted ideas came to him while 'in cloaca' or 'in the sewer'. In 2004, archaeologists in Wittenberg discovered Luther's toilet. Made from stone blocks, the toilet had a thirty centimetre in diameter seat above a cesspit.

One of the most influential figures of Western history, Martin Luther developed the ideas he had begun to explore in his Theses. He came to see that the Bible alone should be the wellspring of religious authority, and salvation came through an individual's relationship with God. Martin Luther's Wittenberg home has become a popular destination for pilgrims; however, those seeking divine inspiration by sitting on the toilet, on display at the museum, have to be prevented from doing so.

NOVEMBER

1 November

'First we heard a rumble', remembered one witness, 'like the noise of a carriage, it became louder and louder, until it was as loud as the loudest noise of a gun.' At 9.40 a.m. on Saturday 1 November 1755 the city of Lisbon was destroyed by an earthquake, followed by a tsunami and firestorm. It was an unimaginable catastrophe that seized the imagination of the whole of Europe.

The ground was torn apart by deep fissures in the middle of the city. To escape the crumbling buildings, survivors ran to the quaysides where they watched as the sea receded into the distance. Shipwrecks were uncovered and lost cargo retrieved. Forty minutes later anyone foolish enough to have gone mudlarking was swept up in a tsunami that flooded the heart of the city. Two more walls of water followed the first.

Lastly came the fire. Toppled candles and lamps simultaneously set countless buildings ablaze. Those flames that survived the tsunamis quickly spread to engulf the wreckage it left. Whole streets were now piles of driftwood and perfect fuel for the fire.

The procession of catastrophes took the lives of up to 100,000 people. Portugal's capital was destroyed, many of its ports badly damaged. It pushed the country deeper into political crisis and hastened its eclipse as an imperial power. But this was also the first natural disaster of this scale to hit Europe since the dawn of the scientific revolution. The quake had a profound effect on the thinking of Enlightenment philosophers. Its nature and impact was studied scientifically, divine causation dismissed (many noted that the disaster had destroyed nearly all the churches but left the brothels, in a different part of town, intact), and lessons were learned. The earthquake was enormously destructive, yet at the same time a foundational moment for modern geology and seismology.

2 November

For centuries the vast Ottoman Empire had controlled the Middle East from the eastern Mediterranean to the Persian Gulf. It had suited British governments that this archaic, crumbling, harmless empire ruled this vital crossroads of Eurasia; better the Ottomans than the Russians or French, but by 1917 British goodwill had run out. Ottoman Turkey had foolishly chosen to back Germany in the First World War, and it had then inflicted humiliating defeats on British expeditionary forces. The new prime minister, David Lloyd George, wanted to carve up the empire and, naturally, take the best parts for Britain.

Also Britain needed allies. The war was at a stalemate. Lloyd George believed the myths about a powerful, international Jewish lobby. So today in 1917 his Foreign Secretary, Arthur James Balfour, signed his famous declaration that sought to secure Jewish support for the war effort and use the Jews to establish British control in the Middle East. On 2 November the British government committed themselves to supporting a 'national home for the Jewish people' in Palestine.

The Zionist movement had been lobbying for the right of Jews, widely persecuted around the world, to move to their ancestral home in and around Jerusalem. The Balfour Declaration committed the world's most powerful empire to achieving that aim. The problem of there being an existing indigenous Arab population was acknowledged. Balfour wrote that 'nothing shall be done which may prejudice the civil and religious rights of existing non-Jewish communities'. Even so, the seeds of a century of conflict were sown, by promising a homeland to one people, in a land already occupied by another.

3 November

Today, on 3 November in 1957, a stray dog from the Moscow streets was aboard the *Sputnik 2* rocket when it was launched. One of three chosen and trained for the mission, she became known as Laika: the first animal to orbit the Earth. Prior to closing the capsule, technicians kissed her farewell, knowing that she would not survive the flight.

While both the United States and the USSR had sent animals on suborbital flights, the impact of space flight upon a living creature was unknown. Many felt it would be impossible to survive the journey, given the physical stresses of the launch and the resultant low-gravity environment, making it essential that a non-human tried it first. Nobody, moreover, had yet designed a craft capable of returning to the Earth from orbit. Preparations for the mission were rushed, after Soviet leader Nikita Khrushchev had suddenly decreed that the launch date should coincide with the 40th anniversary of the Russian Revolution.

Laika's training – a hellish and bewildering ordeal for an animal – involved confinement in progressively smaller cages for almost three weeks at a time, placement in centrifuges to simulate the G-forces of the launch, and in machines replicating the noises of a spacecraft. She was inured to eating a highly nutritious (but scarcely appetising) gel. Her heart rate doubled and her blood pressure increased.

Sputnik 2 was fitted with a 'life-support' system, intended to maintain a constant supply of air and food, and a moderate temperature: little above 15 °C. Laika was fitted with a harness. Chains kept her standing, sitting or lying down. Her breathing, blood pressure and pulse were monitored.

Within hours of the launch, it subsequently emerged, she died from overheating due to a malfunction in the rocket, rather than – as was reported – when the oxygen ran out on day six. Her ordeal was less prolonged than it might have been. As predicted, Laika's remains disintegrated, along with her whole spacecraft, during re-entry to the Earth's atmosphere, on 14 April 1958.

4 November

It was not a riot, it was an uprising. Today in 1839 the last armed rebellion against the government took place on British soil as industrial workers, many brandishing home-made weapons, poured into Newport in Monmouthshire.

By the mid-nineteenth century Wales was becoming the world's first nation in which more people were employed in industry than agriculture. When the economy slowed, as it did in the late 1830s, there was a large, concentrated community of workers who were receptive to radical new solutions.

Chartism was a reform movement with huge support across Britain. Its adherents wanted universal suffrage, a secret ballot and an abolition of a property qualification for MPs. South Wales was seething with unrest, some avowed Chartists, others galvanised by economic distress. There were rumours of unrest following the arrest of Chartist leader, Henry Vincent, and his imprisonment for conspiracy in Newport in August.

Before dawn on 4 November three columns of rebels headed into Newport. The mayor had been tipped off the day before and he swore in 500 special constables and gathered 100 soldiers. At 9.30 a.m. around 3,000 rebels arrived in Westgate Square where they believed Vincent was being held. For thirty minutes a battle raged in and around the Westgate Hotel. Although heavily outnumbered, the soldiers had far more firepower and the rebels eventually broke, leaving perhaps 20 dead and 50 wounded on the battlefield.

Any sense that this was just a normal riot is belied by the fact that the government tried the rebel leaders for high treason. Found guilty, they were sentenced to hanging, drawing and quartering, the last such sentences ever handed down in England and Wales. The Home Secretary commuted their sentences to transportation to Australia.

There is some suggestion that if Newport had succeeded, uprisings would follow all over the country. The mayor of Newport was feted by the propertied classes and was knighted by Queen Victoria. He had crushed Britain's last rebellion.

5 November

The letter was anonymous, but it was unambiguous. 'I would advise you as you tender your life to devise some excuse to shift your attendance at this parliament', the mysterious author beseeched, for 'they shall receive a terrible blow this parliament'. As soon as Baron Monteagle received this mysterious warning he showed it to the Secretary of State, who in turn took it to the king. James I ordered a thorough search of the Palace of Westminster and, in the early hours of this morning in 1605, thirty-six barrels of gunpowder were found. It was enough to obliterate the ruling class of England when it gathered for the opening of Parliament later that day. Standing over the barrels was a man carrying a lantern, dressed in a cloak and hat, his pockets stuffed with slow match. His name was Guy Fawkes.

The Gunpowder Plot was masterminded by Robert Catesby, a tall, athletic, handsome Catholic from an ancient family who dreamed of returning the English people to the Roman Church. His plan was to kill king, lords, bishops and commoners at the opening of Parliament, kidnap James's daughter Princess Elizabeth and install her on the throne as a puppet. He had recruited a small group, including Fawkes, an English-born Catholic who had fought for the Spanish against the Protestant Dutch rebels.

The conspirators easily found an empty, unused undercroft beneath the House of Lords, in the labyrinthine cellars of the Palace of Westminster. Barrels of gunpowder were smuggled in and covered with a layer of firewood and coal. It was here that Fawkes was found and arrested. Two days later James personally authorised torture. After twenty-four hours at the hands of the torturers of the Tower, Fawkes confessed and gave the names of the fellow conspirators. They were captured after a shoot-out at Holbeche House in Staffordshire.

It was one of history's most audacious terrorist plots, and the anniversary became an annual jingoistic celebration of Protestantism and English exceptionalism, the start of a tradition of bonfires, fireworks and revelry that endures to this day.

6 November

There was a child on the throne. Embers of a revolt still smouldered; warlords had tasted freedom and had no wish to bow their heads distant rulers. The government needed friends. Today in 1217 the guardians of the realm for the ten-year-old king Henry III, gathered in St Paul's Cathedral, issued a document that ought to sit alongside Magna Carta as a foundational document of British government: the Forest Charter.

It is largely forgotten now, perhaps because it addresses the concerns of the common man, not the nobility. It represents one of the first times in British history that legal rights for all freemen were carefully articulated.

The Forest was nothing to do with trees. It was land designated for use by the crown, in which the king insisted on exclusive enjoyment of its resources. The deer and the grazing, for example, belonged to the monarch alone. Grasping Plantagenet kings had expanded it to include vast swathes of land, until by 1217 about a third of southern England was Forest. Commoners were unable to graze, fish, hunt, collect fuel or grow the crops they needed to survive.

The Charter reversed the land grab of previous monarchs, and ended barbaric punishments for trespass and other offences. It defined the ways in which common people were able to exploit common land for their survival. Courts were set up to enforce these new laws. The Forest Charter proved to be the most durable foundation of the nation's constitution. It was only superseded in 1971, and at least two of the special courts, in the New Forest and the Forest of Dean, still dispense justice to this day.

7 November

The public could read. There was a hunger for printed news. If the government did not publish their side of the story, bitter experience showed that fake news would proliferate, and threaten the very institutions of government. That is why today in 1665, the *Gazette* was first published, an official government bulletin that has endured for 350 years.

The mid-seventeenth century saw an explosion of newspapers, alongside political instability, civil wars, and the execution of a king. They were not unrelated. Back in 1639 there had been a maximum of five newspapers or periodicals published in England; by 1648, following the outbreak of war and the disappearance of censorship, there were seventy. Paid 'reporters' appeared for the first time. They filled pages with news, rumour, gossip and salacious crime reporting. Although the real news was bad enough for the Stuart monarchy, the avalanche of fake news weakened it and drove opponents to extremes.

King Charles II attempted to reimpose censorship but England's publishing culture was irrepressibly established. So the government published the *Gazette* to make its case in the new arena of print. Issue 'Numb 1' came, like papers still do today, with a slogan on its masthead: 'Printed by Authority'. It contained news of a new bishop of Oxford, appointments of high sheriffs, and intelligence from France.

Over the centuries it would report military victories and setbacks, and officers receiving praise or promotion would be 'gazetted'. It continued to be the official record of government business, and remains so to this day, the world's longest-running newspaper.

8 November

The British public were gripped by the trial and execution of Ruth Ellis, who was found guilty of shooting and killing her boyfriend in 1955. The hanging of this vulnerable, abused woman for a crime of passion provoked a debate that, a decade later, led to the Murder (Abolition of Death Penalty) Act, which was granted royal assent today in 1965. It seems, particularly with hindsight, a profoundly important date in British history.

At the time, of course, a few offences other than murder in principle retained the death penalty – high treason, for instance, or arson in a royal dockyard – but these never required that it be used. It was also provisional: the act contained a 'sunset clause', which made it become inactive unless it was confirmed by Parliament before the summer of 1970. But it was.

The Human Rights Act of 1998 – by which the fundamental provisions of the European Convention on Human Rights were enacted in UK law – saw the death penalty finally abolished in the UK for all offences, though no execution had actually taken place since 1964, by hanging, for murder.

As it stands therefore (and one can hope that it remains this way) the final executions in the UK took place on 13 August 1964: those of Peter Allen, in Liverpool, and Gwynne Evans, in Manchester – both for the murder of John West. The trial of Moors murderers Myra Hindley and Ian Brady, one case that prompted widespread though ineffective calls for the punishment's reintroduction, took place the year after the act.

By this date in 1965 there were eleven European countries that had abolished the peacetime death penalty. As of the middle of 2018 only one remains: Belarus, although Russia's current moratorium is by definition not permanent.

9 November

The North American Air Defense Command was the most sophisticated early warning and air defence operation in history. Its staff and equipment were based under 600 metres of granite hollowed out of Cheyenne Mountain in Colorado. A series of three-storey structures could survive a nuclear attack on its doorstep, protected by massive blast doors, and supported by giant springs that cancelled out shock waves passing through the rock around it.

From this facility, satellites were positioned, nuclear weapons controlled, space objects monitored, and enemy intelligence analysed. It was a staggeringly sophisticated operation designed to allow the United States to survive a nuclear assault during the Cold War. Resilience to a nuclear strike and the ability to launch retaliation was, so the thinking went, what prevented either side from using the weapons. Any nuclear attack would mean Mutually Assured Destruction, thanks to facilities like Cheyenne Mountain. So it was disturbing that a basic error made there today in 1979 almost caused exactly that.

The date 9 November 1979 was not during a time of particularly raised Cold War tension. A technician carrying out some maintenance probably did not realise he was about to endanger the continued existence of the human race. He loaded a test tape into a computer but forgot to switch the system to 'test'. This caused warnings that over a thousand Soviet nuclear missiles were in the air and the president had to make a decision on retaliation in less than seven minutes.

Thankfully it took around six minutes to confirm that it was a false alarm. It was one of multiple occasions when faulty wiring, defective chips, or human error almost tipped the world into nuclear war. We were lucky to survive.

10 November

A man was seated on a mat in his small mud hut in the small town of Ujiji, on the shores of Lake Tanganyika in Africa, when he was lured outside by an unusual commotion. Crowds of people had gathered around a new white visitor, who was carrying an assortment of goods including the American flag. The man pushed through the crowd and walked towards the visitor 'with a firm and heavy tread'. He was tall, tanned, covered in dust but had a well-polished hat. The visitor made his way forward and addressed the man: 'Dr Livingstone, I presume?' On this day in 1871, the explorer Henry Morton Stanley found the missing explorer Dr David Livingstone, the only white man for miles, pale, confused and evidently unwell, after he had vanished for five years, lost in Africa. Two years before in 1869 the *New York Herald* had sent Henry Morton Stanley to find Livingstone

Since the mid century the missionary explorer Dr David Livingstone had sought routes to spread Christianity into the heart of Africa. During his exploration, he pushed east along the Zambezi river, part of a fleet of exploring canoes, led by guides from the Makololo tribe. Near where the modern-day border has been drawn between Zimbabwe and Zambia, Livingstone discovered an astonishing waterfall, which he renamed in honour of the queen, the Victoria Falls. The furthest that Livingstone reached was north of Lake Tanganyika before he lost contact with the outside world.

As he waited for a response from Livingstone, Stanley observed that the man was fragile. Then Livingstone suddenly replied, 'Yes', and then, 'I feel thankful that I am here to welcome you.'

11 November

It was still dark when the men met to sign the Armistice. There were British admirals, two senior French generals, and a German delegation led by a politician who would soon pay with his life for what he was about to do. By 5.20 a.m., today in 1918, they had all signed it. The Germans submitted to the harsh terms of the Armistice. They were in no position to negotiate; their government had collapsed, their nation teetered on the brink of violent revolution.

Within minutes news of the ceasefire was telegraphed around the world. But it would not come into effect for another six hours, at 11 a.m. In a pointless epilogue to one of the bloodiest wars in history around 11,000 men would be killed or wounded that day, a higher casualty rate than D-Day. Generals even continued to order attacks.

The last British soldier to be killed was Private George Edwin Ellison. At 9.30 a.m. he was pushing into the outskirts of the Belgian town of Mons. A shot rang out and he fell, having survived the entire war. He was so close to returning to Leeds to be reunited his wife, Hannah, and their four-year-old son, James. With bitter symmetry this was the same town where the first British casualties of the Western Front had fallen four years before. In the meantime around 1 million British and Commonwealth troops had died, and now the army was back at Mons.

At 10.58 a.m. a Canadian, Lawrence Price, was killed. Then, at 10.59, with a minute to go before the guns fell silent, US soldier Henry Gunther made a suicidal charge against astonished German troops. They reluctantly shot him, the last soldier to be killed in action in the First World War.

12 November

Another monarch, another religious settlement. Today in 1555 Parliament passed the Second Statute of Repeal, a sweeping law that abolished all religious legislation passed in the previous twenty-five years, since Henry VIII had begun dismantling the Catholic Church in England. Henry's zealous daughter Mary and her husband, King Philip of Spain, now also King of England *jure uxoris* 'by right of his wife', regarded this as the most important task of their reign.

Parliament voted for the bill once the members had received assurances that they would be allowed to keep hold of the former monastic lands that so many of them had bought in late King Henry's fire sale of church assets.

After Henry VIII repudiated her mother, Catherine of Aragon, Mary was declared illegitimate and grew up in the shadows of the Tudor court. When her father died, she opposed her brother Edward's anti-Catholic regime, claiming she would rather lay her head on the block than forsake her faith. Then Edward died, and after Mary's coronation it became clear that England would be thrust into further religious turmoil.

Catholicism was restored on this day and Mary actively began to persecute Protestants. She revived former heresy laws and started to burn Protestants at the stake, beginning with Thomas Cranmer, the Archbishop of Canterbury. During her reign, almost three hundred Protestants were declared heretics and burned to death. Many more died in prison and her persecution led to an exodus of Protestant refugees fleeing to the continent. The Catholic restoration under Mary lasted only as long as she did; her heir was her Protestant half-sister Elizabeth who, in turn, introduced her own settlement, also enforced by torture and execution. However, it was Elizabeth's model that endured, and so, somewhat unfairly given the brutal proclivities of all her royal relatives, Mary alone is remembered as 'Bloody'.

13 November

The Vikings were back. After decades of relative tranquillity, the longships were prowling the coasts of England. In the summer of 991 a sizeable force landed at Northey Island in Essex where they defeated Byrhtnoth, ealdorman of Essex, at the Battle of Maldon. The young English king, Æthelred, only just established on the throne after a bloody and intrigue-filled adolescence, agreed to buy them off. They took the money and, unsurprisingly, returned the following year.

By 1001 a large Danish force cruised the south coast pillaging at will, based on the Isle of Wight. A desperate Æthelred authorised a record payment of Danegeld or 'Dane-payment' the following spring. He sought a lasting solution and today in 1002 he unleashed the closest Britain has come to genocide in recorded history. On the feast day of St Brice, according to the *Anglo-Saxon Chronicle*, he 'ordered slain all the Danish men who were in England'.

It is impossible to know just how effective the pogrom was. The large Danish populations in eastern England were probably too strong to be attacked, but in frontier towns or ports where populations had intermingled, the king's orders appear to have been carried out. In Oxford a royal charter from 1004 says that the town's Danes 'striving to escape death' entered St Frideswide's Church 'having broken by force the doors and bolts, and resolved to make refuge and defence for themselves therein'. Then, 'when all the people in pursuit strove, forced by necessity, to drive them out, and could not, they set fire to the . . . church'.

It was a monstrous crime, and worse, a mistake. The massacre had no effect on the Danish raiders, other than enrage them. It is possible that one of the victims was Gunhilde, sister of Danish King Sweyn I. Perhaps in revenge for her murder, Sweyn would later invade England, and send Æthelred scurrying into exile. His attempt to destroy the Danish threat had only emboldened it.

14 November

On this day, in 1666, an experiment took place at Gresham College, an institute of learning in Holborn, London. It was a blood transfusion between two dogs; one of the first successful transfusions that took place in the seventeenth century. This was recorded by an onlooker, from the corner of the room, as he watched medical history made. His name was Samuel Pepys.

Pepys was a naval administrator, MP and Londoner, who kept a detailed diary of life and society. He began his diary on 1 January 1660, after purchasing a fat notebook from a stationer's in Cornhill. He filled its pages with colourful descriptions of everyday life, noting key events of the time, such as the Great Plague in 1665, where he gave a chilling account of the reality of death in the city: 'I saw a dead corpse in a coffin lie in the close unburied – and a watch is constantly kept there, night and day, to keep the people in.' In 1666, during the Great Fire of London, Pepys describes chaos, 'everybody endeavouring to remove their goods, and flinging into the river'. Pepys took a boat to watch the blaze unfurl before him; he was particularly detailed, even expressing concern about the pigeons, who 'hovered about the windows and balconys till they were, some of them burned'.

Pepys's diary also explores colloquial aspects of everyday life, creating a vivid portrait of a man of his time, and his personal exploits; one in particular with his wife's companion, Miss Willet. Pepys describes being in an uncompromising position with Miss Willet, when his wife burst into the room: 'She did find me embracing the girl con [with] my hand sub [under] su [her] coats; and indeed I was with my main [hand] in her cunny'.

Pepys's diary combines the events of his time with the more mundane aspects of the everyday. The diary ends in 1669, possibly after his eyesight began to fail, and Pepys died four years later. His diary is a remarkable document allowing us insights into his life and times. It is a timeless masterpiece.

15 November

On this day in 1492 Christopher Columbus made the first reference by a European to the plant that we know as tobacco, and which has had such a momentous, and damaging, impact upon the modern world. Columbus was keen to explore the island that we know as Cuba, so he sent men to investigate it.

When they came back they reported, with appropriate bemusement, seeing men with burning sticks clamped in their mouths. All over the Americas, during the decades afterwards, European explorers reported the Indian habit of 'drinking' tobacco (or of chewing it) in the belief that this would protect them from various diseases. One told in amazement of the custom of stuffing leaves into a pipe, lighting them, then sucking 'so long that they fill their bodies with smoke until it comes out of their mouth and nostrils as from a chimney'. 'Drinking' the smoke, they were told, kept the Indians warm and in good health. European doctors worried – needlessly, it has turned out – that the habit would put them out of business.

Early reactions were affected by the two types of tobacco plant, one of which – 'tall tobacco' – burned with a milder and more pleasing smoke. This, initially, grew commonly in South America but not further north. Only later was it transplanted to Virginia, for instance, where it was found to flourish, and the supply of this tobacco began the craze for the substance.

By 1614, in London, there were reputed to be around 7,000 shops selling tobacco. Thousands of tons were imported, and it was noted early on that the habit was hard to stop. King James I famously disliked it, but hostile voices were few – and the studies that showed it to be harmful rather than beneficial had to wait for over three centuries to be recognised.

16 November

The king was dead. For once this did not provoke a fight. When Henry III died today in 1272 in Westminster, for the first time ever the crown passed automatically to his oldest son, who became Edward I as his father breathed his last breath. This change in the laws of succession meant that on this occasion there was no violent struggle for the crown. It made a pleasant change.

Since the accession of Edward the Confessor in 1042 there had been ten English kings, and plenty of claimants. Remarkably every single one of those ten monarchs had used violence to enforce their right to wear the crown. Harold and William had clashed at Hastings. William II and Henry I had both fought their brother, Robert, and his supporters. Stephen and Matilda fought a dreadful civil war, known as 'The Anarchy'. Henry II had invaded England to press his claim, his son Richard took on his father, while John fought his nephew, captured him and then almost certainly had him murdered. Henry III had clung to the throne in the face of an invading French army and baronial revolt that had all but deposed his father. Kingship in the medieval world tended to be won and maintained on the field of battle.

This smooth transition must have been a welcome relief to the people of England, for whom the death of a monarch was always a time of acute danger. So confident was Edward that even though he was abroad, travelling home from, you guessed it, fighting – he had been on a Crusade in the Holy Land – he took his time and did not arrive in England until August 1274.

It was not the dawn of a new era. Edward was never far from a battlefield. His son was toppled by an invasion (led by his wife) and descendants would fight the internecine Wars of the Roses, which would lead to the obliteration of the Plantagenet royal line.

17 November

Today in 1603 – in the old capital of Winchester – one of the most famous men in Elizabethan England, the courtier, explorer, soldier, spy, and writer (of prose and of poetry), Sir Walter Raleigh, was put on trial for treason. He remained dignified throughout the hearing, while interrogators lost their temper, turning him almost overnight into a popular hero. 'Never,' wrote one contemporary, 'was a man so hated and so popular in so short a time.'

Critical had been the death early that spring of Queen Elizabeth – her demise probably accelerated by her white, mercury-based make-up. As her death approached, secret letters had been sent to her heir, King James of Scotland, portraying him, probably unfairly, as an opponent to James's succession.

'On my soul,' James is reputed to have said when Raleigh welcomed the new king in London, 'I have heard rawly of thee': a pun likely to indicate the pronunciation of his name. Raleigh attended Elizabeth's funeral, but was arrested soon after, implicated in murky plots aimed at encouraging a Spanish invasion. His arrest and imprisonment led him to make a (probably theatrical) suicide attempt using a table knife late in July.

Though pardoned by the king, he was not released and spent years in comfortable imprisonment – with access to a garden, visited by his beloved wife and children – though incarceration scarcely suited him. No sooner was he released, in 1616, than he embarked upon another voyage in search of gold in El Dorado: a final, but doomed, gamble.

Having failed in his mission he returned to England. He anticipated the outcome: reimprisonment in the Tower, this time without reprieve. 'My brains are broken', he wrote to his wife. Admiring the sharpness of the executioner's axe – and retaining his wit and self-possession until the end – he commended what he called a 'physician for all diseases'.

18 November

The general had been born a slave. Jean-Jacques Dessalines worked in the sugar plantations of Saint-Domingue as a child, but today in 1803 he led an attack on his colonial masters which brought a decisive end not only to slavery on the island but to the colony itself. Henceforth it would be the free Republic of Haiti. It was the only time that a European colony was overthrown and replaced by its enslaved people.

Dessalines might well have shared the brutal fate of his forebears in the disease-ridden and tyrannical plantations, but revolution in France had turned the world upside down and he was freed by a decree from the revolutionary government in Paris in 1794. The Caribbean was one of the bloodiest theatres of the Revolutionary and Napoleonic Wars and Dessalines fought for and against nearly every side as alliances were made and broken and all sides wanted the hugely valuable and vulnerable 'sugar islands' of the West Indies.

He fought successfully to secure the revolution but the coup of Napoleon Bonaparte forced him back into the hills. Napoleon's wife was of planter heritage; partly at her persuasion he sent an expeditionary force to reintroduce slavery. The conflict was unimaginably brutal. Both sides carried out atrocities as the war became one of racial annihilation.

The French troops were decimated by yellow fever and in November 1803 were besieged in Vertières on the north coast. In the early hours of the 18th a ferocious frontal assault shattered the will of the French to go on. The next morning the French surrendered and were given ten days to leave the island for good. Dessalines declared the Haitian Republic two months later. Europe's dominant military power had been defeated by a force of black former slaves.

19 November

It was on this day in 1850 that Alfred Lord Tennyson became Poet Laureate, succeeding William Wordsworth. It is hard to imagine another occasion when two such eminent poets consecutively occupied this honoured post, even if it scarcely drew from either poet the work for which they are remembered. Certainly it was felt upon Tennyson's death that nobody of suitable stature existed to succeed him.

Wordsworth had been Poet Laureate since 1843, having initially refused the honour on account of his age, until the prime minister reassured him that he would have nothing to do. It was as well. Midway through his tenure, his daughter Dora died, Wordsworth became deeply depressed, and abandoned composition entirely. He became, upon his own death three years later, the only Poet Laureate to write *no* official verses.

A then eminent poet called Samuel Rogers – little remembered – was asked to take the role, but also refused, understandably, on account of his age: he was already in his late eighties. So instead the post was given to a much younger man by the name of Tennyson, who held it – the longest tenure before or since – until his own death in 1892. The origins of the post are vague. Long ago, kings and courts employed bards and poets to entertain and to memorialise.

The first official Poet Laureate seems to have been John Dryden. Late in the eighteenth century Edward Gibbon mocked what he called a 'ridiculous custom'. The traditional salary involved not salt, but alcoholic liquor – Dryden's payment involved a butt of Canary wine in addition to a £300 pension. Tennyson is said to have drawn £72 per year and a further £27 'in lieu of the butt of sack'.

The post of Poet Laureate remains, what it has always been, more recognition for a poet's past work than a facility to engender great new work.

20 November

Today, in 1820, a whaling ship named *Essex* was attacked by a huge sperm whale. The dreadful story of some of the crew's survival was told later to Herman Melville by its erstwhile captain, George Pollard. Melville was gripped and it inspired him to write his famous novel, *Moby Dick*. Melville mentioned later how, to the islanders where Pollard lived, off the coast of Massachusetts, he was a nobody. 'To me', he said, he was 'the most impressive man . . . that I ever encountered'.

Survivors of *Essex* told how, far from land in the southern Pacific Ocean, the ship had been attacked by an enormous whale that had flung surf in all directions, thrashed violently, and rammed the ship 'with tenfold fury and vengeance in his aspect'. While Pollard was not on *Essex* at the time, his boat was the first to return and the captain, too dumbstruck by the sight of the stricken, damaged ship, was initially unable 'to utter a single syllable'.

In the wake of the sinking of *Essex*, her crew had divided themselves between her smaller boats, spending more than ninety days without food and under a blazing sun, until they were forced, upon a fishless sea, into the horrifying ordeal of drawing lots to see which of them would be killed and eaten by his companions. One of the first to suffer this fate was Pollard's own cousin, who refused to complain and who admitted that no one would have liked it better. 'I can tell you no more,' Pollard recounted, 'my head is on fire at the recollection. I hardly know what I say.'

Melville's own tragedy was that he never knew how successful his book would become. Only a few thousand copies were sold during his lifetime and it was out of print when he died in 1891.

2 1 November

This day in 1920 was a Sunday. In Ireland it quickly became known as 'Bloody Sunday' – a date long (and still) remembered as fundamental in the Irish struggle for independence from Britain.

First eleven Brits suspected of being spies were killed by the Irish Republican Army. Then, in a brutal, indiscriminate reprisal, temporary and notoriously ill-disciplined soldiers fired randomly at spectators at a Gaelic football match in Dublin's Croke Park. Twelve were killed, more than fifty wounded. The soldiers were 'Black and Tans' (so-called after their makeshift uniforms) and were often unemployed former soldiers, demobilised – and inured to violence – after the First World War.

On that Bloody Sunday, in spite of unease, after word of the IRA killings filtered out, crowds gathered that day at Croke Park, as military convoys also approached. Plans merely to search the crowd led to unprovoked shooting by soldiers who even their commanders admitted were 'excited and out of hand'. Amid what one paper called 'scenes of the wildest confusion', those killed included a woman about to be married and two young boys.

Both British intelligence, and Britain's cause generally, suffered devastating damage: first in the loss of its agents, then in the PR disaster at Croke Park, and finally in the prolonged exposure of a shameful attempted cover-up.

The fighting, and the killing, only got worse. Over the ensuing seven months around another 1,000 people were killed in a pattern of assassination and reprisal, until a truce was agreed in July 1921. By that stage, an act of parliament in Westminster had partitioned Ireland, an Anglo-Irish Treaty was signed in December that year, and in 1922 the 'Irish Free State' was created: though of course the violent unrest – civil war and the largely religious, 'sectarian' division – was not resolved.

22 November

Today in 1963 – a day remembered by almost everyone then alive – US President John F. Kennedy was shot dead in Dallas. It was a Friday.

Kennedy had decided to visit Dallas because of frictions within his Democratic Party, using the publicity to launch his bid for re-election the following year. A public cavalcade was planned, taking the president from a local airbase to his lunchtime meeting with local leaders at Trade Mart (after which he would return for an evening event).

Having moved slowly through crowds estimated at more than 150,000 people, the cavalcade reached Dealey Plaza, five minutes from their destination. The palpable enthusiasm caused the governor's wife, with Kennedy in the car, to turn and observe, 'Mr President, you can't say Dallas doesn't love you', to which he replied, 'No, you certainly can't.' They were his last words.

Passing the Texas School Book Depository, Kennedy was shot more than once – most witnesses recalled three shots – and though the vehicle sped quickly to the nearby Parkland Memorial Hospital, the president was dead on admission.

Not long afterwards, Lee Harvey Oswald, answering a police description, was questioned by an officer, whom he shot at. Though overpowered and arrested, his case never came to trial because he in turn was fatally shot, as he was moved between jails, by the owner of a Dallas nightclub called Jack Ruby. Oswald was admitted to the same hospital to which Kennedy had been taken two days earlier.

Vice President Lyndon B. Johnson had accompanied Kennedy to Dallas, riding in the cavalcade two cars behind. Early that afternoon, on board Air Force One, he took the oath of office, with Kennedy's widow – still wearing her blood-spattered clothes – by his side.

Few believed initial findings that none, other than Oswald, had been involved, and the questions, and conspiracy theories, have raged ever since.

23 November

The fugitive Pope re-entered Rome. His return, today in 800, was made possible by the man who rode alongside him in the procession, Europe's most powerful monarch since the Caesars: Charles I, King of the Franks, King of the Lombards, known as Charlemagne, or Charles the Great.

The year before, Pope Leo III had made his way towards the Flaminian Gate in Rome, when he was set upon by a group of armed men. They fought to tear out his tongue and gouge his eyes but were intercepted just in time by Charlemagne's garrison troops. The attackers fled and the Pope was left unconscious. Understandably terrified of remaining in the city, he fled north to Charlemagne's court in Paderborn.

After their joint entry to Rome, Charlemagne announced that a council would investigate any charges against the Pope. It was brought to a swift conclusion. Leo was exonerated and his opponents exiled. Two days later, a grateful Pope placed a bejewelled crown upon his head and declared Charlemagne the Holy Roman Emperor. It was a powerful assertion by both parties. The Pope was claiming the right to anoint emperors and Charlemagne was placing himself squarely in the tradition of universal empire.

His conquests were certainly impressive enough. He was the uncontested ruler from Denmark to northern Spain and from southern Italy to the Channel coast. Inspired by classical example he fostered a culture of learning, known as the Carolingian Renaissance. But while his vast domain was too unwieldy for his successors, and it fragmented into French and German territories, Pope Leo's title and the idea of a Holy Roman Empire would endure for a millennium, tempting generations of would-be conquerors with the prospect of rebuilding Charlemagne's patrimony.

24 November

After a long morning dig, American palaeoanthropologist Donald Johanson, and his graduate student Tom Gray, walked back across desert scrubland to their Land Rover.

The pair were with other scientists at Hadar, in the Rift Valley in Ethiopia, an area believed to have been the cradle of humanity – where the very earliest human beings first evolved – and therefore likely to contain the very earliest human fossils. Today in 1974, rather than simply retracing their steps, Donald and Tom opted to return to their vehicle by a different route from the one they had used that morning – standard good practice, maximising their land coverage.

As they did so they suddenly paused. Sticking up from the surface of the sand was what looked like a fragment of bone: probably that of an animal kill, but worth investigating. As they scraped the sand away, it became apparent that it was in fact an extremely old forearm bone (a *proximal ulna*, to give it its proper name). They continued to search, finding also a skull, a pelvis, some ribs, a femur and a jawbone – all identified as comprising the skeleton of a hominid: an early human.

A couple of weeks later, after many hours of patient excavation, 40 per cent of a single skeleton (there were no duplicate parts) had been found. It would become perhaps the most famous of all palaeoanthropological discoveries, of profound importance for our understanding of the evolution of our earliest ancestors. This creature walked upright – was *bipedal* – less like a modern chimpanzee and more like a human. As dating techniques have improved, an age of approximately 3.2 million years has been established.

During the excited celebration of that first night the scientists drank, and danced, and listened to music. A Beatles song kept playing – 'Lucy in the Sky with Diamonds'. And so it was that the skeleton – identified, correctly, as a female, on the basis of the pelvic bone – acquired the name that has stuck ever since: Lucy.

25 November

England had a new queen. Today in 1487 her coronation marked not just the start of a new reign but a symbolic end to the Wars of the Roses and a unification of the houses of York and Lancaster. The Archbishop of Canterbury, Thomas Bourchier, placed the crown on the head of Elizabeth of York, eldest daughter of the former king, Edward IV, niece to the overthrown Richard III, sister to the vanished Princes in the Tower and wife to the new king, Henry Tudor.

The crown she won through marriage was hers by right anyway. Elizabeth had a better claim than anyone after the disappearance and likely murder of her two younger brothers in the Tower of London. She narrowly escaped marriage to her uncle, Richard III, when he was defeated and killed by Henry Tudor at the Battle of Bosworth. During that campaign, Elizabeth was detained at Sheriff Hutton Castle in Yorkshire, a solitary figure walking the grounds as she awaited her fate, separated from her mother and family. The victorious Henry VII promptly returned Elizabeth to her mother and petitioned Parliament for her hand in marriage, realising Elizabeth's pedigree immeasurably strengthened his dynastic pretensions.

They were married in September and her union with Henry began the Tudor dynasty, the most famous dynasty in British history, and the one from which all subsequent monarchs are directly descended.

Elizabeth became the ideal of queenship. Kind, loyal, beautiful, charitable and giving birth to a brace of sons. The scholar Erasmus described her as 'brilliant'. Her marriage to Henry VII was apparently happy; they had eight children and there seems to have been genuine admiration between them. On her death in 1503, the king is said to have retired to a private room and asked to be left alone in his mourning. He never remarried.

26 November

Vlad III, or Vlad Dracula, became prince and ruler of Wallachia in Romania three times, and today in 1476 was the last. He clung on until his death shortly after, in 1477. Notorious for his cruelty, he was awarded the posthumous nickname 'Vlad the Impaler' as an ode to the method he famously adopted to dispatch his enemies.

In 1456 a group of Ottoman envoys was granted an audience with Vlad III, then ruler of Wallachia. During the meeting, the envoys refused to remove their turbans, citing a religious custom. Vlad commended them for their beliefs and offered to assist them by ensuring that their turbans would always remain on their heads; he reportedly had them nailed to their skulls.

Around the same time, the lands surrounding Wallachia were in a state of turmoil due to warlords fighting each other. Vlad invited hundreds of them to a banquet, at which he had them all impaled, leaving them to die long, lingering deaths. Vlad's methods of execution became renowned and he used them to discourage his enemies, most famously in 1462, when he left a field of impaled corpses as a deterrent to the pursuing Ottoman army.

After a period of exile and imprisonment in Hungary, Vlad returned to claim the throne of Wallachia, for a third time. Months after, in the middle of a battle against the Ottomans, he was killed and his retinue massacred. Allegedly, Vlad's body was cut into pieces, and his head sent to their sultan, Mehmed II. It is disputed to this day where Vlad was buried, evoking vampire mythology surrounding his corpse. Bram Stoker was inspired by his terrifying reputation, resulting in the birth of the literary villain Count Dracula.

27 November

On this day in the year 1620, the English crew and passengers went ashore in North America from a ship called the *Mayflower*. Though it was not the first time that English men and women had set foot in North America (one indigenous man came to meet them who spoke some English *and* who had lived in London), it was a moment that has come to define the modern history of the United States.

Those on board the *Mayflower* spent some time at sea but in sight of the shore. By the end of November it was three weeks since their first sighting of Cape Cod. At first, realising their navigational error, they attempted to sail south to Virginia – their intended destination – though after battling impossible conditions they decided to head back to the original harbour, where shallows prevented the large ship from approaching the coast.

They saw enough to be staggered by the richness of both aquatic and bird life, the latter greater in number, they said, than 'ever we saw'. On 27 November, the captain, Christopher Jones, organised an expedition to explore the adjacent land, looking for a site well suited to settlement. In an open 'shallop' thirty-four of them (ten sailors) rowed towards the continent. Even so, they could not get very close and had to wade for a distance through the cold water (at a time of year when the climate in general *was* 'freezing cold').

The indigenous population of the continent had been much thinned by European diseases, but still fires glinted at night in the dark, making it clear the land was inhabited. It was a meeting of cultures that became more intense as time passed, and which changed both worlds fundamentally and for ever.

28 November

He had crushed a mutiny, lost one of his precious ships in a storm, another to desertion and he had felt his way through an uncharted passage strewn with navigational hazards. And today in 1520 Ferdinand Magellan and his three remaining ships entered a new ocean. The spring weather was gentle, the sea was still and peaceful, so he named it the 'Pacific'.

Magellan, an aristocratic Portuguese explorer who had fallen out with his king and defected to Spain, wanted to finish the job started by Columbus. He too wished to sail west to find the Spice Islands of the east. They had left in September 1519, and wintered in what is now southern Patagonia. There he was forced to kill some of his mutinous captains, and maroon another one. The executed men were impaled; Sir Francis Drake found their whitening bones decades later.

In late October he had started to probe into the nearly 350 miles of passage that now bears his name (Straits of Magellan). One of his ships turned around and sailed back to Spain where the captain was immediately imprisoned. On 28 November the crews of the three remaining ships became the first Europeans to enter the eastern Pacific Ocean.

Magellan would never see Europe again. After crossing the Pacific he and his men arrived in the Philippines, the first Europeans to do so. During a battle with local inhabitants he was hacked to death. Juan Sebastián Elcano took command in his place and after heroic leadership brought just one ship, the *Victoria*, back to Seville. They had completed the first circumnavigation of the earth. Of the 237 men who had been aboard Magellan's ships when they set off three years before, there were only 18 survivors.

29 November

The *Zong* raised anchor and departed the shores of Africa in September 1781 with a cargo of 470 slaves. The captain of the ship, Luke Collingwood, was aware of the high value of slaves, and he filled his ship to beyond its capacity and embarked on what would be a long, uncomfortable and possibly perilous voyage. On this day in 1781, a significant portion of the slaves on board were murdered.

The *Zong* had not been at sea long before trouble arose. Due to cramped, insanitary conditions, slaves began to die from disease and malnutrition. The ship floated into an area of the Atlantic known as the Doldrums, where there was little or no wind, and the ship was becalmed under a clear, hot sky. Sickness took hold. Seventeen crew members lost their lives, as well as fifty slaves.

The captain became desperate, and decided to jettison some of the cargo. He had the sick and dying slaves thrown overboard to their deaths, relieving the ship of some of the load and attempting to prevent further spread of disease. In horror and defiance, ten more healthy slaves also threw themselves overboard. Collingwood believed that he had solved the problem, as the slaveholders were able to claim on insurance for their losses. As the *Zong* anchored in Jamaica, an insurance claim was filed, citing a 'lack of water to sustain crew and commodities'.

Despite speculation, the case was closed. However, in 1783 it sparked interest among abolitionists, led by Granville Sharp, a leading figure in the movement. Sharp attempted to charge Captain Collingwood and his crew as criminals, for what he described to be 'a massacre'. He was met with the response, 'Blacks are goods and property . . . the case is the same as if wood had been thrown overboard'. Collingwood and his crew were never brought to justice and it would take decades more campaigning to get the slave trade banned, which it finally was in 1807.

30 November

Oscar Wilde spent his final days at Hôtel d'Alsace in Paris. Suffering cerebral meningitis, he was confined to his bed, where he jovially stated, 'my wallpaper and I are fighting a duel to the death – one or the other of us has to go'. Today in 1900, the wallpaper defeated him and Oscar Wilde, poet and playwright, passed away in his green and gold hotel room, aged forty-five.

Three years earlier, Oscar Wilde had been released from prison after being outed for homosexuality and charged with 'gross indecency'. After Wilde regained his freedom, he was prevented from seeing his two sons and was not even permitted an audience with a priest, later claiming, 'my existence is a scandal'.

Wilde's social status had plummeted after his conviction, which resulted from a libel case he had fought against the Marquess of Queensbury, the father of Wilde's lover, Alfred Douglas. Queensbury had accused Wilde of 'posing as a sodomite', sparking Wilde to sue for libel. This backfired when Queensbury hired private investigators to unearth proof of Wilde's sexual relationships with several male prostitutes. Wilde was sentenced to two years hard labour in Reading Gaol.

His last years were spent sadly, in exile, in Paris, where he borrowed money from old friends, smoked and drank the days and nights away in old haunts like the Moulin Rouge. His demise was tragic, plummeting from the enigmatic and popular writer of *The Picture of Dorian Gray* to a broken man unable to pay for his own lodgings. Oscar Wilde is buried at Père Lachaise Cemetery, in a tomb designed by artist Jacob Epstein.

Despite his sorry end, Wilde is posthumously revered. His life story is central to the painful and prolonged struggle for equality for the LGBT community. Today his tomb is covered with lipstick prints from all who have kissed it and mourned the untimely death of a genius.

DECEMBER

1 December

On this day in 1135, King Henry I died, according to chroniclers, by 'eating a surfeit of Lampreys', which 'mortally chilled the old man's blood and caused a sudden and violent illness'. It is most likely that this was food poisoning.

He was the youngest son of William the Conqueror, and his death left England in turmoil, in a war known as 'The Anarchy'. The succession crisis began in 1135 but was precipitated fifteen years earlier, on the perilous water of the English Channel. In one of the worst maritime disasters of the Middle Ages, the *White Ship*, a vessel carrying King Henry's sons, William and Richard, foundered and sank with a loss of 300 lives.

In November 1120, the king and his party prepared to sail to England from the port of Barfleur in Normandy. The ship's captain, Thomas Fitzgibbons, was keen to show off the newly built *White Ship*, which the king agreed to, allowing his sons to travel on board, as well as many nobles. The king travelled separately and the voyage began well, as wine flowed to passengers and crews alike.

That night, the ship ran its side 'violently' into a rock and capsized. Hundreds were plunged into the freezing water, few knowing how to swim. Those on board the king's ship could hear screaming but nobody knew where it came from. Allegedly, William the Aethling, Henry's heir, almost escaped the wreck in a small boat, but on hearing his sister Matilda Fitzroy screaming for help, he went back. His boat was swamped, and neither he nor Matilda survived. Thomas Fitzgibbons, learning of William the Aethling's death, allowed himself to drown rather than face the king.

After the *White Ship* disaster, only one legitimate heir to the throne remained, the king's second daughter, also named Matilda. Her succession resulted in The Anarchy, plunging the country into fierce civil war, between Matilda, and her cousin, Stephen of Blois.

2 December

Today in 1697, thirty-one years after the Great Fire destroyed Old St Paul's Cathedral, the new cathedral was consecrated. Its architect was Christopher Wren.

Much of medieval London was destroyed in the 1666 fire, and Wren was granted an audience with Charles II to lay out his plans for the new London. His revolutionary designs included tree-lined streets, broad and straight, the opposite to the warren of twisted alleyways of the old London.

Wren was an architect and engineer, but he was also a keen scientist, pioneering the practice of injecting liquid into the veins of live animals. His brains and enthusiasm also saw him play a central role in the establishment of the Royal Society. The society's gatherings attracted some of the greatest minds of the seventeenth century.

Over the course of his career, Wren designed fifty-one new city churches, as well as his masterpiece, the new St Paul's Cathedral. During the planning and construction of St Paul's, he submitted several designs, but it was the 'Great Model' of 1673 that became his favourite, due to the impressive domed top. Even so, the unconventional dome was considered to be 'too Catholic' and Wren had to alter the design. Desperate not to deviate from the structure of the roof he envisaged, he replaced the dome with a cupola and a steeple. This was commissioned, but he was given permission to make 'ornamental changes.' He pushed this latitude to the extremes and built a huge dome over the cupola and got rid of the steeple to build the St Paul's that exists today.

Christopher Wren is considered to be the greatest architect in British history, and after fifty years of relentless service he retired to Hampton Court where he lived until his death in 1723. Fittingly, he is interred in St Paul's Cathedral, where his epitaph reads: 'If you seek his memorial, look about you.'

3 December

It was a big title for a small kid. Today in 1533 a three-year-old was formally declared Grand Prince of Moscow, after the death of his father from blood poisoning. His mother was assassinated and the young boy was left an orphan, without, he later regretted, 'human care from any quarter'. No doubt this loveless upbringing contributed to his later excesses.

To English-speaking history he is known now as Ivan 'the Terrible' – a translation of the Russian word *grozni* for which 'awesome' would seem more accurate, though 'terrible' is appropriate given the bout of insane savagery to which Russia was subjected.

Ivan's coronation in Russia was held in 1547 – at sixteen he was proclaimed 'Tsar of All the Russias' rather than simply 'Grand Prince'. A couple of weeks later he married his first wife, a member of the Romanov family, which came to dominate the imperial line.

The title of 'tsar' was derived from the Latin word *Caesar*. Every opportunity was taken to exploit his connection to the emperors of Rome and Constantinople, including the publication of genealogies that were utterly bogus. Moscow never quite became the new Rome, but Ivan did manage to emulate the excess and megalomania of the Caesars. He killed his son and heir in an outbreak of mental derangement; he tortured and slaughtered the inhabitants of Novgorod after a bout of unfounded paranoia convinced him that the city was poised to defect to Poland.

He destroyed alternative sources of authority, creating a profoundly autocratic tsarist state that welded his ever-increasing empire into a coherent whole but remained completely dependent on the person on the throne. This culture of despotism has proved remarkably durable, surviving even the end of the tsars, civil wars, invasion, Communism and free-market capitalism. Today's schoolchildren are taught to revere Ivan, and there is even a campaign to make him a saint.

4 December

On this day – and during this week – in 1952, London was in the grip of what became known as the 'Great Smog'.

In conditions that were both very cold, and very still, stagnant, polluted air hung motionless over the city, made much worse by the heavy use of coal: the capital had many coal-fired power stations, and people burnt more coal in their homes that usual because of the freezing conditions. Particles of soot gave the fog a distinctive yellowish hue, giving rise to the familiar description 'pea-souper'.

For centuries London had suffered sporadic such episodes, but thick fog on this occasion was worse than it had been in the past. One attempt to estimate the impact of the 1952 smog put deaths in the short term at 4,000 and those attributable to it during the subsequent months at around another 6,000. With bronchial infections widespread, a larger number are believed to have claimed sickness benefit.

With visibility often reduced to only a few metres, driving was difficult if not impossible. Street lights at night failed to penetrate and pedestrians shuffled as if blindfolded. Apart from the Underground, public transport ceased entirely. The fact that cloudy, impenetrable air seeped even into indoor spaces caused the cancellation of theatrical events, which audiences were unable to see as well as hear. 'Smog masks' were widely worn.

In the wake of wartime conditions (and with rationing still in place) a culture existed of non-complaint, but unquestionably the event led to measures for improved air quality: in particular, Clean Air Acts of 1956 and 1968, which banned the use of wood and coal in houses and shifted power stations out of towns. A further smog did occur a decade later but in general the improvement was marked.

5 December

It was a crushing admission of defeat. Today in 1933, Ohio, Pennsylvania and Utah became the latest states to ratify the Twenty-first Amendment to the United States constitution by specially assembled state conventions. 'The eighteenth article of amendment to the Constitution of the United States', it stated, 'is hereby repealed': the only occasion upon which a prior amendment has been abolished.

That prior amendment is known simply as Prohibition – the banning of the production, importation, transportation or sale of alcoholic drinks. It had been implemented for the best reasons, to save people from the influence of alcohol, but it had unleashed a wave of crime and corruption.

Bootlegging, the making and selling of illegal alcohol, was embraced by criminal gangs who fought each other and the law to protect their markets. The police became mired in corruption scandals. The poor raged at the rich who had stockpiled wine in their cellars and could afford to drink in secret speakeasy bars. Presidents Wilson and Harding famously moved their wine cellars in and out of the White House as they entered or left office. Even one-time supporters like John D. Rockefeller changed their minds; he noted that 'respect for the law has been greatly lessened; and crime has increased to a level never seen before'.

The advent of the Great Depression lent another argument to overturn the ban. The government badly needed revenue and the black market was generating millions of dollars that could be redirected to state coffers.

All this made Roosevelt's campaign to reverse Prohibition one of his less challenging political manoeuvres. Even so, many people argue that the lessons from the period have not been thoroughly absorbed. America's persistent prohibition on illegal pharmaceuticals has likewise led to a flood of violence, police corruption, mass incarceration and a huge, unregulated black market. Policy change feels inevitable; at least this time it will not require a constitutional amendment.

6 December

Halifax was packed. Nearly every ship crossing the Atlantic had to call into Canada's most important harbour to join a convoy heading to the UK or simply to have their cargoes checked if they were neutral. Today in 1917 the Narrows leading in and out of Halifax was particularly busy. At 7.30 a.m. the anti-submarine nets had been lifted and traffic could commence. The Norwegian ship *Imo* was in a hurry. The bureaucracy and delays of wartime were infuriating to a captain and crew from a non-combatant nation. She entered the Narrows well above the speed limit and swerved this way and that to avoid other ships.

The French ship *Mont-Blanc* was barely making headway, steaming at 1 knot when she saw *Imo* apparently on a collision course. Both ships cut their engines and steered aggressively to avoid each other. It was a very near miss. Then, the *Imo* blasted her horn and reversed her engines, which sent her bow crashing into the starboard hold of the *Mont-Blanc*.

The French ship was laden down with high explosives and highly flammable fuel, destined for the Western Front. The collision punctured barrels of fuel, sparks from the disengaging ships ignited it and the fire spread. The terrified crew abandoned ship as the people of Halifax gathered on the shore to watch the drama. At 9.05 a.m. the fire set off the ship's cargo of high explosives. The shock wave was felt over hundred miles away. A deck gun was blown 3.5 miles through the air. A tsunami smashed into the quayside, fires were started across the city.

Nearly 2,000 people were killed, including the captain and first officer of the *Imo*, 9,000 were injured, and every single building for a mile and half was flattened or badly damaged. It was the largest man-made explosion before the nuclear age, and until the nuclear bomb was dropped on Hiroshima it was the international standard by which blasts were measured.

7 December

The three men spent longer on the Moon than anyone in history, yet very few of us have ever heard of them. Today in 1972 three astronauts, Eugene Cernan, Ronald Evans and Harrison Schmitt, were launched into space aboard Apollo 17, attached to a Saturn V rocket.

It was the first night launch – the three men blasting into a dark Florida sky – as well as the final mission in a long and largely successful programme that had seen humankind land upon the surface of the Moon for the first time. Apollo 17 spent a remarkable three days there, and returned with a large quantity of lunar rock. This mission remains the last time that humans landed and walked on the Moon.

After a Russian, Yuri Gagarin, became the first man in space in 1961, the United States was spurred on by a fear that it was falling behind in the 'space race'. President Kennedy felt under pressure to respond, so he announced a US goal of 'landing a man on the Moon and returning him [a safe bet at the time] safely to the Earth' by the end of the 1960s.

It involved a massive commitment – $25 billion, well over $100 billion today, the largest ever made by a nation in peacetime, employing at its peak some 400,000 people. Thus far the programme stands alone not only in achieving manned Moon landings but in sending manned spacecraft beyond the low Earth orbit of satellites and the international space station.

Between Apollo 11 in 1969 – the first lunar landing which carried Neil Armstrong et al. – and this one, twelve astronauts have walked upon the Moon, on six missions. Only the Apollo 13 mission had to be aborted after a technical failure, though its astronauts were safely returned to Earth.

Today, renewed superpower competition, eccentric billionaires and technological advances have all reawakened the ambition to visit the Moon. Perhaps this time, it will be used as a pit stop for deeper exploration into the solar system.

8 December

The Avon Gorge carves a deep trench from Bristol to the sea, an artery that brought the world's trade but also a chasm too wide for any single-span bridge, too deep for any supporting piles. Or so it was always believed. Today in 1864 the Clifton Suspension Bridge opened. Engineers had overcome nature's obstacle by pushing the limits of the possible.

On 8 December 1864 the new bridge was lit with magnesium flares, appearing like a fiery apparition high in the sky. A brisk, wintry West Country wind blew them out but it could not suppress the excitement of the 150,000 people who gathered to watch the all-day festivities, the marching soldiers, bands and a parade by working men's associations.

In 1829 a competition had sought to find a solution to bridging the gap. The Admiralty insisted that the bridge be high enough to allow tall-masted vessels to pass below. A 23-year-old engineer, Isambard Kingdom Brunel, stepped forward. Henceforth he would always describe the bridge as 'my first love, my darling'.

He would abandon the traditional idea of a stone bridge. The longest single span in the world was only 60 metres and the gap he needed to bridge was 250 metres. Instead he would use new materials, like iron, to create what would be the longest and highest bridge in the world. His two towers would be joined by mighty chains; from these chains the bridge would be suspended. Those chains were so firmly anchored that they stretched for an astonishing 20 miles underground.

Brunel died before seeing his beloved project completed. His colleagues, William Henry Barlow and John Hawkshaw, finished it partly as a homage to the deceased titan. Today the bridge is a symbol of the city of Bristol and a memorial to the pioneering engineers of the Industrial Age.

9 December

'The mind is its own place, and in itself can make a heaven a hell, a hell a heaven . . .' Three hundred and fifty years ago, 10,000 lines of blank verse were published, telling the story of the fall of man. *Paradise Lost* has shaped English literature and its creator, John Milton, regarded as one of the pre-eminent English authors, was born on this day in Cheapside in 1608.

Milton was a radical thinker, a prolific pamphleteer for republicanism, and after the death of Charles I he was elevated as a diplomat with the title of Secretary for Foreign Tongues. Milton mourned the death of Oliver Cromwell and subsequently began his epic poem *Paradise Lost* as an attempt to make sense of a fallen world; in Milton's own words, 'to justify the ways of God to men'. Milton started *Paradise Lost* in the mid-1650s, and over the course of a decade it was dictated to a scribe as he slowly went blind. His enemies considered this to be a kind of divine justice.

Paradise Lost inspired writers such as Mary Shelley, Keats, Wordsworth and Philip Pullman, and the art of William Blake. It is undoubtedly one of the greatest poems in the history of world literature. But Milton was lucky it was published at all. He had been a leading supporter and propagandist for the Republic. The restoration of King Charles II sent him into hiding. His works were burned and he was arrested. After some debate he was included in a general pardon issued by the new king and his Parliament. Charles opted, on the whole, for conciliation rather than retribution.

The case of Milton shows the wisdom of this course. Not only did he publish one of the great works of literature in the years that followed, but he lived a quiet life and posed no threat to the restored regime. His execution would have been a pointless act of savagery that would have only cost Charles support. His pardon illustrates a canny political sense, so lacking in Charles's father and younger brother.

10 December

On this day in 1868, the world's first traffic lights – furniture of the road system which have since, of course, become universal – were installed in Parliament Square, in Westminster, London. It was at the junction of Great George Street and Bridge Street, to address the large amount of traffic crossing Westminster Bridge. During the day they worked by semaphore. At night coloured gas lamps were used.

These were not, however, automatic. An attendant was required to operate the system (which was hardly new given that directing of traffic by individuals was a common phenomenon). And it was not without teething problems. Less than a month after being installed, leaking gas caused it to explode in the face of a man working on it, and he was badly burned.

There were not, late in the 1860s, petrol-driven cars on the road: these had not yet been invented. There were, however, growing numbers of horse-drawn carriages, which it was widely felt, presented a danger to pedestrians. John Peake Knight was an engineer working on the expanding railway network. He proposed that the signalling system used by the railway tracks might also be utilised on the roads: a semaphore system by day, and red and green lights by night.

Having been initially hailed as a great success, the accidental explosion in Westminster caused the system to fall into disuse, reappearing only in the United States – using the un-illuminated instructions 'STOP' and 'PROCEED' – very shortly before the First World War, and becoming widespread in London only in 1929 when electric signals were introduced.

The red–green colour scheme has become universal: gone are the statues, columns, bells or semaphore of early incarnations, replaced by a dull but utilitarian standardisation.

11 December

On 3 November 1936, King Edward VIII formally opened Parliament without wearing the Imperial State Crown, since no coronation had yet taken place: one was planned for late spring the following year. For most of that year, though – from his father's death on 20 January – he had been king, proclaimed the day afterwards.

Yet this opening of Parliament would be one of his last royal duties, because only a couple of weeks later, today in 1936, Edward's reign as king formally came to an end, the same date on which James II had vacated the throne almost 250 years previously, in 1688. After a long period of uncertainty, Edward made his final choice: between being King-Emperor of the largest empire in history, and the woman he loved.

By 11 December the formal decisions had been taken. Wallace Simpson's divorce had been approved. King Edward had notified his prime minister, Stanley Baldwin, of his intention to marry her – and to abdicate if his government opposed the move. His family had been informed. A week before, he had told Baldwin of his decision to abdicate, and the previous day, he had signed the instrument of abdication.

Interviewed on BBC radio that evening, he was introduced as 'His Royal Highness, Prince Edward'. Poignantly, he declared: 'you must believe me when I tell you that I have found it impossible to carry the heavy burden of responsibility and to discharge my duties as King as I would wish to do without the help and support of the woman I love'. Sir John Reith, who conducted the interview, noted privately afterwards how Edward had 'smiled very nicely and rather sadly'.

In his subsequent loyalty and marital fidelity Edward fully justified his words, while attitudes towards marriage at least have shifted in his favour.

12 December

Isabella took the news of her brother's death lightly. As a precaution, today in 1474 she shut herself up in the Segovia Fortress, perched on a rocky crag above the confluence of two rivers in the Guadarrama Mountains of Castile. The news of Henry IV's death had reached her and she had a decision to make.

Henry had been a weak king as his unflattering nickname might imply: 'the impotent'. By his second marriage he had one daughter, but the paternity was strongly disputed and she was widely rejected as his heir. So partial were those who testified, that it is impossible now to be sure of the truth: impotent, infertile, homosexual, or none of the above?

Isabella was twenty-six years younger than her half-brother Henry. Locked in discussions all day with leading nobles, the 23-year-old decided to declare herself queen and emerged in dazzling finery the following day preceded by a courtier with a sword held upright by its point. This was a coup to snatch the Castilian throne; 'some in the crowd muttered that they had never seen such a thing', wrote a contemporary.

Opinions of her quickly changed. As the first Queen Regnant in modern European history, she faced down rivals on the battlefield, and did more to shape early modern Spain and what would become its empire than nearly any other individual. One observer later in her reign wrote, 'This queen of Spain, called Isabella, has had no equal on this earth for 500 years.'

From childhood Isabella had been freely proffered in the marriage market, but remained unattached and demonstrated firm reluctance to be committed against her will. In the end she did secretly promise to marry Ferdinand of Aragon, though the fact that they were second cousins necessitated a papal bull to permit the union. When this was obtained the marriage could take place and in their union lies the origin of modern Spain. Together they completed the conquest of Islamic Andalusia, and dispatched Christopher Columbus to the west. Few monarchs, kings or queens, can match Isabella's impact on the course of history.

13 December

It was late in the year to sail into the Atlantic but today in 1577 legendary sailor Francis Drake did just that. He left Plymouth (for a second time, having been forced back once by bad weather) on his famous circumnavigation of the earth. It was the second time the feat had been achieved, and the first by a captain who conducted the entire journey himself, as captain. He became a national-hero to the English – bolstered after his prominent role in the defeat of the Spanish Armada – in Spain, not surprisingly, he was branded a pirate.

Acclaimed after his success at robbing treasure fleets in Central America (the Spanish Main), Drake was asked to sail up South America's Pacific coast, to attack Spanish ships there. His fleet was drastically reduced. After leaving with six ships, by the time he rounded the bottom of South America and entered the Pacific (one of the first Englishmen to do so) he had only his own, renamed *Golden Hind* having left as *Pelican*. In spite of smaller numbers, though, she fearlessly assaulted Spanish ports and ships as she sailed north, seizing vast riches.

Reaching the coast of modern California, Drake landed in June 1579 – claiming land he called *Nova Albion*, New Albion – before heading south once more to catch winds that would carry him west across the Pacific.

By the time he had worked his way back to the Spice Islands, west once more to the Cape of Good Hope, then up Africa's western coast to Sierra Leone, it was more than a year later – late in July 1580 – and by the time he reached Plymouth (with fifty-nine of his original compliment of 164) it was almost the end of September.

Queen Elizabeth was entitled to half his cargo. Its value exceeded the crown's income from all other sources for that entire year.

14 December

In ninth-century China, a powerful faction of eunuchs, castrated men, dominated court politics. On this day, in 835, a palace coup attempting to overthrow eunuch power was foiled, resulting in chaos and bloodshed, and known as the Sweet Dew Incident.

The plot was initiated by Chancellor Li Xun and General Zheng Zu, who secretly conspired with Emperor Wenzong of the Chinese Tang dynasty. Both the chancellor and general were formerly allies of the substantially powerful eunuch Wang Shoucheng, but as his control and influence at court grew, so their resentment grew. By summer 835 the plot to eliminate the eunuchs had been hatched.

It was on this day that Emperor Wenzong was informed that sweet dew had descended on a pomegranate tree outside Hanyuan Hall, denoting a sign of divine favour. The dew was examined and considered to be false. The emperor ordered that the eunuch Qui Shiliang and other eunuch officials should be invited to examine the sweet dew, where they were met by the emperor's forces. Leading eunuchs escaped the attack, kidnapping the terrified emperor in his litter. Qui Shiliang ordered 1,000 soldiers to attack. Around 1,000 officials, guards and civilians were slaughtered by the eunuch army. The city was thrown into anarchy. Homes were being pillaged for royal officials in hiding, and people began to use the opportunity to loot the city.

Li Xun fled into hiding in the mountains but was intercepted. Rather than being handed over to the eunuchs he begged to be beheaded. The officers agreed and it was Li Xun's head that was finally delivered. Zheng Zu shared the same fate; he was beheaded and his head displayed as well.

The plot to remove the eunuchs from power, had the opposite effect. The eunuchs controlled the government for the rest of the Tang dynasty, significant control and even determining the imperial line of succession.

15 December

The baby born today in AD 37 was a boy. He had no real prospect of being remembered almost two millennia later. Few are. As it is, though, not only is he remembered, he is one of a very select handful of individuals for whom one name alone, so long afterwards, is sufficient to identify him: Nero.

He is not, of course, *well* remembered. Far from it: that single name is a byword for lechery, treachery, cruelty, debauchery, extravagance and almost every quality that is equally unpleasant – not all of it, it has to be said, on good authority, but when the charge sheet is as extensive as Nero's, it scarcely matters whether a crime or two is crossed off the list. The fact that it is unlikely he had any personal responsibility for the great fire that devastated Rome (being miles away at the time) does little to jeopardise his seat among the monsters and tyrants of history.

Many of his personal qualities Nero had plainly inherited from his ruthless, murderous mother, Agrippina: a younger sister of the bad, mad Caligula and with a similar temperament to her brother, even if there was little sibling love between the two. Agrippina married the Emperor Claudius as his fourth wife; he was her uncle though incest was scarcely the worst of her crimes, having poisoned her own second husband – Nero's biological father – and his third wife too. Nero's father is also remembered as 'brutal'. His genetic inheritance was far from being fortunate.

Having been persuaded to favour her son Nero's succession as emperor over the rival claim of his own son, Claudius may then have also been poisoned by his homicidal wife. The early years of Nero's rule were surprisingly moderate and benign. But his violent insanity shone through (he is thought to have murdered his own mother, who it is hard to pity) and it is this that comprises his lasting legacy.

16 December

Many of the men dressed as Mohawk Indians. It was a statement. They were throwing off their British identities and proclaiming themselves as Americans. Their protest, made today, in 1773, marks the symbolic start of the American Revolution: the 'Boston Tea Party'. A riotous act which has shaped the way Americans see themselves, as defiant citizens rather than docile subjects.

In May that year a British parliamentary Tea Act had permitted the East India Company to import its tea into the North American colonies, and to sell it there tax free, thus undercutting local merchants – who, not surprisingly, were livid.

In Boston the royal governor planned to accept tea delivered by three ships: the *Dartmouth*, the *Eleanor*, and the *Beaver*. But in the darkness, late on 16 December 1773, as many as a hundred and thirty men, boarded the ships and hurled the tea chests – all 342 of them, 90,000 pounds in weight and worth around £1 million in today's money – into the harbour.

The British Parliament's decision to punish Massachusetts until it made payment for the damaged tea, by such means as closing Boston Harbour, only drew the American colonies together, and brought war closer – it actually broke out just over a year later. Even today the notion of a 'tea party' is associated in America with radical action against tyrannical imposition.

Following the Boston Tea Party, drinking tea was considered to be unpatriotic. Its consumption declined during and after the Revolution, as people chose coffee as their preferred hot drink. Coffee drinking and distrust of government's are a twin legacy of the period that has endured.

17 December

It was a short flight, but a massive leap forward. Today in 1903, Orville Wright made what is now considered the first-ever *powered* flight in North Carolina. He flew 37 metres in 12 seconds.

The American Wright brothers – Wilbur and Orville – had been obsessed with the idea of flight ever since their father had bought them a foot-long toy helicopter, which they rebuilt when it broke. Subsequently the pair ran a bicycle maintenance shop, capitalising on what was a new craze, and using the proceeds to fund their own growing interest in flight.

What was unusual about the Wright brothers' philosophy was the emphasis they put upon the importance of control, while others focused upon developing engine power. This, they insisted, was the critical, unsolved part of what they called 'the flying problem'.

Their attempt to resolve this was the invention of three-axis control, which remains standard in aeroplanes to this day: 'pitch', 'roll' and 'yaw'. Early on they decided – and their experience in a bicycle shop reinforced their view – that a pilot needed to 'bank' or lean his craft into a turn, just as a bird did, and the rider of a bicycle.

Their early experiments focused upon gliders, which they built, studied and tested. Initially Wilbur, the elder brother, did all the flying, but gradually this shifted. In the end it was simply a matter of tossing a coin to see who would be at the controls.

Finally, towards the end of 1903, they felt ready to attempt to install an internal form of power – having to build their own engine in order for it to be light enough. Into a freezing cold headwind, Orville piloted the plane. It was 10.35 a.m. and the plane flew at under 7 mph. It was, literally, a ground-breaking moment.

18 December

The anonymous pamphlet sold out within three weeks. It was a stunning defence of the French Revolution, which appeared to be sliding towards extremism and violence. Edmund Burke had written a powerful condemnation of events in Paris and the author of this pamphlet struck back ridiculing his attachment to tradition, which was simply a fig leaf for the continuing rule of a corrupt aristocratic oligarchy.

The publisher reprinted, this time with the author's name. Today in 1790 the second edition of *A Vindication of the Rights of Men* was published 'by Mary Wollstonecraft'. The most trenchant and celebrated criticism of Burke had been written by a woman. Instantly, the reception cooled. Critics now found it too passionate, contrasting it with Burke's methodical 'reason'. Other reviewers simply objected to a woman engaging in a form of media and on topics they were traditionally excluded from. 'The rights of men asserted by a fair lady!' quipped one reviewer.

Despite the barbs Wollstonecraft's reputation was made. She was now able to, just, support herself as an independent intellectual. Two years later she wrote one of history's earliest works of feminist philosophy, *A Vindication of the Rights of Woman*.

In it, Wollstonecraft insisted that women were equal to men and ought to have the same rights. Education lay at its heart. Denying women an education ensured that they could not participate in business, law and politics, and then that ignorance and inexperience was used to justify their further exclusion in a closed loop of prejudice and permanent subordination.

Wollstonecraft died at just thirty-eight, having taken on the patriarchy, the establishment, the sexual mores of polite society and, eventually, even the French Revolutionary authorities. Denunciations of her unconventional life eclipsed her work until it was rediscovered by a generation of feminist activists in the twentieth century who ensured that she is now remembered as one of Britain's greatest political philosophers.

19 December

He was easy prey for satirists. When William Pitt was appointed prime minister today in 1783 the gags wrote themselves. One poet quipped, 'A sight to make surrounding nations stare / A kingdom trusted to a school-boy's care.'

King George III was driven to desperation by the loss of the American colonies and determined not to promote Charles James Fox, whom he despised. He decided on the young, serious, aloof, scion of a great political dynasty as his prime minister. William Pitt was only twenty-four.

Pitt was 'younger' indeed, even if the description was meant only to distinguish him from his father (also William Pitt, also a prime minister). Both precociously brilliant and physically frail as a child, Pitt had been inserted into Parliament three years earlier via a 'pocket borough', a seat entirely in the control of a grandee, although he had impressed with an impromptu, much-praised speech shortly afterwards.

When Pitt took office days before Christmas, he was lampooned for leading the 'mince-pie administration', one which would last only as long as the festive period. In fact it lasted for seventeen years, making him only second to Robert Walpole as the longest-serving prime minister in history.

He began by rebuilding government finances after the catastrophic American Revolutionary war and calmed the febrile culture of partisanship. The second half of his premiership saw him confront an existential threat to Britain that compares with the darkest days of 1940.

Although he never fought in the front line, the war killed Pitt. He worked himself to death, building and paying for coalitions to counter the phenomenon of Revolutionary and Napoleonic France. In 1806, with no end in sight, he died, aged forty-six. Victory, albeit a decade later, owed much to his fiscal and administrative genius. He is remembered as a great prime minister, not simply as a younger one.

20 December

'The King' rarely put pen to paper. But he loved his country, and he wanted to help. And he wanted a badge. Today in 1970 on a flight to Washington, DC, Elvis Presley borrowed a pen and American Airlines-headed paper and wrote to President Richard Nixon, offering 'any service I can to help the country out'. Ideally, he suggested, he should be appointed 'a federal agent at large'.

He drove straight to the White House when he landed and hand-delivered it. A Nixon aide, and massive Elvis fan, saw an opportunity for his boss who was hopelessly unpopular with younger voters. Elvis was invited back for a 12.30 p.m. meeting in the Oval Office.

He turned up, naturally, in his signature sunglasses and a flared jumpsuit. He had brought a gift, a Colt .45 pistol. He told the president that he thought The Beatles were behind the 'anti-American spirit' that seemed to be gripping the nation's youth. He also told the commander-in-chief, with spectacular hypocrisy, that 'those who use drugs are also at the vanguard of anti-American protest'.

That brought Elvis on to the purpose of his visit. He loved collecting badges. He was pining for one that would give him the status of a federal agent. Nixon rustled up a badge and Elvis was thrilled. He reached across and gave the unlovable Nixon a bear hug.

That was the end of one of the most incongruous meetings in American history. The rock 'n' roll idol and the deeply unfashionable politician; the King and the Crook. Perhaps they recognised in each other the deep dissatisfaction of the person who achieves their wildest dreams and finds only emptiness.

21 December

Today, in 1898, a scientist from Poland called Marie Curie – working in Paris with her husband, Pierre – discovered a new element, which they named 'radium' because of its natural lustre or 'radioluminescence'.

Nobel Prizes are rare honours. Marie, her husband, their daughter and her husband, and their second daughter's husband have shared four between them. Marie herself won two (the only woman to do so) and she remains the only person to win prizes for two different sciences: in her case, for physics and for chemistry. It is an astonishing haul.

Born in Warsaw in 1867, Marie was proud of her Polish roots – her maiden name was Skłodowska – at a time when Poland had not been an independent country for most of a century, but divided up between Austria, Prussia and Russia. Another element discovered by the married couple was given the name 'polonium' in direct tribute to her homeland.

Focused and driven, Curie was used to tolerating hardship and poverty, conducting her work in ramshackle, leaking outbuildings. Working with naturally occurring minerals called 'pitchblende' and 'chalcolite', Curie noticed that their 'radioactivity' (she coined the term) was more than might be expected if merely due to the uranium present. 'This fact,' she wrote, 'is very remarkable, and leads to the belief that these minerals may contain an element which is much more active than uranium.' She was right, even if the quantity in which it appeared was far smaller than she had thought.

She had no idea that the radioactivity she was constantly exposed to was harmful. In 1934 she died from blood and bone marrow damage, which she had developed as a result, the year before her daughter and her daughter's husband shared the Nobel Prize for Chemistry, just as she and Pierre had done for Physics over thirty years earlier.

22 December

He was a solitary thinker. His contemplation was rewarded, he reported, with a vision that would radically change the course of history. Today in 609 is the date often given on which the Prophet Muhammad received his first revelation: when the Angel Gabriel appeared to him in a cave on Mount Hira – near the town of Mecca in Arabia – and dictated what became the first verses of the Koran.

Shaking with the force of revelation, he is supposed to have dictated the text afterwards, from memory, to a scribe. Tradition has it that after these first revelations came a gap of three years, before they came regularly again for the following decade.

Much about this ancient history is debated. In some places the year 609 is asserted, in others 610. Also, he has been held to have been about forty years of age, but it has been argued he was actually nearer sixty.

Accounts claim that as a young man his chest was miraculously opened for clots to be removed, then sealed again; that he took to contemplative wandering in the surrounding hills. But it is all legend rather than history. Of Muhammad's early life, one leading scholar writes that 'we know almost nothing that can properly be called knowledge'.

The task of writing a detailed history of the Prophet's life is effectively impossible.

One thing is certain. Very few individuals in world history can claim to have exerted a comparable influence upon human culture. Muhammad built a community of believers bound by a zealotry that saw them overcome first their fellow Arab tribesmen, and then, within a generation of his death, two of the world's leading empires, Persia and Rome. The emergence and explosive growth of Muhammad's belief system, Islam, is one of the most important phenomenons in the history of ideas. Today, 1.8 billion people worldwide identify as Muslims, an identity born in a Arabian cave only 1,500 years ago.

23 December

In a long line of kings, the queen stands out. Today in 583, very unusually, a queen acceded to the throne in the Mayan city-state of Palenque, a flourishing place at the time, though it subsequently became overgrown and absorbed by the surrounding jungle. She is known, among other monikers, as Yohl Ik'nal.

In what now is southern Mexico, tombs, and monuments, fine sculpture and architecture have all survived and been reclaimed, along with hieroglyphic inscriptions that tell historians much about this remote period. It is believed, though, that even now perhaps 90 per cent of the ancient city of Palenque remains concealed beneath the jungle; one day, with luck, it will be revealed.

While dynastic lists have been deciphered, the circumstances of Ik'nal's ascent to the throne are shrouded in mystery. She was the first queen of the dynasty. She came to the throne around a year after the death of her predecessor. What occurred in the interval? Nobody knows. Towards the end of her reign Palenque suffered defeat at the hands of a neighbouring power, but either she or her successor reasserted their independence.

Her importance was considered sufficient for her to be depicted upon her grandson's (or great-grandson's) sarcophagus, and sculpted on the wall of his tomb, in spite of the fact that female rulers were in general not given equal status – and expected to adopt male characteristics as they occupied the throne.

What became of Palenque? Evidently, during the eighth century it declined, as did other Mayan city-states. A small, agricultural population clung on in the ruins, before the site was abandoned altogether, to be rapidly reclaimed and grown over by the forest.

24 December

The most famous event in the history of art took place on this day in 1888 in the sleepy town of Arles in the south of France. In a fit of mania, the artist Vincent Van Gogh severed his own ear from his head, wrapped it in paper, and delivered it to a young woman named Gabrielle at a brothel on Rue du Bout d'Arles.

For over a century, the truth behind this famous act has been speculated upon, until in 2016 when research proved the story to be true. A detailed letter and diagram by a doctor named Félix Ray, who treated the artist, was discovered clearly demonstrating that the ear was cut from top to bottom. Not half of the ear, as has been previously suggested, but its entirety. After years of investigation it was discovered that former theories that Van Gogh's ear was given to a prostitute were untrue.

In 1888, a young woman named Gabrielle Berlatier, a farmer's daughter, had attracted the attention of Van Gogh. Gabrielle worked as a cleaner at the brothel to earn enough money to pay for medical bills that her family incurred after receiving the new anti-rabies vaccination after being savaged by a rabid dog; an attack which also resulted in severe scarring on her arm.

It has never been proven what compelled Van Gogh to give his ear to Gabrielle, although it is suggested that he was affected by her trauma and physical defect, becoming briefly obsessed by her. He was discovered unconscious the next day and rushed to hospital, where he allegedly woke with no recollection of the event. Van Gogh eventually took his own life in 1890 at the age of thirty-seven. Gabrielle went on to marry and live into old age, leaving her encounter with the world-famous artist to develop into a popular mystery.

25 December

The decision to ban alcohol for students at Christmas showed a laudable optimism by the authorities at the Westpoint Military Academy in the United States, albeit a detachment from the real world that was slightly alarming in men who were preparing the next generation to defend the country.

By 1826 there was a concern that the 260 students were drinking too much and the staff announced that the Christmas eggnog would be alcohol free. Eggnog was not then the genteel tipple of an ageing aunt, but an explosive cocktail that made today's Martinis look like small beer. George Washington mixed his eggnog with rum, sherry, brandy and whiskey.

As the instructors should have known, forbidding alcohol only added to its lustre. Gallons of whiskey were smuggled in, the students' fieldcraft employed to the full as rowing boats with barrels of spirits were piloted across the Hudson River and into the barracks.

On Christmas Eve, Captain Ethan Allen Hitchcock, presumably guilty of some grotesque wrongdoing in a previous life, was the member of staff on duty. He tried to suppress the drinking parties, but hydra-like they multiplied. Just before dawn a rioting horde of cadets attacked his room, one of them even fired a pistol.

The riot was still in full swing when the cadets were called by the drumbeat of reveille at 6.05 a.m. The Christmas morning parade was an odd mix of the well rested, smartly turned out, and the obviously drunk. There were gaps in the ranks thanks to the most enthusiastic rioters still smashing the place up.

Order was restored by nightfall and a thorough investigation expelled around ten ringleaders. Many of the cadets would go on to have notable careers on the battlefields of the US Civil War, but there is no clear correlation, as you might expect, between the rioters and the Confederate Rebels. Then again adolescent alcoholism is so endemic, it is not a reliable guide to future political orientation.

26 December

His preferred lawyer refused on the grounds of being too old and too fat. The defendent, Citizen Louis Capet, formerly His Most Catholic Majesty, King of France and Navarre, Louis XVI, turned to Raymond Desèze to save his life. Desèze agreed, reluctantly, and today in 1792 he launched his defence with a stunning, three-hour-long plea to the court.

In the preceding weeks, Louis had listened to the case against him. A long list of crimes had been read out as he sat in the same armchair from which he had granted a constitution in 1791 in the vain hope that the compromise would save his crown and his life. The National Convention, already the legislative and executive branches of the Revolution, would now hear the case against the former king. The 850 deputies, meeting in the Salle du Manège, or indoor riding academy in the Tuileries Gardens, would decide his fate.

Desèze had been given a fortnight to prepare. It is said that he abjured sleep for the three previous nights as he perfected his arguments. He attacked the legality of the entire proceeding; according to the 1791 constitution, the king was immune from prosecution. He condemned the National Convention for sitting as judge and jury, and finally argued that Louis had in fact restored liberty to the French people through his reforms. Above all, he reminded them, Louis 'brought to the throne no wicked weaknesses, no corrupting passions. He was economical, just, severe. He showed himself always the constant friend of the people.' Think, he warned, how history 'will judge your judgement, and that the judgement of him will be judged by the centuries'.

A pretty speech, but all in vain. In mid-January deputy after deputy got up to deliver his judgement. Of the 721 present, 693 voted to convict, a handful abstained, others had pressing business elsewhere. On 21 January he was executed by guillotine after a dignified final address in which he wished the French people well. Despite the hagiography of his eloquent lawyer, Louis died better than he had reigned.

27 December

It was the deadliest avalanche in UK history. Blizzards, gales and heavy snow created the perfect conditions for a tragic loss of life. Today in 1836, an avalanche crashed into a street full of family houses. The location of this alpine phenomenon? Not the Highlands of Scotland or the craggy peaks of Snowdonia, but the pretty town of Lewes, in Sussex, only a few miles from the south coast.

South-east England is famous for its gently rolling hills, but in Lewes the River Ouse has carved a gap in the South Downs and created a canyon of sorts with cliffs to east and west of the path of the river. The appropriately named Cliffe Hill lies on the east bank. It rises over 150 metres above the town. A line of workers' cottages sat at the base of the cliff, flimsy, cheap dwellings inhabited by some of the poorest members of the community.

On Christmas Eve 1836 the country was blasted with heavy snow. A gale on Christmas night pushed snow on the top of Cliffe Hill into a huge cornice which hung over the houses beneath. The poor householders had nowhere else to go, particularly in the depths of a freezing winter. They remained in their houses despite the snow hanging directly above them.

At 10.15 a.m. on 27 December the cornice collapsed. A witness reported: 'The mass appeared to strike the houses first at the base, heaving them upwards, and then breaking over them like a gigantic wave. There was nothing but a mound of pure white.' Neighbours scrambled to rescue the victims before they froze or suffocated. Seven survivors were hauled out, but eight people died, one of them a two-year-old toddler.

It was not long before people moved back into the ruined street. Houses remain there to this day alongside a pub called the Snowdrop. They cannot say they have not been warned.

28 December

Today in 1895 two siblings known as the Lumière brothers put on their first paid public screening of a film – or 'motion picture' – at the Grand Café in Paris. Films plural. They were not, though, optimistic about what it might lead to, calling it an invention 'without a future'. To them it seemed that pioneering work on colour photography was more significant than these moving black-and-white images. A decade later they followed their instincts by abandoning film altogether to focus upon colour photography. They went on to develop the first practical photographic colour process, the Lumière Autochrome.

In southern France, Louis and Auguste's father had a photographic studio before he established a factory that manufactured photographic plates. This struggled at first, teetering upon bankruptcy, and from a young age the Lumière brothers worked long, unpaid hours along with other siblings. They displayed, though, an early fascination with the technology and a great facility for invention, designing machines capable of automating the production process, as well as developing a new and extremely successful type of photographic plate, transforming the factory's fortunes. Later, they began to experiment with creating 'moving' pictures – using perforations in the film as a means of drawing it through both camera and projector.

The first film of the ten shown at the end of 1895 was titled *La Sortie de l'Usine Lumière à Lyon* ('Workers Leaving the Lumière Factory at Lyon'). It was forty-six seconds long and was recorded that spring. Though others were trying to create moving images at the same time, it was the Lumière brothers' screening at the Grand Café that is held to mark cinema's birth as a practical artform, whose future of course was vastly greater than they guessed.

29 December

'Will no one rid me of this turbulent priest!' Henry II of England is believed to have articulated these words in 1170, spurring four of his knights to ride at speed to Canterbury, where on this day they butchered Thomas Becket, in front of the high altar in the cathedral. He had gone there to hear Vespers.

Thomas Becket and the king had once been firm friends. However, in 1163, the pair fell into bitter dispute over the Church's authority, Becket claiming it to be above the king's. The argument spilled over into 1164, when, at Northampton Castle, they argued publicly. Insults such as 'Whoremonger' were used, forcing Becket to flee to France, where he remained in exile for six years, before the king grudgingly offered a compromise that allowed Beckett to return to Canterbury in 1170.

Now, only months later, Henry's rage had sent the knights to his cathedral. Thomas Becket knelt before the high altar, as one of Henry's knights struck him hard on the shoulder. He received the blow without falling, after which the other knights unleashed their full might on the unarmed spokesman of God. Thomas Becket was murdered, in the most sacrilegious display of brutality by a crushing blow that cracked open his skull and sent his brains spilling onto the cathedral floor. Allegedly, his final words were: 'For the Name of Jesus and the protection of the Church I am ready to embrace death.'

Henry II was mortified when he heard of the murder in Canterbury Cathedral, immediately insisting that his words were not meant to have been taken literally. The murder caused outrage, forcing Henry to repent publicly by wearing sackcloth, rolling in ashes, and starving for three days. The Pope leapt into action to condemn the act and Thomas Becket was proclaimed a martyr; three years later, he was formally canonised and his shrine became one of England's foremost sites of pilgrimage.

30 December

The bizarre complexity of his murder is appropriate for a man who remains unfathomable. It was today in 1916 that the bearded Russian mystic and imperial adviser Grigori Rasputin was murdered. He was poisoned (given cakes laced with cyanide), shot four times, badly beaten, and eventually flung from a bridge into a freezing river.

Little is known of Rasputin's early life: from a peasant family in Siberia, he was illiterate into adulthood. A pilgrimage undertaken when he was already a married man and father transformed his life, and he became a 'holy wanderer' – teetotal, vegetarian, apparently absorbed in devotion.

Word of his unusual charisma spread. He gained introductions to aristocratic members of the tsar's circle. Late in 1905 he met the tsar himself, Nicholas recording in his diary that he had 'made the acquaintance of a man of God – Grigory, from Tobolsk province'.

What really cemented Rasputin's royal connection was Tsarina Alexandra's belief that he could miraculously treat her son's haemophilia and stop the bleeding that could kill him. The tsarina was unpopular, especially after the outbreak of war, when her German background attracted criticism.

Rasputin was tainted by association with her. It is hard to separate malicious rumour from fact in all the stories of depravity about him, though his excessive interest in confronting sin through direct engagement in it – whether sexual or drink-related (he abandoned his teetotalism) – is well attested.

To conservative, aristocratic opponents his influence upon the hated tsarina, together with his lowly origins and dubious lifestyle and beliefs made him deeply resented. This was the context in which the plot was hatched to murder him. In the end his death did nothing to correct the course of imperial Russia; it would have taken a lot more than the death of a mystic to save the dysfunctional tsarist state.

31 December

The brewery was dilapidated. Arthur Guinness got it for a bargain. Today, on the last day of December in 1759, he agreed to take the lease for 45 Irish pounds per year: a constant rate that would in theory remain unchanged for the duration of the lease: 9,000 years. Rather a good deal, it seems now, less than 400 years in.

Had he, one wonders, provided the refreshments before the terms of the lease were agreed? Had he had a premonition that the drink that now bears his name really was very good for you indeed, increasing life expectancy massively and making only a lease of this length sensible? In fact the lease is used now primarily as a canny marketing device, the brewery having bought the land outright and long since expanded well beyond the original four-acre site.

Interestingly, while Guinness as an alcoholic drink might be associated now with light indulgence, in its original inception it was actually intended to improve public morals rather than the reverse. At the time the most widespread alcoholic drinks were gin, whiskey and 'poteen' – a potent, illicit, home-distilled liquor, its name stemming from the Gaelic word 'pota' for pot. A glass of Guinness, then an ale, was a mild alternative and much healthier of course than unclean water. And it was much better for people than gulping down hard liquor.

Also interesting, given Ireland's divided history, are Guinness's Protestant connections – the new drink was even christened 'Guinness's black Protestant porter'. Arthur Guinness was a Protestant and a Unionist. Catholics would not even be hired until well into the twentieth century, and were fired if they revealed themselves. Today, the hunt for revenue has banished sectarianism, an overlooked virtue of capitalism. Guinness is guzzled much further afield now; 200 million pints are drunk annually in America, and it is virtually the national drink of Nigeria. Arthur's beer is one of the world's most familiar brands.

6 January 1066:
Westminster Abbey hosted a royal burial and coronation in the same day

21 September 1170:
Dublin stormed by Richard de Clare

11 July 1212:
A fire engulfed London killing 3,000 and destroying the medieval city

26 October 899:
Death of Alfred the Great, first King of the Anglo-Saxons

23 June 1314:
Robert the Bruce beat the English

14 June 1381:
Rebels stormed the Tower of London

17 March 461:
Saint Patrick, the patron saint of Ireland, died

29 March 1461:
Britain's bloodiest battle, which culminated in Edward of York declaring himself king

| 40BC | 400 | 600 | 800 | 1100 | 1200 | 1300 | 1400 |

6 March 1204:
Chateau Gaillard falls to the French

15 March 44 BC:
Julius Caesar assassinated in Rome

24 June 1374:
Crowds of people were affected with choreomania, which causes victims to dance uncontrollably

19 September, 634:
Damascus fell to Khalid ibn al-Walid and his Muslim army

30 May 1431:
Joan of Arc burned at the stake

15 July 1099:
Crusaders brutally took Jerusalem

12 December 1474:
News reached the future Queen Isabella of the death of Henry IV

14 December 835:
In Beijing's Imperial City, a coup against the politically powerful Eunuchs was foiled

26 November 1476:
Vlad Dracula becomes prince

12 October 1492:
Christopher Columbus arrives in the Americas

BRITAIN

15 January 1559:
Queen Elizabeth I crowned at
Westminster Abbey

5 November 1605:
The Gunpowder Plot was discovered

21 March 1617:
Pocahontas buried on the banks of the Thames

11 Oct 1649:
Cromwell's brutal Wexford massacre

1500   **1600**   **1700**

27 November 1620:
Mayflower
landed

2 April 1725:
Giacomo
Casanova
was born

14 February 1797:
Nelson enters the
limelight with
victory over the
Spanish

7 February 1569:
Spanish Inquisition arrived in
South America

28 April 1789:
Mutiny on the
Bounty

24 September 1529:
Suleiman the Magnificent's forces
attempted – but failed – to take the
seat of the Habsburgs

26 January 1788:
First time the British
flag was raised in
Australia

31 October 1517:
Martin Luther nailed his Ninety-
five Theses to a church door

8 September 1504:
Michelangelo's *David* was
unveiled at the Palazzo
Vecchio in Florence

16 December 1773:
The Boston Tea Party

REST OF WORLD

4 November 1839:
Last armed rebellion against the government on British soil

9 June 1865:
Charles Dickens was a passenger on a derailed train

11 May 1812:
Spencer Perceval became the only UK prime minister to be assassinated

8 April 1879:
The British able to buy milk in glass bottles for the first time

1800	1810	1820	1830	1840	1850	1860	1870	1880	1890

10 September 1824:
Simón Bolívar given supreme authority to end the War of Independence

28 December 1895:
First movie screening by the Lumière brothers

24 May 1844:
Samuel Morse sends the first telegraphic message

10 May 1869:
The final spike was hammered in to the railway line that connected the West Coast and East Coast of America

12 July 1807:
Napoleon Bonaparte attacked by rabbits

10 March 1804:
Napoleon sold France's US territories to America, doubling its size

25 April 1859:
Work began on the Suez Canal

21 August 1897:
Felix Hoffman invents heroin

18 November 1803:
Enslaved people of Saint-Domingue overthrow their European colonisers

4 January 1853:
Solomon Northup was granted his freedom after more than a decade as a slave

21 December 1898:
Marie and Pierre Curie discovered radium

BRITAIN

2 February 1901:
The funeral of Queen Victoria

8 June 1913:
Suffragette Emily Davison killed in a fatal collision with the king's horse at Epsom

6 February 1918:
Some British women finally got the vote

21 November 1920:
A Bloody Sunday in Dublin

21 June 1948:
500 Caribbean passengers arrived on *Empire Windrush*

31 January 1953:
Britain and its North Sea neighbours hit by a catastrophic flood

30 July 1966:
England won the World Cup

21 January 2008:
The FTSE 100 collapsed

1900   1910   1920   1930   1940   1950   1960   1970   1980   1990   2000   2010

14 January 1967:
Beginning of the 'Summer of Love'

7 May 1954:
French defeated by the Vietnamese

8 May 1946:
Two Estonian teenage girls blow up a Soviet war memorial in an act of resistance

6 May 1937:
Crash of the *Hindenburgh*

16 February 1922:
Archaeologists enter Tutankhamun's tomb

28 June 1919:
The Treaty of Versailles signed

17 July 1918:
Russian Imperial Romanov family murdered

26 September 1905:
Einstein's theory of relativity published

REST OF WORLD

Bibliography

1. Ackroyd, P., P., *Thames: Sacred River* (Chatto and Windus, 2007)
2. Boardman, J., Griffin, J., Murray, O., *The Oxford History of the Classical World* (OUP, 1986)
3. Cannon, J., *The Oxford Companion to British History* (OUP, 1997)
4. Crimp, T., *A Brief History of Science* (Constable, 2001)
5. Davies, N., *Europe: A History* (Bodley Head, 2014)
6. Evans, R., *The Pursuit of Power: Europe 1815-1914* (Penguin, 2016)
7. Frankopan, P., *The Silk Roads* (Bloomsbury, 2015)
8. Fuller J.F.C., *The Decisive Battles of the Western World I & II* (Granada, 1970)
9. Gilbert, M., *The First World War* (Weidenfield and Nicholson, 1994)Harper, K., *The Fate of Rome* (Princeton, 2017)
10. Gillingham, J., *Conquests, Catastrophe and Recovery* (Vintage, 2014)
11. Hibbert, C., *The English, A Social History, 1066-1945* (Grafton, 1987)
12. Holland, T., *In the Shadow of the Sword* (Little, Brown, 2012)
13. Holmes, R., *The Oxford Companion to Military History* (OUP, 2001)
14. Inwood, S., *A History of London* (MacMillan, 1998)
15. James, L., *The Rise and Fall of the British Empire* (Abacus, 1994)
16. Johnson, D., and Nurminen, J., The History of Seafaring (Conway Maritime, 2007)
17. Keegan, J., *Warpaths: Travels of a Military Historian in North America* (Pimlico, 1995)
18. Koch, H.W., *The Rise of Modern Warfare, 1618-1815* (Bison, 1981)
19. Konstam, A., *Historical Atlas of the Viking World* (Thalamus, 2002)

20. Lieven, D., *Empire* (John Murray, 2000)
21. MacMillan, M., *Peacemakers* (John Murray, 2001)
22. MacMillan, M., *The Uses and Abuses of History* (Viking Canada, 2008)
23. Mallinson, A., *The Making of the British Army* (Bantam, 2009)
24. Massie, R., *Dreadnought: Britain, Germany and the Coming of the Great War* (Cape, 1992)
25. Oliver, N., *The Story of the British Isles in 100 Places* (Transworld, 2018)
26. Overy, R., *The Complete History of the World* (Times Books, 2010)
27. Parker, G., *Global Crisis: War, Climate Change and Catastrophe in the Sixteenth Century* (Yale, 2013)
28. Rodger, N. A. M., *The Safeguard of the Sea* (Harper Collins, 1997)
29. Rovelli, C., *Seven Brief Lessons on Physics* (Penguin, 2015)
30. Schama, S., *A History of Britain 3* Volumes (BBC Worldwide, 2002)
31. Sebag Montefiore, S., *The Romanovs* (Weidenfeld and Nicholson, 2016)
32. Snow, P. and MacMillan, A., *War Stories: Gripping Tales of Courage, Cunning and Compassion* (John Murray, 2017)
33. Tombs, R., *The English and their History* (Allen Lane, 2014)
34. Tombs, R., and Tombs, I., *That Sweet Enemy: Britain and France The History of a Love Hate Relationship* (Pimlico, 2007)
35. Willis, S., *Fighting Ships 1750-1850* (Quercus, 2007)
36. Winder, S., *Danubia: A Personal History of Hapsburg Europe* (Picador, 2013)
37. Winston, R. (ed), *Science Year by Year* (Dorling Kindersley, 2013)

Acknowledgements

If you've got this far, it's fair to say that you are a history fan. Years ago I realised that those of us afflicted to spend our lives with one eye always on the past needed a place where we could satisfy our desire for proper history. And so, with a fantastic team of people, I started HistoryHit, a place where history fans could come for audio, television, books, talks and tours, and to meet other enthusiasts.

Our podcast network now reaches millions of people. We filled the 5000-seat Albert Hall to commemorate the 75th anniversary of the Dambusters Raid. We have also started a new television channel, where we stream some of the world's best-loved history documentaries, alongside the new material we are filming all the time – think of it like Netflix for history. It is less than a year old but has already attracted thousands of subscribers and been nominated for a top industry award.

As a big thank you for buying this book, we would like to offer you a three-month trial membership of HistoryHit. You'll be able to watch the channel, enjoy exclusive audio and TV programmes unavailable anywhere else and come along to all sorts of live events and talks, from our now-legendary historic pub crawl to going along on archaeological digs. See page xv for all you need to sign up.

I couldn't have written this book without the support of the team at HistoryHit. Justin Gayner insisted on Napoleon and the rabbits; while Tom Clifford, Helen Carrie, Amara Thornton, Natt Tapley, Dan Morelle, Cassie Pope, James Carson, Felix Maynard, Becky Rothwell, Chris Bailey and Justin Hardy all joined in with their own areas of expertise and knowledge. Thank you, in particular, to the brilliant and talented James Evans and Helen Carr and our heated debates that must have sounded deeply eccentric to any ear-wiggers, but that resulted in all kinds of interesting discoveries and stories. Thank you all.